Ken Keis' new book **Why Aren't You More Like Me?** *is a superb analysis of the impact of Personal Style—one of several that impact personality development—and how knowledge and awareness of that style can make a significant difference in the way we live our lives. More than a great read for a general audience, this book is an invaluable reference resource for professionals in the helping professions and for those who use assessments in their work. I intend to use it often in my work as an executive and leadership coach and management consultant.*

Dr. Ray Williams
President, Ray Williams Associates
Co-Founder, Success IQ University

*Ken's book is a **must read** for any leader, parent, partner, or individual who wants to improve his or her personal or professional effectiveness. It is full of in-depth knowledge that will change the way you understand yourself and others—forever!*

Jill Lublin
Bestselling Author of **Guerrilla Publicity**

In his groundbreaking new book **Why Aren't You More Like Me?** *author Ken Keis has created the ultimate resource to help individuals and organizations maximize their strengths through understanding their unique Personal Styles. Although style does not predict a career—a point wisely noted in this book—knowing what makes people tick is definitely linked to outstanding productivity, profits, and a happy workplace. A **must read** for anyone pursuing higher levels of success.*

Les Hewitt
Bestselling Author: **The Power of Focus**

D0048785

I was one of the early adopters of Ken's programs and have been a big believer in the effectiveness of the content and strategies contained in **Why Aren't You More Like Me?** *Ken lives and breathes what he teaches. He is sincerely interested in helping people do more with their lives.*

Communication and sales skills can be improved dramatically when you know who you are talking to and how they want you to communicate with them.

No gimmicks or copycat concepts here. You can trust Ken Keis and the CRG group.

Jim Janz
International Entrepreneur and Businessman

Most textbooks written by academics on assessment in general—and personality assessment in particular—tend to put me to sleep. Fortunately, the ideas in this book come from professionals in the business world as well as higher education. I find **Why Aren't You More Like Me?** *very reader-friendly, the suggestions for improving workplace relations practical, and the publication comprehensive.*

Richard Knowdell
President, Career Research & Testing, Inc.

why aren't you more like me?

KEN KEIS
with Everett Robinson

Enriching People's Lives

CRG Consulting Resource Group International, Inc.
PO Box 418 Main,
Abbotsford, BC Canada V2T 6Z7
www.crgleader.com

Design and typesetting by William Glasgow and Neil Klassen, Judson Lake House Publishing

Cover Design by Yvonne Parks at www.pearcreative.ca

Editing by Val Wilson, Imagine Enterprises, Inc.

Library and Archives Canada Cataloguing in Publication

Keis, Ken

      Why aren't you more like me? discover the secrets to understanding yourself and others by Ken Keis with Everett Robinson — 3rd edition

1. Personality.   2. Self-actualization (Psychology).   3. Interpersonal Communication.   4. Behavioral assessment.   I. Title.

ISBN: 978-1-897300-03-9

Printed in Canada by Friesens Corporation, Altona, MB, Canada

Printed on Forest Stewardship Council certified paper which is acid free and ancient forest friendly and has been processed chlorine free.

Table of Contents

Acknowledgements

A book does not come into being without a team supporting the author.

I am thankful for the contributions of many individuals.

It all started with Dr. Terry Anderson, founder of CRG and the creator of the *Personal Style Indicator*. Terry took the time to mentor me over 20 years ago. That was a turning point.

Thanks also to Everett Robinson, MA, who wrote the first two editions of this book and is co-author of several of the CRG assessments that established a foundation for the content of this book.

To Eleanor Parkinson, project manager, who has been connected and loyal to CRG for over 22 years.

To my editor Val Wilson, who has worked with me since 1985; her dedication is without equal.

To all the other CRG team members who have supported this process, from creating the special Website so you can take your online assessment, to getting printing quotes and sending out promotional mailers.

Your efforts are appreciated!

Of course, thank you to the many clients who provided stories and case studies about the transformational power of our style and values models. This book would not have been possible without you.

Nor could I have written it without the support of my family.

Thanks to my son Tim, a gifted musician whom I reference more than once in this book as an example of the way style affects our lives.

And to my daughter Stephanie, the productive organizer who prepared many promotional mailings for this book.

And to my life partner, my wife Brenda, who encourages and loves me just the way I am.

Thank you all!

Foreword

by Terry D. Anderson, PhD

This Third Edition of **Why Aren't You More Like Me?** takes an innovative look at how Personal Style affects most areas of life. It will bring the reader closer to understanding why some individuals are happier and more successful than others.

We know from research over the past 10 years that people who have developed social sensitivity and self-awareness are living more satisfying lives—and are more effective leaders. The literature on social and emotional intelligence has made that quite clear.

Ken Keis has labored for months to bring depth and breadth to this edition. It is, I believe, unsurpassed in the field of Personal Style assessment and in the development of style versatility. This book reveals knowledge that can be instantly applied to your inner self-discovery, your relationships with family members and friends, your co-workers, and your career and life planning.

This book isn't simply a one-time read. You will find yourself reaching for it over and over again for help as new challenges arise in your life and your work. It is a resource you will consult frequently. The materials are well organized; you can look at the table of contents and quickly source the pages that apply to an issue or problem you are facing.

In building upon the established work of other authors and experts, Ken has made a significant contribution to the literature on Personal Style. He has created a field manual for learning to live and work more effectively.

I encourage readers to keep this book close by—and refer to it often!

Terry D. Anderson, PhD
PROFESSOR, CONSULTANT, EXECUTIVE COACH

Author: *Transforming Leadership:*
Equipping Yourself and Coaching Others
to Build the Leadership Organization

Introduction

*Life is like a jigsaw puzzle but you don't have the picture
on the front of the box to know what it's supposed to look like.
Sometimes, you're not even sure if you have all the pieces.*

Roger Von Oech

I grew up in an environment where my family and schools did not appreciate my outgoing Personal Style. Frequently, I was told to behave in a different way than I preferred or was comfortable with. I was not accepted the way I was.

You may be old enough to remember the saying "Kids are to be seen and not heard." That was said to me often. I was not encouraged when my Grade 9 English teacher told me I would not amount to much, given my lack of discipline and poor language skills.

As a result of all the negative input, I became insecure in my teens, questioning whether I was okay as a person—even doubting if I was worthy of being alive.

Has that happened to you or to people you love?

Sadly, many people wander through life without direction, not knowing that powerful wisdom is available to help them lead happier and more satisfying lives.

My goal is to have each and every person who reads this book acknowledge, appreciate, and most of all honor the uniqueness we each bring to this life.

It does not matter if you are 15 or 75. You have been created with a life *purpose* and a unique Personal Style and values—preferences that frame the way you interact with the world.

> **Only through the awareness of our own distinctiveness can
> we live our lives intentionally and purposefully
> and take the appropriate action.**

We are all distinctive and different. I will show you how to see the best in what others have to offer and how to live and work harmoniously with people who think and behave differently than you do. That includes your partner, your kids, boss, co-workers, clients, family, and friends.

This book will actively guide you to build better relationships with others, while helping you increase your overall success.

I will outline important benchmarks and development models to equip you to live the rest of your life *on purpose,* while honoring the differences in others.

Thank you for the privilege of assisting you. May you find the insight and knowledge that will transform your life.

CHAPTER 1

Self-Awareness:
The Key to Transformation

Unless you know what it is, I ain't never going to be able to explain it to you.

Louis Armstrong

Awareness: An awareness of one's own personality or individuality

In my younger years, I was not self-aware. I learned the power of self-awareness during my first few months at college. It was my first time away from home and out of town and let's say I let loose. I became boisterous and loud in an attempt to be the center of attention. My quest was to have people like me, but the outcome of my actions was the opposite—*Oh, no! Here comes Ken!*

About 3 months into my first semester, I had a chance to sit down with one of the sharp girls in our dorm. Thirty minutes into our conversation, she said, "You are not a jerk after all. In fact, you are a really nice guy."

In complete shock, I asked her what she meant.

"Ken, you are loud and sometimes obnoxious. You try way too hard. It really is quite irritating. But in this conversation today, you are calm, interesting, and focusing on our discussion."

I was immature and unaware that my actions were driving people away, not bringing them closer.

You don't have to be in college to become self-aware.

When my son Tim was in Grade 8, we started to coach him on the impact his Personal Style was having in his environment. We were creating self-awareness in him.

Tim's style is active and verbal, contrary to the learning model in education that wants students to be compliant and quiet.

A lot of tension had developed between my son and one of the young, less experienced teachers. Her response to Tim's verbal nature was to try to put tighter controls on him, which exasperated the situation.

> **The teacher was not aware of her Personal Style or her instructional style and how it was negatively affecting the learning environment.**

We coached him to manage his verbal nature and tone it down a bit. We did not want to change who he was; we wanted him to be aware that his verbal energy was disrupting the class.

Less than a week later, he burst through our door at home, excited to tell us that class was going a lot better. I asked how he was achieving that excellent result. "Dad," he said, "I learned how to shut up!"

Tim was so proud of his ability to manage himself by being self-aware. If a 13-year-old can do that, anyone can.

Here is an important question for you.

If nothing changed in your life in the next 5 years, would that be okay?

I mean everything in your life—your health, your relationships, your friends, career, feelings of fulfillment, achievement, and so on.

Let's move the calendar ahead 5 years.

- You are the same person.
- The conditions in your life are the same as they are today.

Is that okay?

For the majority, I suspect it is not.

> **One definition of insanity is to continue to do the same things over and over, expecting different results.**

If you want different results, you must **change** what you are doing and/or the way you are doing it.

I am here to show you how to change old habits and/or learn new strategies to better understand yourself and others.

Are you willing to change to increase the fulfillment and achievement in your life?

Before you can act with **purpose** and direction, you must understand what you need to change and how to go about it.

When we are not self-aware about our own preferences, gifts, talents, and tendencies, it is impossible for us to act *intentionally*. If we are not aware, we are living life—day after day and year after year—oblivious to our natural thought patterns and beliefs.

All of us have met people who are completely unaware that their behavior and conduct are inappropriate. They have no clue that they are clueless.

A frequent traveler, I spot *unawareness* on every trip … people who stop at the bottom of an Up escalator, staring into space, with no idea that a line of fellow travelers is forming behind them, and people who let their carry-on bags hit each seated person in the head as they make their way down the aisle in the aircraft.

In his book *Excuses Be Gone*, Dr. Wayne Dyer said it well.

> **"The reason awareness of awareness is so powerful is that it immediately puts me in touch with a dimension of myself that knows that Here in awareness, all things are possible."**

Dr. Dyer went on to quote a Harvard Study that tracked 84 female room-attendants working in different hotels.

The women were divided into two groups.

1. For the control group, it was business as usual.
2. The second group was told their work was "exercise."

The control group experienced no physical improvement, despite engaging in the same activities as the second group.

The second group of ladies who recognized their work as exercise experienced significant health benefits. In just 4 weeks, they dropped weight and lowered their blood pressure, body fat, and body mass index.

That study reveals that our attitude—which is linked to our awareness—can have profound effects on our well-being.

Awareness of our beliefs is one thing. What about awareness of our style preferences and all the implications they have in every part of our daily lives?

A study conducted by Talent Smart discovered that less than 30% of the population has a solid understanding of their own Personal Style preferences.

Thus in that study, about 70% had no inkling of how they appeared to and interacted with others. They had little idea of their strengths and skills; without knowing what they were, they could not implement them properly.

The 70% who were oblivious about their Personal Style had considerably more difficultly handling stress and interpersonal relationships.

In comparing people's levels of awareness about their style and their ability to achieve the things they found most important in life, the study found the following.

- Satisfaction with life increases dramatically when individuals are self-aware.

- People who are self-aware are far more likely to reach their goals.

- Aware individuals take time to first learn then understand their Personal Style so they can better respond to life's challenges and opportunities.

- Because they understand their situation and can identify the people that will help make them successful, they can more easily implement the right strategies.

- They understand their limitations and adjust their attitude and behavior accordingly, to minimize any negative impact.

- They know what they really want; through their awareness, they are motivated to take the best steps and actions to get where they want to be.

> **Self-awareness is so predominant for success that it transcends age, intelligence, education, profession, and job level.**

The Talent Smart study found that 83% of top performers are high in self-awareness—no matter the industry or profession, yet just 2% of low performers possess that critical skill.

The reality is that individuals who understand their style preferences and tendencies are much more likely to play to their strengths at work and at home, limit the negative impact of their deficiencies, and get the results they desire.

> **When you become aware, you cease being a victim**
> **of your circumstances. You own your own space.**

Square Wheels

Used with permission © Performance Management Company, 1993
Square Wheels® is a registered servicemark of Performance Management Company
www.PerformanceManagementCompany.com

When you look at the image of the wagon with the square wheels, what do you see and think?

- What do the square wheels represent as a metaphor for our lives— at home and at work? Some might use words like *struggle, difficult, inefficient, challenge, hard, toiling, stuck*—even *silly*.

- What about the people behind the wagon? What do they see? Only the back of the wagon! What is their perspective on life and this situation? For sure, it's limited.

- What about the person pulling the wagon? What is he thinking and experiencing? Is he wondering if anyone will come along to help? He's not looking around to see if there is any way to improve the situation.

- And what about the round wheels inside the wagon? What do they represent? Do words like *opportunity, improvement, easier way, upgrade, progress,* and *a different way of doing things* come to mind?

Some questions must be asked.

- Why are they stuck—the leader and the followers?
- Why don't they put the round wheels on the wagon or at least consider doing that?
- How far away are the round wheels? The wheels are readily available, but the leader and the followers are unaware of the opportunities.

Have you ever met someone who is dealing with a problem and the answer to his dilemma is obvious—right in front of his eyes—but he still doesn't get it? The answer he seeks is right there but he can't—or won't—see it. He is completely oblivious to the opportunity.

I admit in the past to being quick to judge when individuals did not see the obvious. I now understand that it was not obvious **to them**. Rather than standing in judgment, let's have compassion while coaching and helping people to see the possibilities.

After more than 20 years of serving others in the field of personal and professional development, I see many situations like the one depicted in the next illustration.

A caterpillar tractor is now pulling the square-wheeled wagon!

- Here's their thinking: *Let's commit ourselves 100% to our square wheels. Let's take what has not been working and do it harder.*

Used with permission © Performance Management Company, 1993
Square Wheels® is a registered servicemark of Performance Management Company
www.PerformanceManagementCompany.com

I see it every week in individuals, families, teams, organizations—even governments—that dedicate themselves to their square wheels. They embrace the certainty of misery rather than the misery of uncertainty.

If you look closely at the second illustration, you'll notice that arrows are sticking out of the caterpillar driver's back. The blind devotion to broken and unproductive habits causes pain to everyone concerned.

So what about you?

- Where in your life—in personal and interpersonal effectiveness and career fulfillment—are you holding onto square wheels?

- Where have you blindly—without conscious intention or awareness—stayed committed to your square wheels?

Here's my challenge to you . . .

Everyone has a few square wheels—myself included. Rather than protecting the status quo, I am encouraging you to start looking for and using round wheels. As you can see, the round wheels are within reach—if you choose to embrace change and use new information.

I will provide round wheels for you in this book. If you find the message helpful, please share it with others, to assist them with their awareness and to help them use round wheels on their journey along life's path.

Self-awareness without action is not beneficial to anyone. Like anything else, if you don't use it, you lose it. By exercising your knowledge, you have the opportunity to transform not only your life, but the lives of others along the way.

CHAPTER 2

What is Personal Style Anyway?

It is surely true that no two people are ever exactly alike.
It is equally true that in certain ways, all people are the same.
This seeming paradox is the vessel that contains the concept
of personality.

E. J. PHARES

Personal Style: Your natural predisposition (born that way) to perceive, approach, and interact with the environment. Your environment includes Time, People, Tasks, and Situations.

Have you met someone for the first time and there seems to be an instant connection or chemistry between you? Have you wondered why you had an instant bond with a complete stranger?

What about the opposite? You have no previous history with a new person, yet you really cannot stand him or her? Your interactions seem forced and awkward, and you cannot get away fast enough!

Why the difference?

We tend to be attracted to individuals who are like we are. One of the roots of our responses to potential relationships is our Personal Style.

By exploring Personal Style preferences, you learn about the needs of others and how to approach those needs so that people feel understood and appreciated.

When your behavior as a leader or individual meets the needs of others, your credibility level rises. People begin to perceive you as someone who is not driven by self-centeredness, with no consideration for others.

> **Regardless of any special abilities we may have, the way we conduct ourselves with others always influences our credibility with them.**

The Whole is the Sum of the Parts

We've all experienced differences in others. For example, some people enjoy engaging with complete strangers at a bus stop, yet others would never do that. Some have the ability to focus and build models all day, yet others would rather have a root canal than decipher the directions for the model, let alone spend time building it.

> **Neither response is right or wrong. They are simply different perspectives on similar opportunities and events.**

A Foundation of Preferences

Underpinning all the layers of learned behavior is the anchor of personal preferences. It is your innate predisposition—you were born that way— for behaving in certain ways. That is called Personal Style.

Personal Style is not only predictable, it forms a base line or foundation from which our life operates. As a result, Personal Style can be understood with relative ease and managed intentionally. Even individuals of 14 or 15 years of age can embrace the concept, just as my son did at only 13 in his classroom environment.

Your Personal Style is reflected in your natural tendency to prefer, despite other influences, a particular manner of perceiving, approaching, and interacting with the environment around you. Those preferences form the working definition of Personal Style that will be used throughout this book.

A DEFINITION OF PERSONAL STYLE

Personal Style is Your Natural Predisposition to:

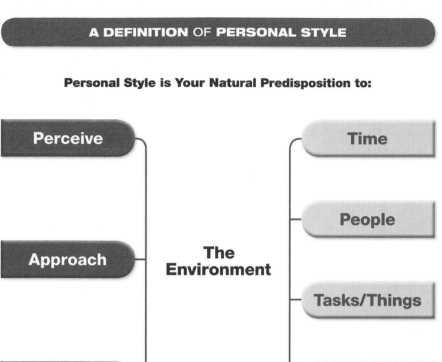

Personal Style affects the way we experience, sense, and see any situation and it controls what will capture our attention. Personal Style influences the plans, approaches, and strategies we use, what we want to achieve from a situation, and where we will place the most value afterward.

Please pay very close attention to this statement.

**Personal Style is not the same as personality.
It is part of your personality.**

The two are very much connected, but they are not the same.

Personal Style acts as an underlying base upon which other factors build. Like the deep foundation of a tall building that supports the rest of the structure, your Personal Style provides the basis for the way you prefer to engage your environment.

A Key for Understanding Self and Others

Although Personal Style is merely one category of the factors that determine the development of your personality, this particular category has a surprisingly pervasive and enduring influence on your life. In fact, it affects your personality and behavioral choices from birth until death.

How can that be?

It is obvious that all individuals in the same situation do not respond in exactly the same way. Even though environmental circumstances may be identical for all the people involved, they often react totally differently.

A key to understanding this fascinating human truth can be found through examining the definition of Personal Style more closely.

The term *natural predisposition* means you are born with tendencies that form an unchanging part of your personality—a part that remains the same throughout your life. We call this your Personal Style.

This part of your personality dominates the way you think, which in turn influences the way you decide to behave, which in turn determines the way you interact with others.

For example, it is clear that from birth, children do not react to stimuli in the same way. Like adults at any age, children exhibit Personal Style differences because they cognitively process information differently. That can be explained by taking a closer look at three human processes: **Perception**, **Approach**, and **Interaction.**

> *What we perceive comes as much from inside our heads*
> *as from the world outside.*
>
> WILLIAM JONES

- First, we perceive what is going on around us by gathering and interpreting the information supplied by our senses. **Perception** is the interpretation of what we record. Each individual gives personal meaning to the information that enters the brain, thus making the data subjective rather than objective.

- Using our Personal Style filter (our bias), we make decisions on how to approach the environment. **Approach** includes both moving away from people and things in the environment, and moving toward them. It also includes not doing anything—remaining in an observation position. While we are behaving in those various modes, we continue to record information and perceive what the data means to us personally. As that happens, new decisions are made for the way we will interact with the stimuli.

- Finally, we **interact** with the environment. That occurs the moment we stop observing the stimuli and become directly involved with it. Again, as interaction occurs, new information is recorded and filtered, and new perceptions are formed. The perceptions influence our approach, which in turn affects our interactions.

That engagement occurs subconsciously most of the time. One of the purposes of this book is to build awareness about Personal Style so you can *intentionally manage it* and *make it work for you*, not against you.

Most people have no idea that those three processes are occurring in their thinking, nor are they aware of how many times and how fast they occur during any hour in their lives. As we noted earlier, in the study of people who did not know about their personal preferences to **Perception**, **Approach**, and **Interaction**, *only 2% were able to realize their potential.* In that case, ignorance is not bliss!

> **Understanding your Personal Style and the styles of others is essential to living a satisfying, fulfilled, and successful life.**

People, for the most part, are not "tuned in" to the fact that their Personal Style is controlling them.

What does our environment include as it relates to our Personal Style?

Personal Style is your natural predisposition to perceive, approach, and interact with the **environment**, which includes **Time, People, Tasks,** and **Situations.**

Let's look at each item separately.

1. Time

Time, the first major element, is a persistent source of interaction. Most of us (not all) are aware we have only a finite amount of time in each day, week, and year. We can never speed up time or slow it down. We must continually pick and choose what we will do—and will not do—with our fixed supply of time.

Time can influence the type of decision-making we make and, for some, can generate high levels of anxiety, especially when important matters are at stake. Our daily tasks of commuting to work, getting the family chores done, and fulfilling other obligations can wear on a person.

Can you think of someone who, no matter what obstacles are placed in her path, is always on time for events or appointments?

Can you think of someone who, no matter what, is always late for his obligations and has an excuse each time?

Why are some people always on time and others are not? One reason is that each individual has a specific Personal Style orientation toward time.

2. People

We learn—some better than others—how to live, work, and get along with many different people throughout a lifetime. Interacting with people can be very rewarding. Our interactions can, however, create stress and tension because we must meet needs, wants, and values other than our own.

That dynamic begins when we are young, in our families of origin, and continues to affect us as we grow older, in social situations such as school and in the workplace. The dynamic doesn't stop when we marry and have our own children or acquire them in a blended family situation.

If you are a parent, you have had many enjoyable moments with your children. Each child is special in his or her own way and can add much love, joy, and delight to your life.

Children also can add challenges.

- An adult can become completely unglued when interacting with a headstrong 4-year-old in a grocery store.
- Not all adults are able (ready) to handle the dynamic that develops when children become teenagers.

Relationships can be draining or gratifying. Depending on their Personal Style preferences, some individuals will be more effective in coping with the effects of daily interaction with others. Knowledge helps provide the necessary tools to limit the strain some people experience in their relationships and it also provides ways to maximize the highs.

3. Tasks

The third environmental element we must manage and experience is tasks. A major focus of human existence is working to accomplish the various developmental tasks of life. The effort we make to accomplish those tasks—both paid and unpaid—is called *work*. We must learn to work if we want to get anywhere in life. For example, we must work to clothe and feed ourselves and our loved ones, to build shelters from the weather, create new products, or enjoy recreational and personal activities.

In daily living, tasks are ongoing. Some are repetitious and time-consuming; others are not. We often work hard to improve processes and systems for making our efforts more efficient. We create tools to assist us with our tasks so our work becomes easier and can be accomplished faster.

Can you think of someone who easily and fully engages his tasks? It could be a mechanic turning a wrench or an accountant reviewing the month-end statement. They have chosen jobs that focus on tasks rather than interaction with people.

What about others who try to avoid tasks as much as possible? Their work station is a mess, their car is cluttered, or their home looks like a tornado just hit. But they always have time for a coffee with you (people) and no time to get the cleaning (tasks) done.

> **The key point is that some individuals prefer to work on tasks more than to connect with people.**

4. Situations

The last environmental element is the contextual situations in which we find ourselves. Situations almost always consist of a combination of the foregoing three elements—Time, People, and Tasks. They constitute both the specific and the general conditions of a person's life.

You apply your unique Personal Style to your daily activities. You might be on time for the $100-a-ticket hockey game, but late for your child's school concert. You might be able to focus for 2 hours on your favorite video game, but become distracted after 5 minutes when answering email at work.

It is impossible to pass through life without being tested by the many conditions that confront us.

- Some might get the promotion they always wanted, but then must manage the additional time stress and responsibilities.

- In marriage, the dynamics of living with another individual can enhance the relationship, or the accompanying stress can threaten the couple's personal peace and calmness.

Events will affect people in various ways for different reasons. There are many factors in life whose influence has a bearing on our personalities and how we choose to cope with **Time**, **People**, **Tasks,** and **Situations.** For the most part, regardless of the circumstance, your Personal Style will exert the greatest influence over the way you handle those four central elements in your life.

We have very strong preferences for the way we personally juggle time constraints, satisfy the demands of other people, accomplish daily tasks, address life's opportunities, and handle challenges. Together, those preferences constitute our Personal Style.

A Lifetime of Influence

You are born with your Personal Style and it does not change over time. Somehow, it is preset from birth and remains static throughout your lifetime, a consistent part of your personality.

Thank goodness for that. Otherwise, our Personal Style would flip-flop and change and we all might have full-blown neurotic tendencies. If our Personal Style were not consistent throughout our lifetime, we would be totally different people at age 30 than we were at age 10 or 20.

Many researchers have indicated that our Personal Style is linked to the natural biochemical balances present at birth that all work together to form our unique perspectives, preferences, and behavior.

In that respect, Personal Style is similar to an individual's physical identity. Although our faces and bodies undergo changes over time, we retain basic physical characteristics through the various stages in our lives. A continuity of resemblance links who we are at each and every age. The same holds true for our Personal Style.

> **This anchor called Personal Style brings stability and continuity to our life.**

An indication of the persistent manifestation of Personal Style occurs when we meet someone again after a period of many years. At class reunions, for instance, we soon recognize something of the people we used to know—even though changes in appearance, health, or other outward differences are immediately noticeable. We are amazed at how much and yet how little a person seems to have changed from the individual we once knew.

Part of the excitement—and dread—of attending class reunions stems from anticipation. Will we be able to recognize others? And, more important, will they know who we are? Our personal engagement increases as we realize that the core part of a person does not change much—even after 10 or 20 years. We connect with the familiar and the stability it adds to our interactions with others.

The stability your Personal Style brings to your life is very important. You can count on taking your Personal Style with you the rest of your life.

Though our bodies may be bent by the years and our opinions changed by the times, there is a basic core of self—a personality—that remains basically unchanged.

Z. RUBIN

CHAPTER 3

Developing the Whole Person: You!

I want freedom for the full expression of my personality.

Mahatma Gandhi

Are We Nature or Nurture?

Are we a product of **nature** (born that way) or **nurture** (input from our environment)?

The answer is Yes. *We are a combination of both nature and nurture.*

Many years ago, I completed a personality assessment from one of our current competitors; it tried to box me into a specific type. The report read like a military tribunal; it projected that I would act and conduct myself in a very specific way, with little room for flexibility or professional development. Not only was the report mostly incorrect, it felt oppressive and burdensome.

Many people reading this book have had similar experiences with other personality assessments. The reason we felt trapped by their assessment descriptions is that most test designers fail to acknowledge in their process that we are both nature and nurture.

> **Each person is born with many parts that form the whole (nature); we gain knowledge and beliefs (nurture) as we live our lives.**

The Uniqueness of You

Your personality is exclusive to you alone. No one else in the history of time has been or will be exactly as you are.

To turn out the same way you have, other people would have to live your life exactly as you have lived it. They would need to possess, from the moment of conception, the same genes that determine—among other things—the color of your eyes, the shape of your ears, and the texture

19

of your hair. They would have to be brought up under exactly the same conditions you experienced in childhood, play all the games you played, suffer all the falls you took, and learn all the lessons you learned.

In fact, they would need to experience everything in precisely the same way you have to produce a person with your unique hopes, fears, desires, values, and characteristics. Even then, your gifts, talents, and abilities are genetically yours; there is little likelihood any two individuals will ever be exactly the same.

During an episode of *Star Trek, The Next Generation,* Commander Riker was beamed up from the surface of a planet. Unknown to the crew, a mirror image of Commander Riker was reflected back to the surface.

Up to that point, the two were identical individuals in every way. For the next 5 years, however, the second Commander Riker survived under hostile conditions on the planet. When *The Enterprise* returned and discovered the second Commander Riker, it was clear the men were no longer identical. Their experiences over the 5 years had shaped them differently, even though they were clones when the duplication occurred. This demonstrates that every event in our lives uniquely shapes us.

It is extremely difficult to assess just how important any one factor has been in creating your personality. How much weight can be given to any single factor?

There's no simple answer, and the presence of so many factors makes it all the more complex. One of the factors that has influenced—and continues to affect—your personality is your Personal Style.

To explain Personal Style's special influence, let's examine the role it plays in your life.

Your Personal Style is the foundation for your interpersonal style; the totality of you as a person is called your PERSONALITY.

Your Personal Style strongly affects everything you choose to do and the way you choose to do it. Even though you may have learned how to display behavior that is unrelated to your Personal Style, your style always has an impact on your decision-making; it serves as a filter system through which all your learned behavior must pass.

All the inputs, conditions, characteristics, and socially learned and expected behaviors you have acquired, plus your Personal Style, combine to create your unique **Personality**.

To acknowledge people's diversity and provide a framework for development and understanding of self and others, we created the Personality Factors Development Model™.

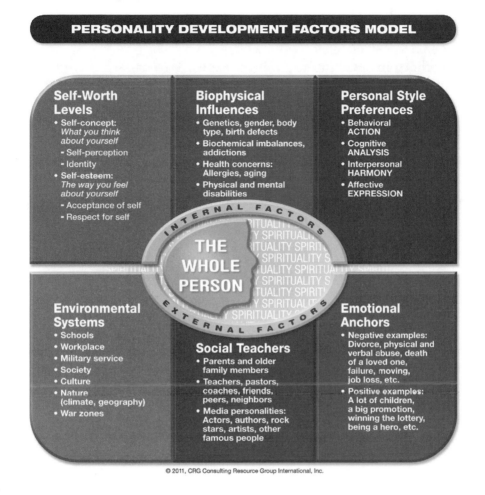

PERSONALITY DEVELOPMENT FACTORS MODEL

Self-Worth Levels
- Self-concept: *What you think about yourself*
  - Self-perception
  - Identity
- Self-esteem: *The way you feel about yourself*
  - Acceptance of self
  - Respect for self

Biophysical Influences
- Genetics, gender, body type, birth defects
- Biochemical imbalances, addictions
- Health concerns: Allergies, aging
- Physical and mental disabilities

Personal Style Preferences
- Behavioral ACTION
- Cognitive ANALYSIS
- Interpersonal HARMONY
- Affective EXPRESSION

INTERNAL FACTORS

THE WHOLE PERSON

EXTERNAL FACTORS

Environmental Systems
- Schools
- Workplace
- Military service
- Society
- Culture
- Nature (climate, geography)
- War zones

Social Teachers
- Parents and older family members
- Teachers, pastors, coaches, friends, peers, neighbors
- Media personalities: Actors, authors, rock stars, artists, other famous people

Emotional Anchors
- Negative examples: Divorce, physical and verbal abuse, death of a loved one, failure, moving, job loss, etc.
- Positive examples: A lot of children, a big promotion, winning the lottery, being a hero, etc.

© 2011, CRG Consulting Resource Group International, Inc.

A Holistic Approach to Your Personality Development

You'll notice the three factors in the top half of the model are called Internal Factors; they affect your personality "from within" because they emanate directly from inside your body or mind. The factors in the bottom half are called External Factors; they are more dependent on stimulation from phenomena "from outside" yourself.

These factors represent the different kinds of influences present to some extent in the lives of all human beings, regardless of gender, race, or culture. The strength of the influence coming from factors within each of the categories may vary for each individual.

Let's look at each factor in the model and examine how each influences your personality development and that of others.

Starting from the top-right corner of the model and moving counter-clockwise, the first factor is **Personal Style Preferences**.

Personal Style Preferences

As outlined in detail in the previous chapter, Personal Style defines the naturally occurring preferences people have for engaging with whatever they find in their environment—their unique and consistent ways of reacting to their surroundings. Their preferences are reflected in their various needs, wants, and values.

The origin of these preferences is unclear, but recent scientific research is offering some clues. Based on conclusions drawn from studies of the functions of various parts of the brain, Personal Style may be closely related to different types of information-processing within the brain. Personal Style is observable very early after birth; that suggests our preferences are genetically based.

If indeed Personal Style is natural, then likely it is strongly related to biochemical functioning in the brain.

It should be noted, however, that the question of whether Personal Style is an inherited trait remains open; children often possess styles quite different from the styles of their parents and siblings can have opposite styles. Some research attempts to link Personal Style to birth order, but that cannot easily account for discrepancies, such as why all first-born children don't fit the same patterns.

We do know children reveal a Personal Style that will remain unchanged throughout their lives; the style a person has at age 2 will be evident at age 80.

> **Let us be clear. We are stating that your Personal Style stays consistent throughout your lifetime. That is not necessarily true for your personality.**

Personality is the totality of who you are.

Personal Style is just one part of you—an important part, nevertheless.

We also know that each individual tends to process information (think) in a distinct way. That means that although people see and hear the same information, they may interpret the information differently. Those interpretations are called perceptions.

Let's say you have bought an older home and decide to renovate it. You plan to move some walls, update the cabinets, install new flooring, paint the walls, and replace light fixtures. You are keeping the original outside walls and the same foundation.

The frame and foundation represent your Personal Style—constant and unchanged. The inside changes reflect the constant upgrades created by your beliefs, your experience, your thoughts, your education and learning, the significant events in your life, and so on.

- You were born with the part of your personality we call Personal Style. And your Personal Style does not change over time.

- Other parts of your personality do change, through learning and experience.

> **As a result, your personality has both**
> **flexibility and stability throughout your life.**

Biophysical Influences
In 1988, I was moody and had severe emotional swings. One minute I was motivated and excited, the next I just had to go to bed and sleep. My doctor said I was manic depressive and put me on the antidepressant *lithium*. About a week into treatment, I was ready to crawl right out of my skin—I was irritable and not feeling at all well.

A friend said, "Ken, you don't have a depression problem. It sounds more like a biophysical condition." At my insistence, the doctor conducted a glucose tolerance test (GTT). (After giving you pure sugar to drink, they draw blood every 30 minutes for 6 hours, to measure glucose levels in your bloodstream.)

The test revealed I had extreme hypoglycemia, a blood sugar condition. When I consume sugar, my pancreas does not produce insulin in the correct proportion, which causes all kinds of complications. Because of the wild swings in my blood sugar, my personality became significantly different. It was a biochemical state. It had had nothing to do with depression.

That is a simple illustration of how something can affect our biophysical system and have a big impact on our life. A more serious illustration of the way biophysical influences impact personality is found in the area of addictions. It is proven that heavy and repeated alcohol and/or drug use can be very detrimental to your overall health, even causing brain damage, which can result in permanent personality shifts or changes

Our biophysical influences can cause each of us to engage life differently. In the Biophysical factor, we include any and all biological and physical influences on your personality and on your body that occur during your lifetime.

Even before we are born, factors such as our genetic inheritance from our parents are at work, determining a host of physical characteristics such as our gender, height, and skin color. Any and all biochemical changes that occur within the body fall into the Biophysical category.

Doctors and naturopaths focus most of their attention on the elements of the biophysical factor. Biophysics is the "window" through which they tend to look at personality and behavior. They have strong evidence that the mind-body connection is one of the most important links to understanding human behavior.

Let's say you are a healthy and vibrant person and you get the flu. How differently will you engage the environment? During that period, friends call with an invitation to a party but you decline because you are not up to it; you choose to stay home. Once you recover from the flu, your personality goes back to normal.

Other Elements under **Biophysical** Influences
that Can Influence Personality and Behavior

Genetics	Gender	Stress-Related Illness
Illness	Body Type	Health and Wellness Conditions
Birth Defects	Addictions	Biochemical Imbalances
Allergies	Bodily Malfunctions	Physical and Mental Challenges

Recently, a medical doctor said that in North America, no health care system can support our current lifestyles; we have such poor wellness levels. At the time of this writing, 34% of the population is obese, and over 70% of people are overweight and unfit.

Even if you had a personality that wanted to be active, high energy, and engaging, it would not be possible if you had biophysical conditions that would not permit it. How can a person play sports or be active with his kids if he gets winded simply walking across a room?

Research links cognitive abilities to wellness and weight. People must change their biophysical condition before their can implement other desired changes.

Are any biophysical influences hindering your ability to engage life the way you want? If your answer is Yes, what are those influences costing you in terms of your lifestyle or your quality of life? What are you willing to do about it?

_____

_____

_____

_____

If you would like to find out more about your stress and wellness levels, investigate CRG's **Stress Indicator and Health Planner** assessment. We help you measure your stress and wellness levels using 120 questions in five strategic categories: Personal Distress, Interpersonal Stress, Health and Wellness Stress, Time Stress, and Occupational Stress. To learn more, please go to www.crgleader.com.

Self-Worth Levels

You and I could have a similar Personal Style but, if one of us has high self-worth and the other has low self-worth, we could respond differently to similar events.

- Self-worth is the part of the human personality that determines personal value and importance.

- It is the area of our thinking that evaluates our behavior, appearance, feelings, thoughts, and abilities.

- It outlines both the level of appreciation we have for ourselves and the way we feel about our inherent worth—what we believe we need to be or do to have value as a person.

> **Does it really matter if your sense of personal value**
> **(self-worth) is high or low?**
> **The answer is Yes, absolutely!**

Self-worth is a basic human need that is essential to normal, healthy development. High self-worth helps provide flexibility, strength, and a capacity to regenerate. It relates to increased levels of mental health, life success, and happiness.

Research has shown that individuals with lower self-worth have a lesser ability to contribute to society than people with higher self-worth. Low self-worth undermines all areas of human interaction and diminishes resilience in the face of life's problems. Low self-worth can stunt psychological and emotional growth.

Our level of self-worth is an extremely powerful factor in our personality development and behavior. It represents the important role that our feelings about ourselves play a role in determining aspects of our personality. Our sense of security is linked directly to our level of self-worth.

> **The majority of research overwhelmingly supports the opinion that there are strong overall benefits to having high self-worth.**

Self-worth is not only a source of motivation and personal energy to engage life, it reveals areas of psychological vulnerability. Dr. Nathaniel Branden, author and researcher of *Our Urgent Need for Self-Esteem*, sums up our thoughts in this quote.

> *Self-worth provides the experience of being able to cope with the basic challenges of life and being worthy of happiness. It consists of two components.*
>
> *1. Self-Efficacy: Confidence in our ability to think, learn, choose, and make appropriate decisions*
>
> *2. Self-Respect: Confidence in our right to be happy and the belief that achievement, success, friendship, respect, love, and fulfillment are appropriate to us*

The basic challenges of life include fundamentals such as these.

- The ability to earn a living.
- The ability to take independent care of ourselves in the world.
- The competency to form human relationships that are mutually satisfying.
- The resilience that allows us to bounce back from adversity and persevere in our aspirations.

Most of the research suggests that our self-worth is in constant flux, changing in response to the many dynamics that present themselves in our lives. We never achieve high self-worth permanently; we are always actively re-establishing it during our entire lifetime.

We see a fluctuation of self-worth in individuals who are laid off or fired from long-term positions or when personal relationships fail. In numerous cases, seemingly high self-worth individuals can fall apart.

It is possible to reduce the impact that various events could have on an individual's self-worth levels, if the person understands the situation and has specific approaches for maintaining and increasing self-worth levels.

As self-worth goes up, so does our sense of trust that somehow we can cope with the environment. When it decreases, we lose confidence that we can be successful in our environment.

For instance, a person with a high level of self-worth may overcome a negative environment and become successful, while a person with a lower level of self-worth may fail within positive surroundings.

> **Note that self-worth is learned.**
> **It does not exist at birth.**

In our opinion, most self-worth is a product of nurture, not nature. It develops in us during very early childhood. It is strongly affected during adolescence and adulthood as people and events react to our personalities and behavior.

To some extent, self-worth is developed by factors in all the other categories. It is especially influenced by factors within the social-teacher category. We come to behave toward ourselves in much the same manner that significant others have behaved toward us.

For instance, if parents are persistently critical about what they consider to be failings or imperfections in their children, when the children become adults they may have difficulty appreciating the skills and the attributes that they possess.

If the reactions of significant others are *positive* toward who we are and what we do, our self-worth levels begin to increase and strengthen. If their reactions are *negative*, we can become weaker and our sense of value as a person decreases.

While the foundations of our self-worth can be established as young as age 7 or 8, the fact remains that in the mind, each individual is in a constant state of self-evaluation of his or her worth.

> **The important point to remember is that our self-worth levels are learned and whatever has been learned can be unlearned.**

Note: Personal Style theory can be a major advantage in building self-worth. We have found it affirms individuals about who they are. Thus, they can change their unreasonable or erroneous expectations and simply accept—and be—themselves.

If you would like to learn more about your self-worth levels, consider completing our *Self-Worth Inventory,* which measures self-worth in five categories: Self, Family, Peers, Work, and Projected Self. To learn more, please go to www.crgleader.com.

Environmental Systems

This category includes any form of experiential stimulus we receive from the environment around us—a stimulus that does not belong specifically in any of the other categories. That includes all the general influences we experience in our lives as a result of being members of certain social, cultural, and ethnic groups.

It also refers to any form of environmental stimulus, other than the influence of people who have functioned in some way as significant role models for us. For instance, while a person's whole family unit would be included here, the role played by a specific relative would belong in the social-teacher category.

We are strongly influenced by the environmental systems that surround us as we grow up. The first such system is our family of origin—the family unit in which we are raised from birth to young adulthood.

In looking into the environmental-systems category, I am interested in how my personality was affected by my exposure to, as well as my observations of, the interactions of my family.

Children are often the family's audience. Much of our childhood time is spent watching what is occurring within the family unit, rather than actively participating in it.

Within that category, we are interested in information such as how Mom and Dad communicated, problem-solved, argued, made up after an argument, showed affection, discussed sexual issues, and took vacations.

Also important are other interactions within the family, such as how an older brother got along with Mom, a younger sister with Grandpa, or Dad with his in-laws. All those kinds of everyday family interactions created an environment that shaped our perceptions of, and attitudes toward, family life and—more important—life in general.

The fact that over half of marriages end in divorce has fragmented families, leaving a negative environmental experience for many children.

Other environmental systems include schools you have attended, towns or cities where you lived, the countryside where you grew up, the society and cultures that influenced you, military service, and associations and organizations to which you belonged.

Even climate conditions and acts of nature can have an impact on the way you look at life. Climate can affect you and your responses. It is well known in long-night northern winters that many people suffer from seasonal affective disorder (SAD). They need exposure to sunlight for a certain length of time each day or they start to feel lethargic, moody, and depressed.

What about growing up in a war-torn area or a place of high civil conflict? That certainly will affect your perceptions and responses and shape your thinking, compared to being raised in a peaceful area.

Every day, there are, on average, 50 different armed conflicts going on in the world. Those who survive the experience are usually strongly affected by the violence and the horrifying conditions they have witnessed. Often, their personalities and behavior reveal major shifts as a result of exposure to war, evident in many of the soldiers who served in active duty in the various theaters of engagement.

The following factors are examples of Environmental Systems.

Families of Origin	Step Families	Foster Families
School Systems	Places of Work	Geographic Settings
Organizations	Climatic Conditions	Communities
Natural Catastrophes	Religious Groups	Cult Groups
Cultures	Military Service	

Social Teachers

I grew up on a dairy farm and was taught to work hard. Taking time off was a treat. My parents like to tell me they worked 14 years without a single day off. When I went back to the farm after college and wanted to have a couple of weekends to myself each month, they quickly adjusted my work schedule to 2 half-days a month.

As one of my early employers, my parents taught me that hard work comes first and there is little time for play. In every position I have held since, I have put 100% into my efforts—no matter the working conditions or the pay being offered. The work ethic was instilled into my mind long ago as an important value.

Social Teachers are the people we imitate . . . anyone who has had a direct or indirect influence on the way we currently perceive, approach, or interact with the environment. Those influences can be positive or negative. For instance, copying the conduct of social teachers has been shown to influence a broad range of behavior, from aggressiveness in children to the way children reward their own performances.

This social learning process is called modeling. We use other people as role models and develop an understanding of which behavior is desirable and which should be avoided.

Frequently, the learning occurs indirectly and often without our being aware of it.

> **Much of the way we behave on a daily basis is learned from watching and imitating other people's behavior.**

The American Academy of Pediatrics (AAP: www.aap.org) confirmed that a child's input reflects his or her output. Social teachers can be video games, social media, music, and the like. Exposure to media violence through television, movies, music, and video games can contribute to a variety of physical and mental health problems for children and adolescents, including desensitization to violence and aggressive behavior, nightmares, fear, and depression. Here is their statement.

American Academy of Pediatrics

Music plays an important role in the socialization of children and adolescents. Popular music is present almost everywhere, and it is easily available through the radio, various recordings, the

Internet, and new technologies, allowing adolescents to hear it in diverse settings and situations, alone or shared with friends.

Parents often are unaware of the lyrics to which their children are listening because of the increasing use of downloaded music and headphones. Research on popular music has explored its effects on schoolwork, social interactions, mood, and effect, and particularly behavior.

The effect that popular music has on the behavior and the emotions of children and adolescents is of paramount concern. Lyrics have become more explicit in their references to drugs, sex, and violence over the years, particularly in certain genres. A teenager's preference for certain types of music could be correlated or associated with certain behaviors.

As with popular music, the perception and the effect of music-video messages are important, because research has reported that exposure to violence, sexual messages, sexual stereotypes, and use of substances of abuse in music videos might produce significant changes in behaviors and attitudes of young viewers. Pediatricians and parents should be aware of this information.

Furthermore, with the evidence portrayed in these studies, it is essential for pediatricians and parents to take a stand regarding video content and music lyrics.

Input Equals Output

The social-teacher category includes the people who raised us from birth—in most cases, our parents. It includes other family members with whom we frequently came into contact, especially those who are older than we are. That would include all our peers while growing up and other significant individuals such as teachers, pastors, and athletic coaches.

Even media personalities, historical figures, authors, sports celebrities, and movie stars might be included in that category, if they had a significant impact on our thinking and behavior.

A list of social teachers who might have had some lasting impact upon our thinking, personality, and behavior include the following.

Parents	In-Laws	Girlfriends
Brothers	School Teachers	Boyfriends
Sisters	Coaches	Actors
Grandparents	Friends	Rock Stars
Aunts	Peers	Supervisors
Uncles	Neighbors	Authors
Cousins	Religious Leaders	Artists

> **Even today, your values are being shaped and influenced by the input you are allowing into your space and mind.**

It's time to be brutally honest with yourself.

Who are you allowing as input or social teachers for yourself and/or your family?

- What kind of books or magazines did you buy—if any—last month? Are they positive and educational or frivolous, like *People* magazine and the *National Inquirer*?

- If I looked at your library, what would I find?

- What about other media—TV, music, DVDs, movies? What was the content? How much time did you spend in each of those media? North Americans watch 5+ hours of TV a day. That's a lot of input.

- If you have children, what input are you allowing them to absorb?

What about family and friends? Can you educate them on the impact of the input they are allowing into their lives?

Even if both of us have identical Personal Style preferences, we can have different values because of our social teachers. One of us could be a police officer, the other a criminal.

Emotional Anchors

This category consists of any experience that has in some way caused us a strong emotional recall or response—positive or negative. After a major event shocks or affects our systems, we are never the same again. The memory of it penetrates beyond our reasoning into our subconscious and leaves us "different" from who we were before the event happened.

Here's a recollection of mine . . . it was almost my very last act.

Growing up on the dairy farm, we were always conscious of safety around farm equipment. My father was harvesting silage—cutting grass for winter storage.

One day after school, I hitched a ride in one of the silage wagons that had chains and sharp spikes **for unloading** the silage (feed for cattle) at the storage location. The driver pulled the silage wagon up to a powerful blower that threw silage six storeys high. In the process, he had forgotten I was in the silage wagon. He had already turned on the belt that fed the blower and was about to turn on the silage wagon. I knew I had to get out of the wagon or I would be injured or killed.

As I jumped out, I slipped onto the conveyer belt that fed into the blower. I was 2 seconds away from death when a hired hand pulled me off the belt. Needless to say, I never rode inside another silage wagon.

That experience is an emotional anchor for me. It has made me extremely safety conscious and cautious around any type of equipment. Just ask my kids. My three favorite words are safety, safety, and safety.

Emotional experiences may not start out negatively, but they can end up that way. For example, a woman who gives birth to triplets may be overjoyed at first, but due to the extra amount of work involved in taking care of three infants, she might end up feeling quite resentful because she has no time to herself. While she loves each one of the children, the overall experience has become an emotional anchor.

Notice I said *might* end up feeling resentful. The same experience may not have the same effect on another individual. For instance, one person who has been in a very serious auto accident may be emotionally scarred for life, whereas another person may quickly get over the accident and still enjoy driving.

A few years ago, a firefighter saved a 5-year-old who had fallen into an old abandoned well. That seemingly simple act of courage turned into a disaster for the firefighter.

As media outlets from around the world called to interview him, he began to get attached to the attention. Before long, his attitude (ego) toward his colleagues became too hard to handle and he was fired from his position. Even his family abandoned him, leaving him with nothing. A seemingly positive event turned into a negative emotional anchor.

> **An emotional anchor is any event or memory that causes a strong emotional response—positive or negative.**

As a teen, I was very involved in the youth 4-H program. At 16, I earned a trip to Toronto for the national conference and was selected to speak to over 400 delegates and sponsors at the awards banquet. I vividly recall the nerves and the excitement I felt! After that experience, I knew I wanted to be a speaker and a communicator to large groups. That is a strong and positive emotional anchor for me.

The main point is that after we have an intense emotional experience, our personalities and behavior can change in some way; we do not remain the same.

Are you aware of how you have been affected by your experiences?

Examples of Emotional Anchors

Negative possibilities: Divorce, physical abuse, death of a loved one, failure, moving, job loss, natural catastrophes

Positive possibilities: Raising a lot of children, a promotion to your dream job with much more responsibility, winning the lottery and being unable to manage your new-found wealth, becoming a hero

Each individual will respond uniquely to events. Some will be traumatized; others will not. Don't try to judge a situation's impact on another person by the way those experiences might affect you.

Spirituality

In the Personality Development Factors Model, in the center you will notice the facial profile of a person. Beside the profile, the word Spirituality is written many times. Spirituality is part of our model because we recognize that a person's beliefs and spiritual perspective highly influence behavior, choices, values, and life satisfaction.

> **In the end, each person will make his or her own choice about Spirituality. People should be respected on their spiritual journey.**

Spirituality can be a sensitive issue for some people but there is no way to avoid the subject. If we don't mention it, we deny each other access to answers that will bring resolution to our true *purpose* in life—and the base for everything we are and do.

In our Personality Development Factors Model, we are not talking about the humanistic, watered-down version of Spirituality that typically refers to unspecific beliefs. We are referring to the foundational beliefs on which our lives exist and function. That is the deepest level of awareness we can seek to achieve.

Here is the reality. Confirming and determining your true calling and *purpose* in your life includes going on a personal quest to find answers about your Spirituality!

- Are human beings Spiritual? How can we know?

- If we are Spiritual, what does that mean? What is the truth on the subject?

- How can I tell spiritual truth from falsehood?

- Does God exist? Who or what is God?

Those questions and the answers you find will help expand, confirm, or challenge your thinking about your Spirituality. The truth will set you free—only if you seek to know it. Approaching the subject with an investigative, inquisitive mindset is important to the process. Of course in the end, you will make your own personal choice.

Our lives operate under natural laws and truths. Regardless of our opinions about those laws, the laws do not change.

One example is gravity. It exists even if we don't understand or accept it. When people believed the world was flat, their collective opinion did not make it so. The principle of natural law applies equally to Spirituality. Our focus should be on discovering Spiritual truth, not in creating it, because no one can create Spiritual truth—just as no one can create gravity.

A study was released about the factors that most influenced the happiness (lack of worry) and fulfillment of 8-to-12 year olds. Contrary to the researchers' premise, happiness and fulfillment were not always present in a two-parent family, with higher income levels and physical health. The happiest kids had faith in God.

Children with faith were the most content and the best adjusted. Their faith was even more important than the number of parents raising them.

Their spirituality provided hope, grounding, and well-being beyond their circumstances.

All individuals should be respected in their spiritual search process. Each journey is intensely personal, even though the destination is the same—to arrive at a place of Spiritual Truth.

We include Spirituality as part of our Personality Development Factors Model because your beliefs highly influence your choices and success in life.

So . . . what about you? If you are going to understand self and others, the core of your spirituality matters—and matters deeply—to your inner peace, your fulfillment, and your ability to positively impact others.

If you want to learn more about this subject, I have written extended comments and my personal spiritual journey at www.crgleader.com. Search for the *Living On Purpose* ezine, Issue 129.

> **No single Personality Development Factor is more important than another in determining personality and behavior.**

In real life, any category can override or dominate any or all the other categories at any given time, in any given situation.

When one category dominates the others, the others simply don't go away. They are still there and can be used to assist a person to increase his or her current level of self-management.

People are complex and diverse individuals made up of a lot of different factors. The **Personality Development Factors Model** acknowledges that each of us could have identical Personal Style preferences, yet we could be quite different individuals, given all the other factors that have influenced—and are currently influencing—our personality.

CHAPTER 4

What Is Your Personal Style?

There is something about each person, a pervasive style that applies to almost everything he does . . .

Probably it is not just one isolated behavior here or there that gives us an impression, but rather a composite of behaviors that are indicative of a certain style.

ALBERT MEHRABIAN

As far back as I can remember, my parents considered me *different*. Although I know my father loved me, I often felt he wanted me to be someone other than the person I was born to be.

When I was only 9 or 10, he would tell me I talked too much. I know he did the best he could with what he knew, but his negative pronouncements did not encourage me. I started to wonder if there was something wrong with me.

Can you relate to times when others did not accept your way of being and wanted to change you as a person? How did that make you feel?

Perhaps you are the one who does not accept people who are different than you are. Do you want others to think and act the way you do?

Whatever your viewpoint, you will discover your unique Personal Style in this chapter.

An Online **Personal Style Indicator *(PSI)*** assessment is included with the purchase of this book so you can experience the power of self-awareness firsthand. I recommend that you complete it now, before you read the remainder of the book.

If you are unable to complete the **Online *PSI*** at this moment, please continue reading. You can link the information to your Personal Style at another time.

You will need a computer with Internet access and a Web browser. A

56K dialup modem will work, but it will be slow. If you can access the Internet at high speed, you will have a much more enjoyable experience.

Please go to www.whyarentyoumorelikeme.com and click on the icon to redeem your free Online *PSI*. You will be required to create an online learning account so we can link your results to you. Please follow the directions to insert the pass code you will find on the inside back cover of this book. You will need this book during the login and verification process to access and complete your Online *Personal Style Indicator* assessment. The code included with this book is for a single-use only. It is not transferable to others.

The *PSI* is not a test. You cannot fail.

There are no right or wrong responses. It typically takes about 10 minutes to complete the assessment questions. All your results are private. If you wish, you may email your completed assessment to others.

When I completed my first *Personal Style Indicator* over 20 years ago, I finally began to understand my differences and to accept me for who I am. Compared to other assessments I had completed, I liked the simple design of the *PSI* and the way it addressed such a complex subject—me!

I found the *PSI* more accurate and clear than any other assessment I had taken, including the MBTI, DiSC, and the silly assessments based on animals and colors. Quite frankly, I never could relate to the results any of the other assessments produced for me.

As I mentioned earlier, can you recall a time when you have walked into a room and immediately had a connection with someone you had never met before? What about the opposite situation? You meet someone for the first time and something about him or her makes your skin crawl. What is creating those responses to two strangers?

Our personalities are made up of many factors. Our Personal Style, however, strongly drives our perceptions and our connections with others. You will have more chemistry with someone who is similar to you in terms of your preferences and the way you like to interact with the world.

Perhaps the person with whom you don't have chemistry has different preferences than you have, hence the disconnect.

Why is that?

To **really** understand yourself and others, you must be aware of the meaning of Personal Style and that each style dimension has predictive qualities and characteristics. None is better than another. They are simply different. Those differences, however, can lead to conflict, miscommunication, and strife, all which can be eliminated or at least reduced when you understand the essence of Personal Style.

The CRG process uses a four dimension (quadrant) model. We each possess a blend of all four dimensions in various intensities. Your response to the online word list will help you determine the degree to which each dimension is influencing your perceptions of life and your environment.

The blends are called style patterns; each pattern has its own uniqueness. Before I describe the dynamics of CRG's proprietary style model and the way it relates to the 21 style patterns, first we must grasp each dimension in its purest sense.

Imagine I have two glasses of water on the table in front of me. One contains cold water and the other contains hot water. In one large glass, I combine the two glasses of water. Now I have created a glass of warm water.

The CRG style model is similar to that example. To understand your style pattern(s), you must understand the characteristics and qualities of the hot and the cold water or, in the case of CRG's Personal Style, the pure characteristics of each of our four dimensions before they are blended.

Each of the four dimensions has its own influence on the way we view, interact, and behave as individuals. For the most part, the result is not right or wrong . . . just different.

The Four Dimensions

- **Behavioral ACTION**
- **Cognitive ANALYSIS**
- **Interpersonal HARMONY**
- **Affective EXPERSSION**

We each have all four dimensions in different intensities; the intensities of each dimension combine to create your unique style pattern or patterns. As I outline the characteristics and qualities of each dimension, you might identify with some of the comments.

As you read through each dimension, take a moment to highlight the statements you believe to be true about yourself.

I ask that you be completely honest in this process. If you see a statement that reflects your preferences but you don't care for the comment, be real and highlight it anyway.

While you are reviewing and highlighting the qualities of each dimension, are there statements that you are not highlighting for yourself—but that you *would* highlight for others you know well? That is the first step to understanding people who are different than you are.

> **We are giving you permission to tell the PSI who you are,**
> **not the other way around.**

Our approach is designed for you, the learner. That is the reverse of many of the assessment options in the marketplace that are structured for the test-giver.

> **Note:** If you have already completed your Online *Personal Style Indicator*, you have the option to print your report and complete this exercise on the report, rather than in this book.

Now please read through these dimension summaries and highlight what you believe to be true about yourself. If you have your scores from the online assessment, transfer them into the respective box of each dimension. You will be using your scores several times throughout the process. Please keep them handy.

Behavioral ACTION   Your Score

Individuals who score higher in the **Behavioral** ACTION (**B**) dimension like to set goals, accomplish predetermined plans, and be in control of what is going on around them. The **Behavioral** dimension frequently motivates a person to take on larger responsibilities, make quick decisions, and focus on future developments.

This dimension is the source for strategic thinking and action-oriented behavior. These individuals prefer to work alone and can have a strong tendency toward being independent.

Physical energy is a main characteristic of a **B** style. They often perform activities that require hard work and endurance. The **B** style likes challenge and often prefers jobs or hobbies that require some risk-taking.

Behavioral ACTION Tendencies
Facial expressions: Hard to read
Emotions not shown easily or often
Impatient with loss of time and delays
Energy experience: Forceful, powerful, aloof
Very active physically; like doing many things
Fast decision-makers; no hesitation
Hard workers; work long hours; expect the same from others
Silent types; don't talk much

Behavioral ACTION

General Orientation
To tasks:	*Want results now*
To people:	*Seek authority*
To problems:	*Are tactical, strategic*
To stress:	*Double their efforts*
To time:	*Future and present*

Typical Strengths
Act rapidly to get results
Are inventive and productive
Show endurance under stress
Are driven to achieve goals
Can boldly assume authority

Common Difficulties
Can be too forceful or impatient
Can often think their way is best
Can be insensitive to others
Can be manipulative or coercive
Can be lonely or fatigued

Cognitive ANALYSIS   Your Score

A high **Cognitive** ANALYSIS (**C**) score suggests individuals prefer analytical thinking and problem-solving because mental energy is a key characteristic of **Cognitive** styles. They prefer to think rather than do, and tend to constantly question and judge whatever is going on around them.

This dimension influences them to evaluate critically any part of the environment around them, including people. They often appear outspoken or critical, and like to give advice. The **Cognitive** dimension motivates them to be organized and systematic when interacting in the environment.

They have good perception and an ability to think deeply about things. **Cs** like to interact with one person at a time, rather than with a group of people. They are usually very verbal, but only when feeling confident about the situation.

Cognitive ANALYSIS Tendencies
Facial expressions: Obvious, such as frowning
Show anger quickly; tend to hold grudges
Value being on time; expect same of others
Energy experience: Nervous, talk fast
Verbal challengers; critical and opinionated
Mentally active; very perceptive; "thinkers"
Work 9 to 5, then leave for home
Loyal employees; good systems-builders

Cognitive ANALYSIS

General Orientation
To tasks:	*Want quality*
To people:	*Seek security*
To problems:	*Analyze data*
To stress:	*Withdraw*
To time:	*Past and future*

Typical Strengths
Act cautiously to avoid errors
Engage in critical analysis
Seek to create a low-stress climate
Want to ensure quality control
Can follow directives and standards

Common Difficulties
Can bog down in details and lose time
Can be too critical or finicky
Can be overly sensitive to feedback
Can seem to be lacking in courage
Can be too self-sufficient, alone

Interpersonal HARMONY   Your Score

A high **Interpersonal** HARMONY (**I**) score represents practical thinking and social harmony behavior. This dimension motivates individuals
to care about others and helps them work in a consistent and reliable
manner with others. They are very good team players.

A significant characteristic of the **Interpersonal** dimension is emotional
energy, which influences their sensitivity about what others think and
say—sometimes overly so. They tend to put others before themselves,
even when that causes them discomfort.

Because they are oriented toward caring for others, they prefer jobs
where they can serve others. Non-assertive behavior is the primary
characteristic of the **Interpersonal** Style. For example, they can have
difficulty expressing their feelings or opinions in conflict situations.

Even though the **I** will put others before herself, she tends to be shy
around people and prefers not to have group attention placed on her;
she works best with others when the focus is not on her.

Interpersonal HARMONY Tendencies
Facial expressions: Small smiles, attentive
Quiet; do not talk often or for long; shy
Very patient with others; forgiving
Energy experience: Gentle, kind, calm, placid
Consistent workers; steady, not fast
Get very stressed in conflict situations
Don't talk much but love to listen to others
Make decisions slowly; need time

Interpersonal HARMONY
General Orientation
To tasks:	*Are reliable performers*
To people:	*Seek to help others*
To problems:	*Want practical solutions*
To stress:	*Adjust to it*
To time:	*Present*

Typical Strengths
Promote harmony and balance
Are reliable and consistent
Try to adapt to stress
See the obvious that others miss
Are often easygoing and warm

Common Difficulties
Can be too easygoing and accepting
Can allow others to take advantage
Can become bitter if unappreciated
Can be low in self-worth
Can be too dependent on others

Affective EXPRESSION   Your Score

They are creative thinkers and therefore exhibit many expressive types of behavior. Imaginative energy characterizes **Affective** EXPRESSION **(A)** types and influences the **A** tendencies and abilities to express themselves.

They represent the most social of the four character styles (dimensions). **Affective** people love to talk about anything and everything. Although they are very accepting of others, regardless of others' different qualities or lifestyles, they like to influence others through creative ideas and activities. The **A** person will move away quickly from any source of negativity about those creative endeavors.

As eternal optimists and dreamers, they require positive energy from the individuals around them. When people or situations restrain the fulfillment of their needs, especially their need to be free from routine, they will bring their power of influence to bear on the problem, attempting to sway others' thoughts and feelings, or they will change the environment.

Affective EXPRESSION Tendencies

Facial expressions: Big smiles, laughing
Very verbal; talk to everyone; often loud
Trouble keeping time commitments
Energy experience: Creative, funny, upbeat
Lots of ideas for changing, improving
Overpromise and underdeliver
Trouble focusing on one thing for long
Learn experientially; not auditory (ear)

Affective EXPRESSION

General Orientation

To tasks:	*Put people first*
To people:	*Seek to influence*
To problems:	*Are intuitive and creative*
To stress:	*Escape from it*
To time:	*Present and future*

Typical Strengths

Act creatively on intuition
Are sensitive to others' feelings
Are resilient in times of stress
Develop a network of contacts
Are often willing to help others

Common Difficulties

Can lose track of time
Can "overburn" and overindulge
Can be too talkative
Can lose objectivity, be emotional
Can be self-oriented and overly
self-assured

We are starting to create an awareness in you about your Personal Style preferences and the preferences of others who might be different than you are. Without this style information, only 2% of the population has optimized their potential.

The Intensity of Influence

If you completed the **Online *PSI*** and transferred your scores, here is what the numbers mean in terms of influences on your perceptions. You should have found that your highest scores have the most highlights and your lowest scores have the fewest. The higher the score, the more that dimension is influencing your perceptions and preferences in life.

- If you have a dimension with a score of less than 30 (it can be as low as 16), this dimension has a **weak** influence on you; you really do not like to engage life using this dimension. It doesn't mean you can't operate from the dimension but it does not come naturally or comfortably to you.

- If you have a score between 30 and 39, this dimension has a **moderate** influence on the way you perceive and interact with your environment. Obviously, if you are closer to 39 than 30, you are High Moderate. In that case, you are able to operate from this dimension, but typically only in lower stress conditions.

- If you have a score between 40 and 49, this dimension has a **strong** influence on the way you see and connect with your environment. We could say that on a day-to-day basis, you more than likely will use this dimension to make decisions about your life, judge others, and give credibility to behavior that models this dimension.

- If you have a dimension with a score over 50, up to 64, this dimension has a **very strong** influence on the way you see and interact with your environment. I can say with certainty that you would use this dimension to engage your life. We can almost guarantee that you will take this dimension wherever you go, into all your activities and relationships.

> **Most of us are a blend or combination of more than one dimension; those combinations are called style patterns.**

The understanding of the way each dimension functions is critical to your understanding of the power of Personal Style in all areas of *your* life and the life of every single person you engage. Learning how each dimension operates in its purest form is critical to your observational skills.

As part of our "Building Relationships With Style" seminars and our **Assessment Systems Certification** Workshops, where we teach others to teach the *PSI*, we ask people with the same highest dimension to sit together.

I ask the members of each group to respond to four simple questions.

1. What are your style-related strengths?

2. What are your style-related challenges?

3. What could you do to increase your effectiveness personally, professionally, and with others?

4. What pet peeves (behavior that annoys you) do you have regarding others' styles?

> **People are constantly telling us what they prefer and want, but many of us are not paying attention.**

Almost immediately after I divide the group into their style corrals, the tendencies of each of the dimensions manifest within the dynamic of each group.

The **Behavioral** ACTION group gets straight to it, with very little language or talking among themselves. In fact, they are irritated by the silly group activity where I get them to report their findings on a flipchart. There is little emotional interchange; they are focused on the task to complete the assignment.

When it comes to the question about challenges, they don't think they have many. Their response to question 4 almost always includes frustrations with people who are too slow in making a decision, too talkative, too sensitive and touchy-feely, and of course too detail-oriented.

The members of the **Cognitive** ANALYSIS group carefully review the directions of the exercise and the questions, then plan their discussion. They want to do a quality job on their report. They also have very little emotional interchange as part of their process; they are task-focused.

They usually have a long list of style-related strengths and sometimes struggle with listing their challenges.

Their pet peeves typically include exasperation with individuals who lack attention to detail in all areas of life, from reports at work to the way their teenager cleaned up his room. They don't like domineering, pushy, or loud individuals and certainly are not interested in how emotions or feelings might play a part in getting things done.

The members of the **Interpersonal** HARMONY group engage each other carefully with sensitivity. In fact, many times they are all looking at each other to start the discussion because they are deferring to each other.

They ensure everyone is comfortable before they begin the discussion or move ahead. Their discussions are thoughtful; they try to include everyone in the conversation even though this style prefers one-on-one activities, not group work.

I witness hesitation by many participants who are quite willing to stand back and let others speak. Their pet peeves always include critical or domineering individuals, whom they abhor. They also don't like individuals who are focused on themselves and who appear to be self-centered. The one development factor mentioned by every **Interpersonal** HARMONY group I have facilitated is to increase their assertiveness.

The members of the **Affective** EXPRESSION group move to a location in the room, then proceed to talk to each other about just about anything. It may be 5 minutes into the activity before someone says *What we were supposed to do?* They are completely oblivious to time and the task at hand.

Typically, this group is the loudest, engaging with passion and high person-to-person energy. One of the items always on "the improve list" for this group is the challenge of overpromising and underdelivering. They are eternal optimists.

Because life rarely lines up perfectly the way they had envisioned it, they can let others down by not keeping their promises. They don't appreciate people who are boring, too serious, and no fun and individuals who can't make up their minds or who are bullies.

Every single person you have met and ever will meet has a Personal Style. In each and every interchange, they leave clues about who they are and what they prefer in their interaction with you.

Each of us is doing the same thing, whether we know it or not. Knowledge of Personal Style helps create that critical awareness of self and others, so you can be intentional in your choices and your life.

By now, you may be noticing that each style dimension has its own related strengths and challenges. To function as a society, we need each style present to achieve the varied tasks and relationships required for true success.

In the next chapter, I will take you into your style pattern and the implications of the way style dimensions blend together to create your unique pattern or patterns.

> *With a good heredity, nature deals you a fine hand at cards, and with a good environment, you learn to play the hand well.*
>
> WALTER C. ALVAREZ, MD

Personal Exercise

What did you find out about yourself and others?

Did you have a dimension where you highlighted most of the comments and another where you highlighted almost nothing?

While doing that exercise, did you think of a person for whom you would have highlighted most of the comments in a specific dimension but hardly any for yourself?

What insights did you have regarding your style?

How is your style influencing the way you see and perceive the environment around you?

Take a moment to list any insights you gained about yourself and others, as you reviewed the information.

_____

_____

_____

_____

CHAPTER 5

Going Deeper: What Is Your Style Pattern?

All the problems of the world could be settled easily
if people were only willing to think. The trouble is that
people often resort to all sorts of devices in order not
to think, because thinking is such hard work.

THOMAS J. WATSON

Is One Style or Style Pattern Better than Another?

The answer is NO! Each style and style pattern have their own strengths and weaknesses, but not everyone sees it that way. In many instances, society, culture, parents, and organizations want us to change to match what they want from us, rather than acknowledging our personal uniqueness and what we can contribute.

I recall conducting an executive briefing for a local university about the power and merits of having every student and faculty member complete the ***Personal Style Indicator*** as part of establishing an empowered culture. When we stated that every style and style pattern is okay and that each person should be honored for the individual he or she is, one woman broke down in tears, deeply emotionally touched.

During the break, I had a chance to have a private conversation with her. She had just joined the team at the university and was ready to start her new professorship. She had recently emigrated from an Asian country where for 50 years, her culture told her to be someone she was not.

Although her style pattern was very forthright and bold, her previous culture had not embraced equality for women. Thus, for her whole life, her true self was denied and oppressed. **Finally**, in this new environment, she had the freedom to be accepted for who she was. That is what created a strong emotional release for her.

In my experience of working with thousands and thousands of individuals, if the lives they are leading—at work, at play, and in general—do not reflect their unique style patterns, they cannot live fulfilling lives.

> **No style dimension is better than another.**
> **It is simply different!**

The *Personal Style Indicator* provides you with an organized view of the way you perceive yourself, while revealing the likely consequences of your style.

As you become more keenly aware of the consequences, you can plan to develop greater style-flexibility to increase effectiveness at home, at work, or at play. The behavior exhibited by your style varies somewhat from person to person and situation to situation. For the most part and for most people, behavior remains consistent over time.

The general pattern you exhibit is unique and distinct from the patterns of most other people. Gaining deeper understanding of the four style dimensions will help you appreciate the characteristics of each of the styles. You can apply the knowledge later, when you want to adjust your style to be more effective and to build credibility with others.

Even though each style has its strengths, it also can have related challenges. Those challenges can contribute to conflict with self and others.

The Power of Your Style Pattern

A reminder, that we all have all four dimensions in varying intensities.

- The higher the score in any dimension, the greater the influence that dimension has on you and the way that you perceive, approach, and interact with the environment.

- The lower the score, the less influence that dimension will have with you.

> **Each style pattern has its own unique qualities and characteristics.**

Let's say both of us have the highest score of 55 for **Behavioral** ACTION. You have a second-highest score of 45 in the **Interpersonal** HARMONY dimension and I have a second-highest score of 45 in the **Affective** EXPRESSION dimension.

Even though we share the same highest score, we are completely different in our style perceptions because of the influence of the second-highest score. We will have a much different approach to the environment because our style patterns are not the same.

Identifying Your Style Patterns

In CRG's *PSI*, there are 21 possible combinations or patterns.

Everyone has a Primary style pattern, which is calculated by using all your scores that are 40 and above. If you completed the **Online** *PSI*, your score was automatically computed for you.

The Primary style pattern is identified by the highest score first. For example, the following bar graph denotes a person with scores of **B**55, **A**45, **C**35, and **I**25, and the Primary style pattern of **BA.** Why? **B** is highest, then **A**.

Please note: A **BA** pattern is not the same as an **AB** pattern, even though the same two alphabetical letters are present.

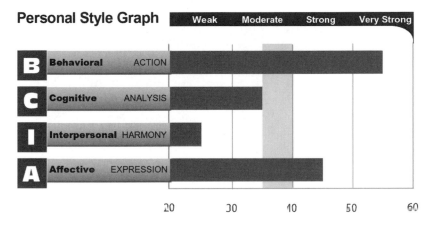

Sometimes it is possible for a person to have two Primary patterns. That is possible when two dimensions over 40 are within 5 points or less of each other. In that case, we could interchange the letters and provide respondents with two Primary style patterns.

We do this so you have permission to tell the instrument (the *PSI*) who you are, not the other way around! Because the scores are so close, only you can determine the part of each detailed description that best fits for you. This approach reduces or eliminates feeling boxed in by comments and statements that might not resonate for you.

In the following example, the person has scores of **B**30, **C**50, **I**52, and **A**28. The person would read both the **IC** and **CI** patterns.

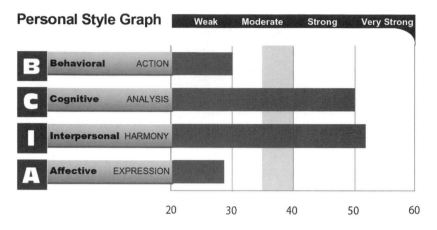

Determining Whether You Have a Secondary Pattern

You might have noticed the shaded area between the numbers 35 and 39 on the bar graph. Not everyone has a Secondary pattern. If you don't have any scores from 35 to 39, you will not have a Secondary pattern. And that's okay. Don't worry if you don't have one.

The Primary pattern includes all your scores 40 and above; a Secondary pattern includes **all** your scores 35 and above. In the previous Primary pattern example, the individual's scores were **B**55, **A**45, **C**35, and **I**25.

This person does have a Secondary pattern because of the **C** score of 35. Thus, the person's Primary pattern is **BA** and the Secondary pattern is **BAC**.

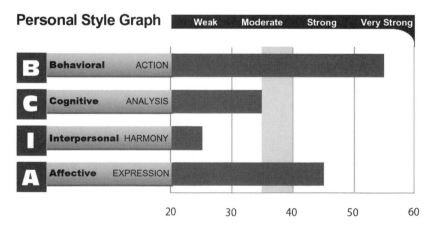

Knowing the Primary and Secondary style patterns of ourselves and others is an important step to being more intentional in all our actions with ourselves and others.

You might have begun to notice that your style pattern or the patterns of others have opposites within them. One part of you is task-driven, yet another part likes people. That can result in internal dialogue where you are uncertain about the right course of action or your preferred course. That is why looking at the combination of your scores over 40 or 35 (style patterns) is so important; the styles combine to create your unique preferences and perspectives.

Style-Flexibility of Different Patterns

One-High Pattern

In this example, only one score is over 40; the other three are below 40. Typically, one dimension is 15 to 20 points higher than the next-closest score.

In the example of **B**34, **C**34, **I**62, and **A**30, the **I** dominates the other three dimensions.

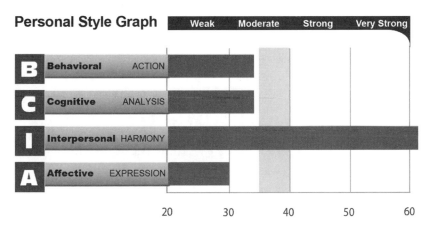

The benefit of that type of pattern is that you can count on the individuals to be very consistent. For the most part, only one dimension is influencing the way they approach and interact with the environment. Even in different environments—at home, at work, or at play—the individuals will behave in much the same way.

Although One-High individuals have great consistency, they are not very flexible. They find it a challenge to shift from their highest dimension. They can operate from the other dimensions but, because of the way they are hard-wired, it is difficult for them to do that. About 10% of the population falls into the One-High pattern.

Two-High Patterns

In this example, two scores are over 40. The two dimensions dominate the weaker dimensions and have the strongest influence on the personality.

In the example of **B**30, **C**30, **I**45, and **A**55, the **A** and **I** dominate the other two dimensions **B** and **C**.

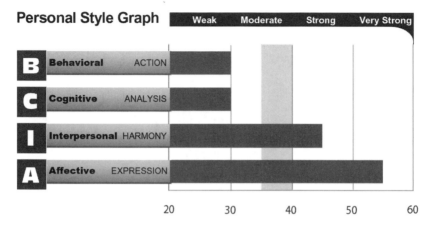

People with these types of patterns demonstrate flexibility between their two higher dimensions; they can "shift" or move from one dimension to the other very quickly. They are not as flexible, however, when moving between their two lower dimensions.

The majority of individuals—around 60% of the population—have a Two-High pattern; they score high in two dimensions and low in two dimensions.

Three-High Patterns (Triple-High)

This is where three scores are 40 or higher. Those three dimensions rule over the fourth dimension and have the most influence on the personality.

In this example of **B**30, **C**42, **I**45, and **A**43, the **CI** and **A** are influencing the individual more than the **B** dimension is.

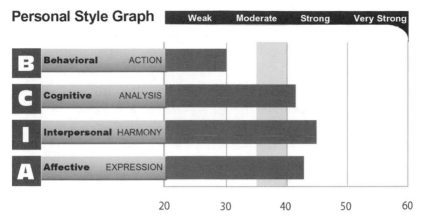

People with these types of patterns have inherent style-flexibility; they can quickly "shift" among their three strongest dimensions. They can respond to a lot of diversity in their life and role without creating stress. They often demonstrate different—and sometimes seemly quite opposite—behavior. About 25% of the population has a Triple-High pattern.

Note: When three dimensions are over 40, the order of the letters no longer matters because the reports are written to reflect a balance among the three highest dimensions. That is different than the Two-High patterns, where the order of the letters is very important.

Four-Even Scores

In this scenario, all four scores are very close (within 4 points of each other) or exactly at the midline: 40-40-40-40.

Note: It is also possible to have a Secondary Pattern that includes all four dimensions when all scores are above 35.

In this example of **B**38, **C**42, **I**41, and **A**39, all four dimensions are within 4 points of each other.

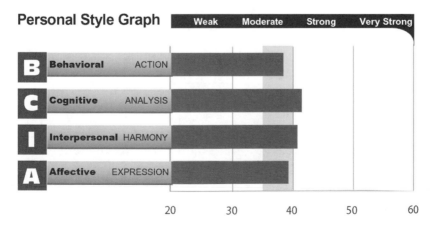

People with this type of pattern have the greatest level of "natural" style-flexibility because the intensity level in each of their dimensions is high enough to match anyone else's highest dimension; therefore, they can understand the way others perceive things.

They often get along with most others but there is one person with whom they may have the most difficulty—themselves!

Imagine that four horses are pulling on a heavy metal ring. That's what the Four-Even pattern feels like, many times to the complete frustration of the person.

- Each dimension is equally trying to influence what the person will say and do.

- Each dimension is equally influencing the way the person perceives the environment, yet each dimension sees the environment through a completely different perspective.

When these individuals learn behavioral context and are able to discern which dimension is needed at any given moment to get the results they want, they are extremely effective. In the **PSI**, about 5% of the population fits into what we call the Synergistic or Four-Even pattern.

Here is a very important point about style patterns. If you add all the pattern percentages together except the One-High, what percentage of the population as a whole has two or more dimensions that influence their perceptions?

About 90% of the population has a style pattern of Two-High, Three-High, or Four-Even. Even more dramatic is the fact that 30% of the population has a Triple-High or Four-Even pattern.

Remember my hot water/cold water example? Combining glasses of hot and cold water created warm water.

Reminder: Patterns where only 1 of the 4 dimensions in the purest form (hot or cold water) is over 40 represents only about 10% of the population.

> **Most of us operate as blends of the four dimensions.**

Years ago, I remember completing an assessment that tried to pigeonhole me into just one dimension. I did not fit. The professional person conducting the assessment tried to argue that the results were valid and I was wrong. In the end, I did not feel honored or respected. It was not a pleasant experience.

That's why so many participants who complete CRG's *PSI* say *Finally! An assessment that captures my diversity and complexity!* In the past, they were categorized wrong by other assessments.

As an example, suppose a person has a **Behavioral ACTION** score of 50 and a **Cognitive ANALYSIS** score of 45. Identifying this person as only **Behavioral** when he also has a **Cognitive** score above 40 does not reflect the truth about his style pattern. The *PSI* would indicate that he has a **BC** style pattern.

Note of Caution when Using Style

Although the knowledge and importance of style is invaluable, we never should pigeonhole individuals or try to stuff people into a personality "box."

When we are provided with crisp, neat categories, the temptation is to use the models as a shortcut for getting to know people. The models were intended to provide clarity and insight about a person's personality, which is constantly changing, somewhat unpredictable, and often a surprise, even to careful observers.

Some people have said of others, "Oh, he's a **Cognitive** type" or "She's an **Affective** type," pronouncing clear judgment of another person's style. That type of simplistic thinking is to be avoided, especially when you share information about style patterns with friends, co-workers, or family members.

That is why I have concerns about assessments in use in the marketplace that use negative nouns to describe styles, such a Dominator, Socializer, Terminator, Anal Retentive, Socially Inept, and others. They are not "building" words.

Some assessments use animals to describe your style. In my opinion, that is equally damaging because they try to dumb-down your Personal Style to a *cute* level. People are way too complex to be categorized by descriptions that are limiting.

> **To live a fulfilling life, you need to play to your style strengths.**
> **Developing your weaknesses is highly overrated.**

Here's what I mean by that statement. If you are born with a natural way of interacting with the environment, trying to be someone you are not will create stress and frustration—as it did with the young female professor.

You are responsible for your behavior and for acting in an appropriate manner.

- Playing to your strengths is freeing and empowering.
- Trying to develop your weaknesses is draining and becomes a burden.

From leadership, parenting, communications, marriage, teaching, team-building, job satisfaction, sports, and much more, your Personal Style and the Personal Style of others touch every part of the fabric of our lives.

To deny the importance of Personal Style is like saying you can live without oxygen.

Personal Exercise

As part of your online report (or in the print format), you received an Interpretive Summary, a mini paragraph outlining the preferences and dynamics of your specific style pattern(s) plus a two-page **In-Depth Interpretation** outlining your pattern's strengths, difficulties, reactions to stress, team functioning, leadership implications, and recommendations to increase your effectiveness.

To get the most benefit from this process, go to your reports and highlight the statements you believe are true about yourself. Ask someone who knows you well to do the same about you, using a different color highlighter.

Do that for both your **Interpretive Summary** and your full **In-Depth Interpretations Patterns**.

Reflect on your **Online *PSI*** In-Depth report(s) and ask yourself these questions.

What are some of the strengths of your style pattern or patterns?

_____

_____

_____

_____

Which difficulties of your style pattern are true for you?

_____

_____

_____

_____

What stress-related issues are part of your style pattern or patterns? What action steps can you implement to reduce any stress you might have?

_____

_____

_____

_____

What insights about working or interacting with others did you gain, as a team member, leader, or family member?

_____

_____

_____

_____

What changes are you willing to consider, to increase your effectiveness?

_____

_____

_____

_____

Note: To view all 21 patterns and their **Interpretive Summaries** and an example of a two-page **In-Depth Interpretations** report, please see Appendix A and Appendix B.

CHAPTER 6

The Power of the Personal Style Model

The truth is that all of us attain the greatest success and happiness possible in this life whenever we use our native capacities to their greatest extent.

Dr. Smiley Blanton

The *PSI* Model

People often ask us how we are able to be so accurate in describing them in the *PSI* **In-Depth Interpretations**. They wonder if we've been secretly watching them from afar.

Personal Style has predictable behavior. The majority of respondents to the *PSI*—about 85%— agree with approximately 85% of the statements made about them in their **In-Depth Interpretation**. The accuracy has to do with the design of the *PSI* and our approach.

When I conduct seminars, I identify the information contained in this chapter as very, very important. When I heard about Personal Style over 20 years ago, it changed the way I looked at myself and others forever. Finally, I had a framework to help me understand why and how others act the way they do. I trust it will give you a framework, too.

Dr. Terry Anderson, founder of CRG, is the brilliant creator of the first version of the *Personal Style Indicator*. He was determined to address his concerns with many of the other assessments in the marketplace, a number of which are still in use today.

Most other assessments are built on a single source or theory, from the work of Carl Jung (1928), W. Marston (1927), J. Grier (1977), or Merrill and Reid (1981).

To produce our proprietary *PSI* **Model**, we took a multi-theory strategy and integrated the best practices and elements of all the leading-edge theory and research in the field.

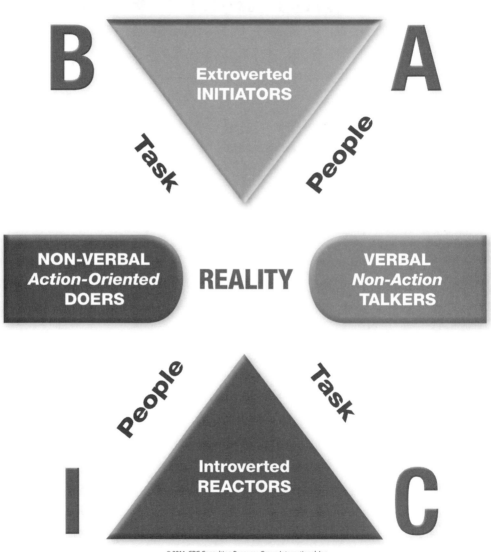

THE PERSONAL STYLE MODEL

B

A

Extroverted
INITIATORS

Task

People

NON-VERBAL
Action-Oriented
DOERS

REALITY

VERBAL
Non-Action
TALKERS

People

Task

I

C

Introverted
REACTORS

© 2011, CRG Consulting Resource Group International, Inc.

All It Takes is a System

The central purpose of the **Personal Style Model** is to illustrate the main similarities and differences in how Personal Style dimensions tend to influence behavior uniquely.

Personal Style Theory maintains that every person is influenced to some extent by all four style dimensions. Therefore, each dimension has an influence upon a person's thinking and behavior, regardless of its level of intensity.

The Personal Style dimensions that are the weakest in intensity are significant to consider because what a person naturally prefers *to avoid* is just as important as what the individual naturally prefers *to approach*.

The **Personal Style Model** is based on three personality continuums. Each can be considered an orientation toward certain types of behavior. All three continuums have two criteria and represent a wide range of continuous behavior.

1. The first continuum is orientation toward Extroversion-Introversion.

2. The second continuum is Non-Verbal and Verbal orientation.

3. The third continuum is People-Task orientation.

The Extroversion-Introversion Continuum: It's Not What You Think!

- If I were to ask for the stereotypical definition of an *extrovert*, what would most individuals say? *Extroverts are people-oriented and loud and like to be the center of attention.*

- What is the stereotypical definition of an *introvert? Shy, inward-looking, and not assertive.*

If you related to the above definitions, I request that you forget them entirely. Our definition of Extroversion and Introversion does not link to an individual's orientation to people or to the source of energy sometimes described as internal and external or to a measure of verbosity.

> **Our definition of Extroversion or Introversion is a person's orientation toward the environment.**

Extroversion can be defined as biologically less sensitive to environmental stimuli.

In our model, extroverts see the environment as an opportunity. Internally, they feel they can tell the environment what to do, not the other way around. They view the environment as an opportunity to be influenced. They are programmed to initiate; they need strong stimuli to gain and hold their attention and motivate them toward action.

They have little fear of the environment and make decisions quickly, with few concerns for making a mistake. They prefer adventure to routine and they like taking risks. They prefer to lead, not follow. Weak environmental stimuli don't hold their attention because extroverts lack the biological sensitivity to appreciate or value a low-stimulus event.

When you look at the *PSI* Model graphic, you will note that Extroversion is placed on the top center of the model. Both **Behavioral** ACTION and **Affective** EXPRESSION have an extroversion orientation. Even though the **B** and **A** are both extroverted, they are extroverted in opposite ways—the **B** toward tasks and the **A** toward people.

Introversion can be defined as biologically more sensitive to environmental stimuli.

In the *PSI* Model, introverts see the environment as a place where you need to be careful and cautious. They internally let the environment tell them what to do, which is the opposite behavior to extroverts. They perceive the environment as a big place that moves fast and is unpredictable. They typically take more time to make decisions. They want to know what the rules are and prefer to follow rather than lead.

They tend to react/respond to environmental stimuli. They can be very sensitive to environmental stimuli and react more quickly to the subtle elements in their surroundings. In fact, they prefer weak stimuli to strong stimuli, which can often overwhelm their "sensing levels." Introverts will choose a tranquil environment over an active one.

In the *PSI* Model graphic, you will note that Introversion is placed on the bottom center of the model and that both **Interpersonal** HARMONY and **Cognitive** ANALYSIS have an introversion orientation. Even though the **I** and **C** are both introverted, they are introverted in opposite ways—the **C** toward tasks and the **I** toward people.

Introverts are people who have a stronger need and preference to "wait and see" before engagement because they are naturally more cautious of the environment. Due to their high levels of sensitivity, they prefer to react and adapt to, rather than act upon, their environment.

Extroversion-Introversion

Introverts are indeed more sensitive to environmental stimuli than are extroverts. Introverts tend to pay more attention to environmental stimuli and make decisions about how to act based on what is going on around them. In contrast, extroverts like to "change" what is going on around them.

Extroverts are less concerned about what is occurring on the outside because they are not easily intimidated by their environments. Therefore, they tend to move into or even challenge the environment more easily; they often are stronger initiators who seek new and more intense stimulation earlier than introverts would.

While Extroversion-Introversion is presented here as a continuum, most people have the potential to think and behave in both an introverted and an extroverted manner, to some extent.

Because all four Personal Style dimensions influence behavior to some degree, every individual is continually being influenced by two external and two internal dimensions. That may in part explain why some individuals can take the initiative and tell the environment what to do in some situations, yet in others, they may defer.

Here's an example to illustrate that point.

I had just finished speaking at a career development conference, when I noticed a participant being scolded by three career counselors. They insisted that his perception he said he was a balance of Extroversion and Introversion—was simply not possible. The position of the counselors who were using a competitive assessment was "You must be one or the other; you cannot be balanced."

Those "experts" had no idea how damaging their comments were. They wanted him to choose **one**. In exasperation, the man asked why he couldn't be "balanced." The counselors' eyes glazed over and they responded "because."

I later met with the man and offered him the opportunity to complete the *Personal Style Indicator*. According to his responses, he discovered his Extroversion and Introversion scores were in fact *balanced!*

> **We all have Extroversion and Introversion in varying levels.**

Here is another illustration to help you better understand extroversion and introversion in your daily life.

Note: We are not condoning that you break the law.

Let's say it's 3 AM on a Wednesday in your town or city. Traffic is sparse and you come upon a red light. You stop and wait. There are no other cars on the road and the light is not changing to green.

What will the extroverts (generally) do more quickly than the introverts? They will look both ways to confirm no one is in harm's way, then proceed through the red light.

Have you done that?

On the other hand, before going through the intersection, someone with a higher Introversion score will wait longer and might even get out of the car to push the WALK button so the light will turn green.

Have you done that?

Observations

The red light is part of the environment. To an extrovert, the red light does not necessarily mean STOP because he wants to tell the environment what to do.

The introvert will defer to what the red light means, which is to stop. He will obey or respond to the environmental stimulus.

The Reticular Activating System (RAS)

To better appreciate the power of extroversion and introversion, it is helpful to understand the biological basis.

- Every human being has two nervous systems—the main communications networks from the brain to other parts of the body.

- Each system plays a vital role in keeping the person interacting effectively with the environment.

The **central nervous system** contains all the nerve networks within the brain and spinal cord. The brain is the command center for the body; the spinal cord acts as a "superhighway" from the brain to the various parts of your body.

The **peripheral nervous system** contains the nerves that are **not** located within the brain and the spinal cord. This system is responsible for transmitting information from the body—the muscles, glands, sensory organs, and so on—to the **central nervous system** and back again.

Every day, electrochemical messages sent from the brain stimulate millions of activities within the body. In turn, the brain receives millions of messages from the body.

The **reticular activating system (RAS)** is a bundle of nerve fibers at the base of the brain stem. RAS is believed to be one of the major reasons that Personal Style differences exist.

> **People react and are motivated differently by environmental stimuli, depending upon the extent of the reticular activation they experience.**

The important influence of these different levels of arousal on styles of behavior is described by W. P. Blitchington.

> In fact, whether you're an introvert or an extrovert depends largely upon your RAS. There are other contributions, to be sure. But people who inherit an "overdeveloped" RAS will be predisposed toward introversion. Those who inherit an "underdeveloped" RAS will likely become extroverts.

In short, environmental factors that stimulate one person to act in a certain manner may not influence another person to behave in the same way, because of developmental or temperamental differences in their reticular activating systems.

An assembly of individual sensory neurons (nerve cells) within the brain stem, the RAS is essential to the central nervous system because it stimulates people to be engaged—whether asleep or awake—and to pay attention to and concentrate on what is occurring within the environment around them.

Dr. David Meyers, Professor of Psychology at Hope College, described it this way.

> Inside the brain stem, extending from the spinal cord right up into the thalamus, is a finger-size network of neurons called the reticular activating system (also called the reticular formation). Most of the spinal cord axons of sensory neurons travel up to the thalamus. Along the way, some of them branch off to the adjacent reticular system.
>
> Thus, when sensory stimulation occurs, the reticular system

is activated. The reticular system transmits information about its state to the cerebral cortex, which in turn arouses the brain. Under the influence of the cortex, the reticular system controls not only arousal but attention.

Some individuals are more sensitive to environmental stimuli and therefore shy away from becoming overly involved in the environment (Introverts), while others are less sensitive and tend to seek out environmental stimuli to maintain active levels of interest (Extroverts). All individuals try to shift their behaviors to the environment in such a way as to increase their level of comfort and to decrease their level of discomfort.

The reticular activating system also affects individual attention levels. Introverts, being overly sensitive to the environment, pay more attention to weaker stimuli (less intense), often withdrawing from stronger stimuli (more intense), which tend to overpower them. That could be why introverts sometimes tend to magnify, distort, and "overreact" to experiences that are intense and/or stressful.

In contrast, extroverts—less sensitive to what is occurring around them—tend to become disinterested by weaker stimuli; they pay closer attention to—and are more engaged by—intensity.

Extroverts sometimes have a tendency to underreact to situations where there is not enough stress or stimulation. Thus, extroverts and introverts often prefer different activities, physical surroundings, and even friends or associates, due to their personal level of sensitivity and response to environmental stimuli.

There are strong suggestions that introverts have more nerve fibers in their RAS than extroverts do, so they take in more data or input from the same event. Metaphorically speaking, the introverts (**CI**) have a bigger radar disk than the extroverts (**BA**). Therefore, introverts are collecting more information in any given moment in time. That also explains the behavioral differences between the two ends of the continuum.

What happens when the hard drive in a computer becomes full? It shuts down or fails. That's what happens to introverts when stimuli overwhelm their system; they personally cannot take any more input. Their physical body actually feels burdened and breaks down (unable to function normally) with a given amount of stimulus. To reduce additional input, they must retreat.

On the opposite side, extroverts (**BA**) are wondering what the problem is. Since they have fewer receivers (a smaller radar disk), the same stimulus does not overwhelm their system, so they can go another few hours and engage more opportunities for input.

One other **very** important behavioral difference between extroversion and introversion is what we call sit-ability. Extroverts (**BA**) have far less sit-ability than introverts (**CI**). What we mean by sit-ability is the body's capacity to stay stationary for a certain amount of time. Extroverts cannot sit still for very long or they will feel they might crawl out of their skin. They have to fidget and get up to move. If you expect an extrovert to stay glued to his work station or to his desk for hours, forget it.

On the opposite end, introverts have far more capability to stay stationary and not have to move.

The dynamic of an individual's extroversion and introversion shows up in life every single day. If you are the parent of an extroverted child and you give him instructions to sit still and not move, what does he do 5 seconds after you turn your back? The extrovert **must** stay active. With a highly introverted child, you can check back in a few minutes to find he has not moved from that space on the carpet where you left him.

In work situations, highly extroverted individuals must get up from their desk on a frequent basis. Supervisors who want those individuals to stay put are not making a reasonable request. On the other hand, extroverts must take responsibility for the impact of their behavior. If it is disruptive to others, that is generally not acceptable.

Years ago, in my all-day workshops, I learned to give permission at the beginning of a session that it is okay to get up any time during the seminar to stretch, grab a coffee, or whatever, as long as it is not a distraction to the class. The result was a comfortable learning environment for everyone and I was not getting bent out of shape when participants needed to move their bodies. My goal is *learning*, not class compliance.

Ironically, in my opinion, one of the environments that least acknowledges the different Personal Styles and learning styles is education—all the way from grade school to university.

If I were to ask you who best fits the *compliant, sit-still, don't move, be quiet* education model, would you say extroverts or introverts? Introverts, of course! They let the environment tell them what to do and they have natural sit-ability.

Although I cite some examples of learning style in this book, it will be a topic for a future book—*Why Don't You Teach The Way That I Learn?*™

I am a past chair of a school board and my wife is a teacher. We constantly see that individual differences are not honored in today's education system. If educators understood the *PSI* Model and applied the information in this book, the success rate of students would dramatically increase and the frustrations of learners and teachers alike would decrease.

Understanding extroversion and introversion differences is foundational to any intentional behavior, life choice, interaction with others, and to the career you will select or have already chosen.

The Second Continuum: Non-Verbal Action-Oriented and Verbal Non-Action-Oriented

Another distinct difference in style characteristics is that some people verbalize far more than others when they communicate. Non-Verbal and Verbal refer to the spoken word **and** the quantity of written words or documentation that a person needs to use when communicating with someone else.

Non-Verbal and Verbal also refer to the amount of language, information, data, or communications a person requires or prefers to use to be understood or provide information to others. The Non-Verbal and Verbal criteria are shown on the *PSI* Model.

> **Non-Verbals can be defined as Action-Oriented individuals who use language less often to influence and persuade.**

Under stress, non-verbals stop talking and start doing. They are action-oriented, meaning they tend to finish what they start. They can judge others by what they have done or are doing, rather than by what they are saying.

Because they are action-oriented, they are very consistent in finishing what they start. They like to "get the job done" and tend to have a high completion rate. One of the reasons the non-verbals get things done is they talk very little while they work. They don't interrupt themselves and others with idle chitchat.

When you look at the *PSI* Model graphic, you will note that the Non-Verbal is placed on the left center of the model. Both **Behavioral** ACTION and **Interpersonal** HARMONY have a non-verbal orientation. Even though both the **B** and **I** are non-verbal, they are non-verbal in opposite ways—the **B**s toward tasks and the **I**s toward people.

For instance, **B**s prefer to be doing tasks rather than talking about how they are going to do them. They give very few details when explaining what they want to accomplish, usually preferring to talk about the desired results rather than the process of accomplishment.

Is are excellent listeners because they prefer not to talk. When they do talk and express their opinions, that shifts the focus onto them. Being shy, they would rather not be watched by others. They also have a high need for harmony; they believe it is better to keep their mouths shut rather than offend someone and possibly start a conflict.

> **Verbals can be defined as Non-Action-Oriented individuals who use language more often to influence and persuade.**

They tend to use many words and can talk very quickly, fluently, and loudly. You might send them a simple email that requires a one-word response and instead, they send you several sentences. Under stress, they are more likely to increase their volume and talk faster or provide more information.

They tend not to be action-oriented; they would rather debate and talk about a topic than do something about it. They can have trouble finishing what they start.

When you look at the *PSI* Model graphic, you will note that Verbal is placed on the right center and both **Affective** EXPRESSION and **Cognitive** ANALYSIS have a verbal orientation. Even though both the **C** and **A** are verbal, they are verbal in opposite ways—the **A** toward people and the **C** toward tasks.

The **C** and **A** people are verbal—they are the talkers and the communicators, but their attitude and approaches to talking differ. The **A**, for instance, talks to all kinds of people about anything others want to discuss. The **A** prefers optimistic themes over negative ones because **A**s are eternal optimists. They always look for and find the "silver lining in the cloud."

They love variety and have a high level of tolerance for people from different backgrounds and situations. They like to talk to these people so they can learn about new experiences they might try one day.

The **A** style tends to smile quite a bit when talking; they are joke tellers who like to laugh at other people's jokes. They will have funny cartoons on their Facebook page and, during online interactions, could have long responses based on a story.

Cs, on the other hand, prefer to talk one-on-one or to just a few people at a time. **C**s are very particular about the individuals to whom they will talk, when they will talk, and where they will talk. They are task-oriented and more serious in their discussions. That means they like to argue, debate, inform, teach, describe, categorize, and organize while they are talking. They also are focused on how correct the information is. They like data and expert opinions, which they often use in their discussions.

They are also much more likely to focus on negative topics or themes. Others actually perceive **C**s to be pessimists, while **C**s perceive themselves as realists who are sounding a warning to others to pay attention or pay the price.

Some highly verbal individuals have taken offense to our suggestion that they can be non-action-oriented. To clarify, I am not saying they aren't busy—they can have a *flurry* of activity. But is it achieving results? Action that produces actual results can be less prevalent in this group than with individuals who are non-verbal.

The Third Continuum: People-Oriented and Task-Oriented

There is an important difference between the way individuals tend to deal with the *people* aspects of the environment vs. the *task* or *thing* side. It would appear that some people are almost completely task-oriented. For whatever reasons, they tend to underfocus on interpersonal issues or events, to the chagrin of others.

Conversely, many others tend to overfocus on the people aspects of their surroundings and have more difficulty becoming task-focused. Those two groups of individuals represent the extremes of the continuum because most individuals have some natural orientation toward both people and tasks.

It is our observation that few people at the ends of the continuum can naturally shift back and forth gracefully from people to task without a great deal of concentration.

Task-Oriented styles are more focused on Tasks than People.

They are more focused on what is being done and how it is being done than on who is doing it or why. They are left-brain dominant, which means they are more likely to be strategic and analytical thinkers.

They are more motivated to complete tasks than be with people. That is often reflected in long hours of work activities and a lack of involvement with most people, except close relationships at home and work. That doesn't mean they don't value people; it's simply that for them, work and tasks come first.

When you look at the **PSI** Model graphic, you will note Task is across the center of the model and both **Behavioral** ACTION and the **Cognitive** ANALYSIS have a task orientation. Even though the **B** and **C** are task-oriented, they proceed with different mindsets—the **B** toward production and the **C** toward quality control.

Because **B**s have a task-oriented production point of view, they want to see results within a specific period of time. Knowing the work objectives, they set clear, obtainable goals, then determine how much time it will take to get the job done. **B**s are masters at that. They are very focused on obtaining authority, on being the leader of the project.

Bs don't like working for others, especially if others are slow and don't know what they are doing. **B**s make decisions and perform very well under pressure. They don't understand why others can't do what they can do as fast as they can do it.

Contrary to popular belief, **B**s don't want to control you; they want to be in charge. That is a big difference in terms of their preferences and behavior. If you get the agreed results, for the most part the **B** will leave you alone. He has little patience to babysit (manage) others.

Because **C**s are task-oriented from a quality control point of view, they want to slow things down and double-check all work to make sure the final product is the best. They are perfectionists and critical of the way other people do things. Their area of expertise is creating orderly and systematic ways of accomplishing work results.

Cs experience high levels of stress if they have to work under pressure for long periods of time. They don't like short timelines for production and are bothered if people don't value their "there is a right way and a wrong way to do things" attitude.

Cs often are overly concerned about making mistakes, especially if the mistake affects what others think of them as workers. They prefer to work alone in situations where they have control over what they are doing. That doesn't mean those individuals are poor workers; they approach work from an introverted task perspective. **C**s like to think about doing things and they like to talk about doing things/tasks, but they really don't like doing things.

When it comes right down to it, they often hesitate or stall because they are afraid of failing or of not getting it quite right. They prefer to figure out how something should be done, then tell someone else how to do it, rather than apply their knowledge to do the task themselves.

People-Oriented Styles are more focused on People than Tasks.
They are more concerned about people first and tasks second. They are especially sensitive to others' concerns and feelings. They tend to be right-brain dominant, which means they are more likely to be practical and creative thinkers. Because they prefer people over tasks, they put the needs of others before any tasks that must be completed.

When you look at the *PSI* Model, you will note that People is across the center of the model; both **Affective** EXPRESSION and the **Interpersonal** HARMONY have a People orientation. Even though the **A** and **I** are people-oriented, they proceed with different mindsets—the **A** is self-oriented and the **I** is others-oriented.

Because **A**s are more self-oriented in their approach to others (while extremely friendly and accepting of others), they usually have some agenda and want to persuade others to engage it. They are natural-born salespeople who love to influence a person into doing what they think will be best for that individual.

As are very good at networking with others. They were born to communicate on the phone or in person and will spend as much time as needed to make their sale. The challenge they face is knowing when it's time to be quiet and stop talking.

Since the **I**s are people-oriented and others-oriented, one of their greatest strengths—which can become a weakness by letting others take advantage of them—is putting others before themselves. They are very good at supporting the efforts and hopes of others to achieve something. They are especially thoughtful and caring, particularly if others are in need.

Is have the gift of compassion and are wired to serve others. They love to take care of people who can't take care of themselves. They often go into careers that allow them to work with children, the elderly, the disabled, and special needs people—those who are ill, dying, or suffering in some capacity.

Your Personal Style Criteria Scores

By this point, you are understanding the power of style and the influence it has on every single person. Taking the information from the three continuums, let's expand on that knowledge and summarize the way the behavior and preferences of each dimension show up in your life and the lives of others.

The **Behavioral** (**B**) dimension tends to be like this.
- Extroverted and Initiators
- Non-Verbal and Action-Oriented
- Task-Oriented

Earlier in this chapter, I defined Extroversion. In the model, **B**s are extroverted—they want to tell the environment what to do—but they don't reflect the stereotypical definition of Extroversion.

In some cases, based on others' understanding of Extroversion/Introversion, **B**s are called introverts because of their non-verbal nature. Nothing could be further from the truth.

Let's say a High **B** is invited to a costume party. The invitation says to come at a precise time and dress in a certain way. In addition, there will be party games and interactive networking so guests can meet with as many people as possible. Plus, guests are not to leave until a specified time.

Although the **B** might not wish to attend, here's what would happen if he did. He will arrive when he wants to arrive—not at the time demanded on the invitation. He will dress the way he wants to dress and only to the point of getting into the event. Nothing more.

He will speak to anyone he wishes and will avoid any silly party games or networking sessions. He will leave when he wants to leave. Some might say he's shy because he does not talk to anyone. The fact is that he is in charge of the environment; he simply does not wish to speak to anyone. He's not shy. He has no interest in mingling.

The **Cognitive** (**C**) dimension tends to be like this.
- Introverted and Reactors
- Verbal and Non-Action-Oriented
- Task-Oriented

Cs confuse people because they are introverted and also outspoken (verbal) and task-driven. Individuals ask me how someone can be outspoken (verbal) but not extroverted. **C**s are into collecting information and getting all the details. When in a meeting or an exchange with others, they will challenge them on the validity of the data as it relates to the task at hand.

In many cases, **C**s collect all the information, verify it, triple-check it, then they don't do anything else with it. The introversion influence causes them to hesitate and their verbal side would rather discuss and investigate the options than actually choose one and get on with it. So, in the case of a High **C**, don't confuse questions and data with action (results). It is merely activity.

In an automotive dealership, I was coaching a sales rep who was clearly frustrated with the High **C** potential client with whom he was interacting. The client had printed all sorts of information from the Internet, including consumer reports, and had done his analysis, yet he still had lots of questions for the sales rep.

Not being a **C**, the sales rep did not realize the **C** buyer needs to gather information before making a decision, and that it might be weeks, even months, before the buyer's need for information was met. Collecting data is reflective of the verbal nature of this **C** style. In addition, the buyer's introversion means he will be careful and cautious and won't want to be rushed into a decision.

The **Interpersonal** (**I**) dimension tends to be like this.

- Introverted and Reactors
- Non-Verbal and Action-Oriented
- People-Oriented

Is can be the one group taken for granted more than all the other styles. They are introverted (responding to the environment), and non-verbal action-oriented. They get things done without making any fuss.

Since they find it more difficult to verbalize concerns and bring up issues, everyone believes they have no troubles but, below the surface, there could be many.

Their drive to get things done is usually in the service of others. Because they are loyal and dedicated, they will fulfill responsibilities they don't even like. Because of their introverted nature, they might not ever mention those negative feelings to others.

I outline in our *PSI* seminars that a High **I** invented the word *sabotage*. Because they are introverted, non-verbal, and people-focused, they will avoid conflict at all costs. But, over time, their denial of their feelings becomes unhealthy. As a result, the feelings must finally manifest themselves. Sometimes, bitter feelings can act out sabotage-related behavior as a type of passive resistance.

The **I** individuals must note that the main people to suffer from not forgiving someone and withholding true feelings are the **I** people themselves. Because **I**s are introverted, those emotions will negatively affect their nervous and immune systems and cause them to physically and mentally break down.

The **Affective** (**A**) dimension tends to be like this.

- Extroverted and Initiators

- Verbal and Non-Action-Oriented
- People-Oriented

A is the dimension that reflects the world's stereotype extrovert. They are outgoing and influence the environment (mostly people) through their extroversion. They are highly verbal and use lots of words to communicate what they have to say. But they can be the person accused of *all talk, no action*.

Again, don't mistake activity for results. They have all kinds of ideas, creativity, and concepts that they want to discuss and investigate, but they will need to develop discipline to move from talking to doing. Although they like to be liked, their extroverted nature can cause them to miss cues as to what some people are really feeling about them.

I recall working with a High **A** who always promised the world but never delivered. He was absolutely committed to getting the task done, yet just about every time, it was not done. He was so people-focused and verbal, he was unable to concentrate on the task at hand. He constantly distracted himself and the others around him.

In the end, he left his role because he was unable to shift his behavior to meet the needs of the job.

Calculating and Interpreting Your Criteria Scores

Each person reading this book has unique personal criteria scores. Let's compute your scores and determine what they mean to you.

First, you need your *PSI* scores from your online assessment. To get your Personal Style criteria scores, we will calculate your *PSI* scores in a different way.

Using the scoring grid, find the two dimensions (your letter scores in each line) and add them together to get your numbers for each criterion.

For your Extroversion score, you will add your **B** and **A** numbers together. For your Introversion score, you will add your **C** and **I** numbers together. For your Non-Verbal score, you will add your **B** and **I** numbers together For your Verbal score, you will add your **C** and **A** numbers together. For your Task score, you will add your **B** and **C** numbers together. For your People score, you will add your **I** and **A** numbers together.

Do that now for each of the six numbers.

Personal Style Criteria Scores

Extroversion	Add **B** plus **A** scores	☐
Introversion	Add **C** plus **I** scores	☐
Verbal/Non-Action	Add **C** plus **A** scores	☐
Non-Verbal/Action	Add **B** plus **I** scores	☐
Task-Oriented	Add **B** plus **C** scores	☐
People-Oriented	Add **I** plus **A** scores	☐

Your totals in each of the three continuums reflect your natural orientation in each area and influence the way you perceive, approach, and interact with the environment.

Balanced Score

If you have scores of 80 and 80 or scores of between 83 and 77 for your Extroversion and Introversion, that indicates you are balanced between those criteria.

Balanced means the two criteria are fairly equal in terms of how powerfully they influence an individual to think and behave. For example, if you have a balanced score in this continuum, in certain situations you would be influencing the environment, telling it what to do. In other situations, you would defer to what the environment wants you to do.

The balanced score numbers would apply to Non-Verbal and Verbal as well as Tasks and People.

Imbalanced Score

That does not mean you have an unbalanced personality; it refers to your scores on the continuums. If you have scores that are 8 points or more apart, that indicates an imbalance between the two criteria; it infers that a dominant side exists for you. Scores starting from 76 and 84, which is an 8-point difference, are an indication of that.

Of course as the difference between the two numbers increases, the more one of the criteria would dominate the other.

I have witnessed score differences as high as 56 points. Scores of 108 and 52 at opposite ends of the criteria would result in that point difference.

Now before you rush to judgment, remember there are no right or wrong answers. In itself, no score can be wrong or negative. The scores simply establish behavior that might or might not be appropriate for the situation.

> **For each of you, every score has implications on how you get things done, the way you interact with others, and the way you are perceived by others.**

Here's an example of how quickly people are able to understand the power of this model.

The following are my Personal Style criteria scores.

Personal Style Criteria Scores

Extroversion	Add **B** plus **A** scores	**100**
Introversion	Add **C** plus **I** scores	**60**
Verbal/Non-Action	Add **C** plus **A** scores	**81**
Non-Verbal/Action	Add **B** plus **I** scores	**79**
Task-Oriented	Add **B** plus **C** scores	**82**
People-Oriented	Add **I** plus **A** scores	**78**

As you review them, you can see my People and Task scores are balanced, as are my Non-Verbal and Verbal scores. That cannot be said about my Extroversion and Introversion scores.

With my score of 100 for Extroversion (remember our definition of Extroversion?), what do you think my orientation to the environment will be? Based on my scores—and I confirm this personally—the word **can't** is not part of my vocabulary. Because I am so extroverted, I don't understand the word No.

To me, No means Maybe and Maybe means Yes. When someone says something *can't* be done, I have no concept of, or respect for, that statement. My extroversion energy says there is ALWAYS a way to influence the environment.

If I use my extroversion perspective ONLY to view and judge others, I can detest individuals who make excuses. If you convert that into behavior and presence, my energy and outward confidence can intimidate introverts when I walk into a room. Some have said things like *Who does he think he is* or *Boy, he's cocky—he thinks he's superior.* Although I have learned to soften my intensity, I am biologically wired to influence my environment—and only accept from it what I want.

While creating and delivering programs for a Fortune 500 client, I co-developed a series of programs for the auto industry for service advisors—the men and women at the service counter who write work orders and take your instructions to confirm what you want done on your vehicle.

One of the sessions included a full-day workshop on "Building Relationships With Style," which included the *PSI* and some of the content of this book. When we got to the section on the *PSI* Model where I was describing the differences between extroversion and introversion, one of the participants looked embarrassed and turned red.

During the break, the gentleman came up to me.

"Ken, I need to apologize to you."

I asked why.

"I want to admit that when you were here conducting the first program, I thought you were overly confident, even cocky. I realize that you aren't really a jerk, as I had thought. Your extroversion is high and my introversion is as high as your extroversion. In my introversion, I did not believe anyone could have that much confidence.

"In fact, I now realize that your extroversion intimidated me and I passed judgment on you. That is where I was wrong and that's the reason for my apology. This information is going to change my life because I see how, with my high introversion, I have let the environment tell me what to do even when I wanted to say No. Now I understand why—and I can do something about it."

That's one example of how the simple yet profound *PSI* Model can help each of us understand how we engage life differently. And although we must be responsible for our personal actions, the *PSI* helps explain how our preferences and our innate nature drive our behavior and perceptions about what is appropriate and acceptable.

Case Study: Applying the *PSI* Model

Knowing what you know so far about style differences, I would like you to determine the potential conflict points for the following group. Then I will outline the outcome so you can see how close your observations were.

I got a call from a longtime friend in the financial industry who wanted my help on a very sensitive organizational issue. A credit union was going through a lot of changes, including the possibility of a merger.

A rift had developed between the general manager of 17 years and the Credit Union Board. The conflict had escalated to the point where they did not know if the general manager would survive the month in his role. The Board was also struggling to make decisions; the survival of the credit union was at stake.

For those unfamiliar with credit unions, in Canada they are cooperatives owned by the members of the credit union. The Board is typically comprised of credit union members chosen in a general election. In essence, the Board manages its own financial institution. Paid staff members take care of the day-to-day operations.

In this case, the credit union was based in a rural area. Most of its members were from the agricultural community.

The Board was under significant pressure to make major decisions about the future direction of the credit union, including a possible merger with another local credit union.

If you go back a few years, the financial industry was going through major retooling and adding new financial products and offerings. The credit union was not keeping up with the changes. To survive, it needed to grow so efficiencies of scale would allow it to be competitive. Staying small was no longer an option.

To establish a common language of communication and understanding, I began my intervention by conducting a workshop for the Board and senior executive staff using the ***Personal Style Indicator*** and the contents of this book.

Within 2 hours, it became very clear that the differences in Personal Style were creating a lot of the conflict between the Board members and the general manager.

- All the Board members had an **Interpersonal** HARMONY and **Cognitive** ANALYSIS pattern, either **CI** or **IC**.

- The general manager had a **Behavioral** ACTION and **Affective** EXPRESSION pattern of **BA**.

Knowing what you know about style differences, what do you think were some of the conflict points from the respective perspectives of the Board and the general manager?

_____

_____

_____

_____

_____

_____

_____

_____

Let's see how many of the issues you were able to identify.

Because the Board members' style-patterns were **CI** or **IC**, those individuals were highly introverted. In the *PSI* Model, that means the environment would control them, not the other way around.

With the **C** and **I** both present, the **C** style needs detailed information to make a quality decision and time to make it. The **I** side of the group was concerned about what all the credit union members would think and they also worried that some members would be upset over their decision. Remember, the High **I** style has an aversion to conflict—and dislikes change almost as much.

The Board chair, with an **IC** profile, had deferred the major decision on the merger for 3 months because, at each meeting, one of the Board members was unavailable. He did not want to hurt anyone's feelings. For one meeting, Johnny was working in the fields; for another, Tom was branding cattle, and so on.

In the meantime, the general manager, with a **BA** profile (highly extroverted), wants to get on with the project. Each month's delay was adding to his frustration. Because High **B** individuals want to be viewed as competent, he took the Board's request for more information *personally*—he thought it meant they were questioning his capabilities. That caused him to be even more defensive.

The reality was that the Board members needed more information to make a respectful, quality decision; their request for more information had nothing to do with the general manager's competencies.

In less than 5 hours, using the power of understanding Personal Style, the conflict was resolved and the Board members and general manager were laughing and joking together. I helped the chair understand that the Board decision *not to make a decision* was in fact a decision *to do nothing*, and that waiting for every Board member might result in the failure of the credit union.

The chair now understood the impact of indecision. Through the power of understanding style, the Board members recognized they needed information but, at some point, enough is enough. More information was not what was needed. A decision was required.

The Board had to accept the fact that not all credit union members would be happy with their choice and that no matter what they did, there would be some conflict.

The general manager acknowledged that the Board's request for more information was not a slight on his abilities. Even though he wanted all decisions to be made yesterday, his interaction with the Board required more patience on his part. He learned that if he wanted to speed up the process, he had to provide more comprehensive information up front.

Not only did we quickly resolve the conflict, we equipped the Board and management with tools and communication processes to increase their effectiveness with self and others—immediately and forever.

My experience has taught me that a lot of conflict between and among individuals is style-related. When different styles interact—without knowledge of the material contained in these pages, of course—they are at odds with each other. That is because their style perspectives and needs are so diverse.

I trust you are beginning to realize that much of our frustrations with others can be contributed to the differences in our styles.

Personal Exercise

What about your criteria scores of Extroversion/Introversion, Verbal/
Non-Verbal, and People/Tasks? Are there insights or surprises for you?

_____

_____

_____

_____

Take a moment to think about how you might be more intentional with
your behavior as it relates to your scores in each of the three criteria.
Personally, I have to soften my extroversion when interacting with an
individual or a group of introverts. We call that style-shifting, which
I describe in more detail later in the book. Or perhaps you are being
influenced by another criterion, where one item dominates you.

I know a person with a score of over 100 for her verbal criteria. Sometimes,
people around her would like to grab a roll of duct tape. She has not
taken the *PSI* and, as a result, is oblivious to the impact her Personal
Style is having in her environment. For the most part, it is negative,
meaning her behavior is lowering her credibility with others.

What insights did you gain from the model that you can immediately
apply to your life?

_____

_____

_____

_____

CHAPTER 7

Style Differences, Similarities, Compatibilities, Incompatibilities, and Challenges

Life is more than a heartbeat or the ability to breathe, eat, see, and feel. An individual's life rotates around the quality of his relationships with other people.

Life is people, and it is not so much what they do for you as what you do for them and what you give each other.

MAXWELL MALTZ

It would have been so much better in my growing-up years if my parents and my siblings had understood our style differences. Instead of being frustrated by our style differences, we could have embraced and celebrated our similarities and differences.

What about you? Are you up to the challenge of understanding the various styles so you can intentionally increase your effectiveness with self and others?

Again, I remind you that we all have patterns and blends of the four basic styles.

As you review the following grid on Personal Style and the Environment, think about yourself and your tendencies AND think about the individuals with whom you interact. Can you recall an instance when the style differences between you and someone else started to increase the tension between you? What might you do differently today? Would you withhold judgment or have more tolerance for people who are different?

Here are the dynamics of the four dimensions.

Personal Style and the Environment

	Behavioral	*Cognitive*	*Interpersonal*	*Affective*
Perception of the Environment	Environment belongs to them	Environment is complex, dangerous	Environment is big and overwhelming	Environment is one big adventure
Approach to the Environment	Direct; little or no hesitation	Slowly, with caution	Slowly, with trust	Immediate, impulsive, and fast
Interaction with the Environment	Takes charge quickly	Verbally questions or tells	Listens, moves ahead with others	Verbally influences others
Energy Displayed in the Environment	Physical action	Mental discussion	Emotional caring	Creative expression
Fear of the Environment	Low	High	Medium	Low
Will to Succeed in the Environment	Strongest	Medium	Weakest	Strong

Because we each have a complex set of factors, I ask that you use the following compatibility grid only as a guideline. These comments should be viewed as possibilities, not absolutes.

Personal Style Compatibility

The following chart is a brief overview of how individuals who are strong in a particular Personal Style dimension might interact with a person who is strong in another Personal Style dimension.

B   Strong Behavioral Types and Other Strong Behavioral Types   B

AREAS OF COMPATIBILITY	AREAS OF INCOMPATIBILITY
Bs respect one another. They like each other's decisiveness and action orientation, and make good friends if both have similar interests. They work well under stress. If they are in agreement on a project, they can team up to bring significant personal capacity to achieve a goal, complete a project, or get results.	Conflict can occur between two **B**s if both want to be in charge and have opposing values and goals. They can be aggressive enemies in conflict situations. In a conflict, because they are extroverted they can spend a lot of time entrenched in their position, wanting the other person to change.

C   Strong Cognitive Types and Strong Behavioral Types   B

AREAS OF COMPATIBILITY	AREAS OF INCOMPATIBILITY
Cs and Bs work well together, if B is the boss and respects C's abilities and views. B's concern for production plus C's need for quality control can result in a mutually beneficial work relationship. They are both task-oriented so they can team up to complement the quality and timeline needs of a project.	Cs and Bs might not make good friends because their interests can be very different and both need/ want control. Conflict is likely if C is B's boss and C is blunt, indecisive, or incompetent. B could be frustrated by C's slower pace and C's need to control others. Cs could be intimated by B's extrovert energy.

B   Strong Behavioral Types and Strong Interpersonal Types   I

AREAS OF COMPATIBILITY	AREAS OF INCOMPATIBILITY
Bs and Is make a good work team when B is in charge and I follows through with the tasks. Bs will like I's loyalty, ability to help people, and ability to get tasks done on time. Is like B's fairness, hard-work ethic, and ability to lead.	Is can be easily dominated by Bs and hurt if Bs are uncaring. The B needs to be sensitive to the I's need for appreciation. If Is are the boss, Bs might see them as weak and, as a result, won't respect them unless the Is can gain B's respect by being more direct and assertive.

A   Strong Affective Types and Strong Behavioral Types   B

AREAS OF COMPATIBILITY	AREAS OF INCOMPATIBILITY
As and Bs make very good team workers if B is tolerant of A's creative and people strengths, and if A lets B teach A how to increase production (get results, not just talk about it) and manage time better.	Bs may not like A's unreliability, inconsistent performance, and verbal nature of all talk, no action. As may not like B's drive for results and low concern for other people's problems and feelings.

C   Strong Cognitive Types and Other Strong Cognitive Types   C

AREAS OF COMPATIBILITY	AREAS OF INCOMPATIBILITY
Cs enjoy deep talks and learning about self, people, and issues. They can be very loyal friends and good co-workers if they share similar values and opinions. They both have a commitment to quality and expertise.	**C**s may have many verbal disagreements and avoid each other. They can be critical of others, but neither accepts criticism well unless trust levels are high. If the **C**s are polarized on how things should get done, grudges can ensue and last a long time.

C   Strong Interpersonal Types and Strong Cognitive Types   I

AREAS OF COMPATIBILITY	AREAS OF INCOMPATIBILITY
Cs and **I**s often work well together and get along socially due to **I**'s need for harmony and **C**'s need for intimacy. They both are family-oriented and honest. **I**s can help **C**s be tolerant and care for others and **C**s can help **I**s be more attentive to details and organizational skills.	**C**s can be too blunt and critical of **I**s, leading to hurt feelings and resentment. **C**s may have trouble with **I**s not being assertive enough, while **I**s may have trouble with **C**'s tendency to be critical. Under stress, **C**s are all about the task before people and **I**s are the opposite, focusing on people, not tasks. That can lead to different priorities and conflict.

A   Strong Cognitive Types and Strong Affective Types   C

AREAS OF COMPATIBILITY	AREAS OF INCOMPATIBILITY
There are few areas of compatibility between these two styles; they resemble the original Odd Couple. **A**s can bring fun to a relationship while **C**s will bring structure and organization. If **A**s and **C**s understand each other's strengths and don't try to force one another to change, they can effectively work together.	**A**s may resent **C**'s inflexible attitudes and behavior. **A**s like to be spontaneous; **C**s are about planning ahead. That can be like oil and water. **C**s may be intolerant of **A**'s lack of commitment and avoidance of work and responsibility. Without tolerance, conflict is likely between such opposite styles.

I Strong Interpersonal Types and Other Strong Interpersonal Types I

AREAS OF COMPATIBILITY	AREAS OF INCOMPATIBILITY
Is work and socialize well together, make good friends, and are reliable co-workers. They enjoy each other at work and at home and like talking and doing things together. They can make a good team for helping and serving others or parenting.	Is can have trouble making big decisions or working out disagreements. They want to avoid conflict. Stubbornness may cause frustration and avoidance. They may sometimes be untruthful to protect others' feelings, letting disagreements or hurt fester over time.

I Strong Interpersonal Types and Strong Affective Types A

AREAS OF COMPATIBILITY	AREAS OF INCOMPATIBILITY
Is and As socialize very well. As add fun to I's practical routine and stimulate I's creativity. Is can help As stay focused on tasks needing completion. They can make a good people-helping team.	As may take advantage of I's caring and unselfishness. Is will feel stress if As are financially or socially irresponsible. As might want Is to take more risk and Is might not be willing to do so, leading to frustrations. This may not be the best team for making big decisions carefully.

A Strong Affective Types and Other Strong Affective Types A

AREAS OF COMPATIBILITY	AREAS OF INCOMPATIBILITY
As are very socially compatible because both enjoy activities, excitement, and variety. They are very people-oriented and like to have fun. As can make a good sales, communication, or people-helping team, when they stay on the task.	As may not finish projects due to their sociable nature and lack of concentration on tasks and time. Impulsive decision-making and spending could cause difficulties financially and lead to overcommitments. As a team, they could have the tendency to start everything and finish nothing.

| Every style has it strengths and each one has its related challenges. |

Earlier, I stated that developing your weaknesses is highly overrated and that you need to play to your style strengths.

Regardless of our style pattern, we need to take responsibility for the impact our behavior is having in our environment.

The following is a summary of some of the typical challenges or blocks each style can have. Again, there is no right or wrong style, just the implications of each dimension as it interacts with the environment.

Typical Behavioral Challenges

Bs can be very independent and well able to take care of themselves; they need others far less than most individuals who are strong in the other dimensions. Yet other people need them, and sometimes they should take more responsibility for adjusting in ways that can meet the needs of others, as well as their own.

If **B**s work at removing or reducing certain blocks, they can be of greater assistance to others. This, in turn, will help them feel more connected to people and less isolated.

1. Let Others In

Bs can often keep others at a distance because of **B**'s need for independence and freedom. They usually want control of any decision-making process that will personally affect them. They like to work alone and often spend much of their time focused on work tasks, which leaves them little time to socialize with others.

Bs need to be sensitive to the fact that they can create unnecessary concerns for others who are trying to relate to them on a more personal level. Not letting them do so may ultimately affect **B**s and the others over the long term.

My father has a lot of **B** in his profile. He spent most of my formative years either working on the farm or volunteering for many community groups. He rarely spent time playing with me or my siblings. Even though we loved each other, a connection was missing.

I missed him at ball games and hockey games. I know my brothers and sister also would have appreciated more of his attention when they were growing up. In our teen years, I believe a lot of our conflicts as siblings came from the lack of connection with Dad during our younger years. There is no question that my father cared for us but his style led him always to be working, at the expense of family relationships.

Children who don't have **B** in their profile will want a deeper connection with their parents or they can feel rejected or unloved; they likely want more time together than a **B** parent might be naturally providing.

2. Reduce Your Pride

Bs are strong-willed and determined in what they believe is right. They seldom vary their opinions. They tend to have a high level of self-regard that can cause stress for others. Very often, they are sorry for making a mistake but are unwilling or unable to admit it because of their non-verbal orientation. Others interpret that behavior as pride, and **B**s lose credibility in their eyes.

Making whatever adjustment is needed to avoid repeating the mistake is the **B**'s way of taking care of the situation. But others do not realize that. **B**s need to be aware that this pattern of behavior may end up hurting others because their orientation to task is much stronger than their sensitivity to people. It can lead **B**s to appear prideful and hard-hearted to others, even when that may not be the case.

There are several reasons **B**s find it difficult to admit they have been wrong and to apologize for mistakes they have made. First, they do not tend to make many mistakes. Second, they perceive apologizing as a sign of submission, weakness, or defeat that could possibly be used against them at a later time. Despite what they think, admitting their shortcomings will not make them helpless. Instead, it will help others see that **B**s care as much about others as they do about themselves.

When **B**s refuse to shift their style for others, and that can occur frequently, other people suffer. They should remember that others are not as "tough" as they are and that others often need more care and attention than **B**s naturally feel comfortable giving. To improve their relationships with others, they could "soften up" to some extent, and let others know that **B**s can be sensitive toward people.

If you are in the company of a person with a strong **Behavioral** style, lower your expectations a little. Don't expect that person to be as warm, sociable, and humble as you may be. Such expectations reveal the desire to change the natural tendencies of an individual. That merely leads to stress and resentment.

3. Share yourself

Bs believe talking about situations seldom solves anything and that action is the best cure for all problems. Being oriented toward independence, **B**s firmly believe it is each individual's responsibility to solve his or her own problems. Hence, they are less likely to seek counseling, medical treatment, or other kinds of assistance than people with other Personal Styles will. While this confidence in their own ability may be noble, it can lead others to believe **B**s don't trust them or care enough to let others help them.

Bs also don't like sharing personal feelings and thoughts. The more they hurt inside, the more they will be apt to withdraw and isolate themselves. They usually take care of their needs first, and later return to talk with others about situations with which they are having trouble. They also tend to be more verbal when they feel good about themselves and when others are discussing work-related subjects. This preoccupation with their agenda and the withholding of personal feelings can give others the impression that **B**s are aloof and do not care—when often they really do.

4. Learn to Meet the Needs of Others

One strength **B**s have as individuals is they can be immovable in their opinions and beliefs. They are sure about what they want and what you can do for them. This quality is of great importance in many different areas of life, such as business and school. Yet in social relationships, it may prove to be the one characteristic to which others have the most difficulty adjusting. **B**s are firm in their beliefs and attitudes. In their eyes, there is little chance that someone who disagrees with them is right.

While **B**s can successfully take care of themselves, we should recognize that they may not be good at understanding what others need, think, or feel. This lack of understanding of others' feelings can prevent them from moving beyond superficial relationships with others who want to be closer to them. While they may have a strong respect for what others have accomplished in their life, they could end up viewing others as strangers, even though deep down they wanted to get to know them.

Typical Cognitive Challenges

Those of you who are strong in this dimension care about others and life very much, yet **C**'s methods of showing care toward others often push people away, which is exactly the opposite of what they wish to accomplish. If **C**s develop their ability to love others in ways that are important to others, **C**s will find the caring and respect they want to receive. The following ideas will help **C**s do that.

1. Anger will not bring you respect.

Cs have a high need for respect. When others reject their opinion or advice, they usually get angry and upset. By getting angry and overreacting in other negative ways, they lose credibility with those they are trying to influence. Their anger is a block that can cost them much more than they realize in their relationships.

They say they don't care about what people think or say, but the truth is that **C**s care very much, which is why they can get so angry in the first place. People seldom get upset about things that are not important to them.

2. Control yourself, rather than others.

Cs have a tendency to want to control others. This can occur because of their strong need for safety and compliance. High **Cognitive** parents, for example, will likely be overprotective of their children because they have a strong need to know they're safe and secure. That necessity can become destructive in the relationship if they do not moderate it. If their requirement to be overprotective is left unchecked, **C**s can become obsessed with keeping tight limits on their children.

This particular block most often occurs in verbal attempts to make others do what **C**s think others should be doing. **C**s can be manipulative by verbally trying to convince others that their way is the right way. When they do this, they often come across as dogmatic and insensitive to others, which makes others feel alienated.

Cs can develop more credibility and be more effective in helping others if they take more responsibility for their behavior, rather than trying to control what other people do.

3. Criticize tasks, not people.

Cs can be perfectionists and therefore usually tend to be advice-givers. They believe that telling others what is wrong with them actually helps others solve their problems. As a boss, the **C** might say to an employee,

"That's not the way you talk to someone on the phone. Let me show you how to do it."

While that approach may get the message across that the employee is using the phone inappropriately, it also can leave the person feeling discouraged. Being "right" is effective in developing credibility only if the **C** is also being sensitive to the other person's needs.

This problem is caused in part by the **C**'s tendency to freely verbalize what he thinks. They also are more sensitive to tasks than to people. They often tend to blame others for not completing tasks the "right" way. When that happens, they can come across as being critical.

For example, after overhearing a business telephone conversation, the **C** might say to an employee, "I don't understand why you say such ridiculous things over the phone." That leaves the employee feeling attacked and believing that the **C** thinks he is brainless. That kind of criticism does not encourage the employee to want to learn a better way of making a phone call.

4. Think and talk less. Listen and do more.

Another **Cognitive** block that hinders **C**'s success in developing relationships is the **C**'s tendency to analyze and verbalize instead of taking action. In relationships, there definitely is a time to turn off your brain—stop talking and listen. A **C** tends to overthink. As they talk, they are trying to sort out what is in their mind. Consequently, they often spend more time and effort thinking about what they are going to say next than to listening to someone else speak. Before reacting with their own "agenda," **C**s need to learn how to listen (attentively) to what others have to say. That could strongly reduce stress in their relationships.

Sometimes, the overthinking process can make **C**s worry about every little detail. As a result, people with strong **Cognitive** styles can have difficulty making decisions. Because their high need for respect pressures them to avoid mistakes, **C**s often don't act in a timely manner and mistakes are made. Instead of gathering the information necessary for the decision and acting on it, **C** people tend to analyze every possible course of action and resist taking any of them.

Typical Interpersonal Challenges

Individuals who are strong in the **Interpersonal** dimension usually need to be more assertive in their daily interactions. Their non-assertive approach to life can actually become a serious obstacle for others who wish to develop relationships with them. If you are a person with a strong **Interpersonal Style**, the following suggestions should be of assistance to you.

1. Stand up for what you believe is right.

A major block for **I** people is their passive behavior. Being naturally humble can be beneficial in many situations, but it can keep others from really getting to know what is important to the **I**. If **I** people want a more "equal" relationship with others, they must be willing to take the risk of sharing themselves with others. Others won't always agree with the **I**s, but they will respect them more for standing up for what they believe.

Learning to be more assertive will be difficult for **I**s because they have such a strong need for harmony, which comes out of their fear of conflict. The thought of standing up and stating what is important to them can frighten them because they are worried someone might become angry with them for doing so. That fear must be overcome if the **I** person is to develop self-esteem.

2. If you can't say it, write it down.

Because **I**s tend not to verbalize, sharing feelings with others—especially feelings about personal issues—is often difficult. Their need for harmony is so strong, when put on the spot they often find their mind going blank; they choke with emotion. They have trouble expressing their thoughts and feelings because they are preoccupied with what others are saying and feeling.

Is could try removing this particular block by writing what they want to say to someone before trying to say it. Then they can either give the piece of paper to the person or verbalize the words aloud to themselves. That allows them time to think of what they really wish to say.

3. Let others take care of themselves.

Another block that can hinder relationships is the **I**'s high need to nurture others. While some individuals may appreciate the **I**'s efforts to care for them, others may have different needs and thus either ignore or misunderstand the **I**'s intentions.

Also, some people may perceive the **I**'s overcaring for them as a sign of disrespect for their ability to take care of themselves; they may resent the **I** for trying to "parent" them with his concerns. That is especially true when the **I** starts to overcare for teenage children in the family.

This type of behavior pattern results from the **I**'s strong need to feel appreciated and to love others. A key way for **Is** to gain that appreciation is to get involved in others' lives. It is natural for them to do things for people. It's very noble and a good way to show their concern for others, as long as it does not become their identity.

They should not want their value as a person to be determined by what they do for others, nor should they let their strong need to nurture control their behavior toward others in such a way that it costs them credibility. **Is** would improve their relationships if they were as caring toward themselves as they are toward others.

4. There's a time and place for stubbornness. This is not it.

Is are very warm and loving people who often think less of themselves than they do of others, but when they have been wronged or feel strongly about an issue, they can become extremely stubborn. They send others non-verbal messages that convey how really upset they are. Unfortunately, others can perceive these messages as signs of passive aggression.

For example, they say nothing and just stand their ground silently, even sullenly. When that occurs, others are less apt to cooperate with them. Even when others are aware of the **I**'s non-verbal messages, they may not understand why the **I** is upset with them. While **Is** think others understand their non-verbal communications, others are more likely to ignore them or misread the message.

Rather than going "on strike," a far more effective method for **I** people is to express their feelings directly. That approach will get their point across sooner and more accurately.

Although there is a risk that others may not change, when the **Is** share their feelings and opinions they are at least letting people know they are not trying to punish them.

Even if sullen silence periodically works for them, withdrawing from others will not gain them any credibility with others in the long run. Others will become tired of being shut out just as quickly as the **I** people will become tired of having others do things that irritate them.

As opposed to remaining stubborn, by standing their ground and communicating their opinions and feelings they will have a better chance of obtaining the appreciation they need.

Typical Affective Challenges

People who want to develop a closer relationship with **A**s often wonder if they are reliable. They seem as if they are and they talk as if they are, but when the pressure is on, where are they? If you are high in the **Affective** dimension, improving yourself in the following areas can help you develop your credibility.

1. Be on time because you care.

One common frustration others may experience is the **A**'s lack of attention to time. They are so people-oriented and creative, they love to stop to talk with people or dream up new ideas, which often distracts them from their responsibilities.

As are often late for appointments and occasionally forget about their appointments altogether. This kind of behavior often leads others to think they don't care about them and that they are self-centered. If an **A** is going to be late or has a change of plans, he should call ahead, before the appointment time passes, to let others know about the delay.

2. Stay out of debt.

Of the four dimensions, the **Affective** dimension has the most influence on an individual's need for pleasure. **A** likes to indulge—play, be active, and entertain. That can sometimes cost more money than he can afford. Expensive activities such as going to parties or eating out regularly can slide the **A** into financial difficulties all too easily.

Going into debt usually doesn't scare the **A** as much as it would scare the **I**. Being naturally optimistic, they believe they can wriggle out of debt with a little creative thinking and financing. Sometimes, that only slides them into deeper financial trouble and causes strain on others who have to live or work with them.

The fact that **A**s cannot pay for something doesn't always slow them down because they are impulsive decision-makers when it comes to doing almost everything. They tend to be generous with their money and possessions because they desire the acceptance of others, which of course they receive by spending money and lending possessions to others.

Consider an **A** when he was 10 years old. He just *had* to have that new bike, with all possible accessories. He assured his father he would take care of it, but his **A** aspect let every kid on the block ride it. Then one day, he forgot it in the street while playing baseball with the guys and it was stolen.

3. It is essential that you finish what you start.

A people have so many ideas and interests that they continually start one project after another—and seldom finish any of them. It's not that they are insincere about completing the tasks; it's just that they are easily distracted by other interests. If **A**s made fewer commitments and followed through on those already made, they would be recognized for their accomplishments.

Rather than overbooking, they need to learn to say No to others. When they promise more than they can deliver, it severely diminishes their level of credibility with others. Instead of getting the acceptance they want from others, they often end up losing it.

4. Work is not a dirty word.

While play is at the top of the **A**'s list of things to do, work is near or at the bottom, unless of course work is play. Since **A**s are people-oriented and focused on pleasure, they would much rather use their time and energy doing things that are fun. When work includes meeting different people and discussing their interests—as does a sales, customer service, or communications position—then work is often quite fulfilling for them. When variety and involvement with people are lacking, the **A** motivation sags and the **A** easily becomes bored and loses interest.

Maintaining sustained effort can be difficult for the **A**s because they tend to lack the stamina and persistence needed to accomplish projects that are arduous or tedious. If others must depend on an **A** to complete work tasks and the **A** leaves the tasks unfinished because he finds them boring, the **A** is placing an unfair burden upon his co-workers. That could also affect the **A**'s family life.

For example, an **A**'s wife may admire him partly because he is kind and sensitive to people, but if he consistently starts jobs and quits them because he's bored, he could put the family into financial difficulties that she may find hard to forgive.

You can see how each dimension has the opportunity to increase effectiveness with others by first acknowledging its own style preferences, then paying attention to the way certain behavior is affecting others.

CHAPTER 8

Do You Really Know What You Value?

By distinguishing types according to their own strivings and values, we are trying to develop knowledge that increases compassion, respect for differences, but also understanding of what we like and dislike in ourselves and others and why . . .

MICHAEL MACCOHY

I recall a time when my values where challenged. My friend Mike called to invite me to a special investment opportunity meeting that was by "invitation only." The investment offering was limited, so it was important to get to that first meeting, if I wanted to be part of it. I committed to attending with Mike on Thursday at 7 PM.

When Thursday rolled around, my wife Brenda called just after 6 PM from her cell phone to ask if I was driving to the kids' concert on my own or did I want her to pick me up from the office.

Wow! I had completely forgotten about the concert. Mike was to arrive in a few minutes. I shared this dilemma with Brenda and asked her to tell the kids that I had given my word to Mike, so I would not be at their concert.

In her wisdom, Brenda said, "No, you tell the kids you are not coming," and she handed the phone to my son. I proceeded to sell Tim on the merits of keeping my word to Mike and that I was planning to go to the meeting. I promised to view the video of their concert with Tim and my daughter as soon as I got home. My son, showing great insight at age 9, said, "Daddy, why don't you just say No to Mike?" I thought about it . . . and of course I attended the concert.

Every day, your choices reveal not only your style preferences, they reveal your core values.

Why the delay on my part to choose the concert over the meeting?

Some false beliefs were influencing my desire to attend the investment meeting.

One was the fear of loss. I was incorrectly framing that meeting as my last chance to ever get into a ground-level development with a high rate of return. I thought there would never be another investment opportunity like that one! When I think about it now, that was ridiculous.

Never again would I have had the opportunity to attend my kids' concert. That was the real truth for me, according to my core values.

What about you?

Do know your values?

Are you using your values to make decisions every day?

What is a Value?

A value is something that has great desirability or worth to you—it is important enough that you spend time trying to fulfill or keep it as part of your lifestyle. A value is simply a label for something that is an imperative for you.

Values are internal and personal to you. You will find you have embraced certain values from your environment and/or social factors; other values seem part of your genetic makeup. Regardless of the potential source or circumstances, the key is to understand that your values are uniquely yours.

Your values reflect a vital part of who you are. Knowing *what* is most important to you and *why* can be helpful for making meaningful decisions in all parts of your life. It is very difficult to make decisions about work, recreation, home, and interpersonal relationships without first knowing what is most important to you.

People who are confused or unclear about their values often have difficulty making the bigger decisions in life because they don't know themselves well enough to decide what would be best for them. That is especially true today with all the mixed messages that pull us in various directions.

For instance, if you value organization, you will work best in an organized environment. If you value pleasure, you will value situations and people who create pleasurable experiences for you. Individuals tend to value different things and types of situations because they have different needs within themselves.

Everything in your life is a reflection of the values you are embracing and living.

The research is clear; the majority of individuals are, at some level, unhappy with their lives.

> **In the area of relationships, a recent study identified that 93% of us feel we have settled for less than what we want, desire, or deserve.**

The Importance of Values Cuts Two Ways

As critical as it is to be clear about our own values, it is equally important to understand the values and related needs of the major interpersonal relationships in your life.

People with different values tend to disagree more than individuals with similar values. Conflicts in relationships, both at home and at work, often can occur because two individuals have opposite views on a situation. Their perceptions and viewpoints are influenced by their values.

For example, a wife who values security may argue with her husband who values recreation; she prefers to use their resources to open a savings account and he wants to buy a speedboat.

Values are intensely personal. That is true for you and for everyone you meet. It is essential to remember that what *you* feel is important (value) might not even appear on another person's radar—and vice versa.

Although that observation seems blatantly obvious, many individuals still don't acknowledge the various values we each hold and the deep implications that values have in *ALL* our interactions with others.

The power of ***values clarification*** is equally as important for learning what other people value as it is for learning what you value.

Each style dimension has related needs, fears, and values. What drives me to behave in certain ways may not drive you. For example, I spent long hours sitting at a computer, writing this book. The decision to use this time to produce a book rather than do something else was inspired by my values, which include both needs and fears.

Those variables will differ for others. Some will be inspired to use their time to complete tasks such as restoring an old car or learning a foreign language. I have little interest in either.

How Are Individuals Inspired to Do One Thing rather than Another?

Understanding the answer is key to understanding other people and ourselves.

> *Inspiration, then, is the impulse which sets creation in movement; it is also the energy which keeps it going.*
>
> ROGER SESSIONS

Theories on internal motivation suggest we are stimulated to engage things that meet our predominant needs and to disengage from activities that don't meet our needs. *When something consistently meets a particular need of ours, it becomes more attractive and valuable to us.*

We value most whatever best meets our needs.

We can tell what is important to us by listening to the "voice" of our feelings.

Feelings are related to needs and values. When you feel satisfied to engage in a particular activity, something about that activity is meeting one of your needs.

When you feel dissatisfied, that activity is not fulfilling your needs. Activities that consistently make you feel positive (happy, joyful, confident, proud) are therefore more important and valuable to you than activities that leave you feeling negative (upset, sad, mad, disappointed, depressed).

Take a moment to review the following list of 21 values. Identify what you feel are your top 7 values in their order of priority for you. List them in the space provided.

As you select your top 7 values, see the big picture—the way your values pertain to **all** areas of your life, not just to your work or to your home life separately.

Note: This list of values is not meant to be all-inclusive; it focuses on behavioral values that are linked to each style dimension.

CRG Values List©

Values	Definitions
Accomplishments	To complete tasks, get results
Acknowledgement	To be appreciated and rewarded for your efforts
Challenge	To live an active and exciting life, achieving targets
Cooperation	To get along well with others, influencing family harmony and teamwork in the workplace
Creativity	To be able to experiment with and develop new ideas and things
Expertise	To be an expert in a special subject or skill area
Friendship	To have valuable friendships
Honesty	To be truthful and have others be truthful, too
Independence	To have freedom of action, to be primarily responsible for making decisions about your life
Instruction	To acquire new information and share it with others
Intimacy	To share close companionship and/or deep affection with someone
Organization	To plan and carry out logical and structured procedures
Pleasure	To be happy, contented, and comfortable with life; to have fun
Quality	To maintain a high standard of work with only a few errors
Recognition	To become well known, obtain awards, and attain a special status
Responsibility	To be in charge, lead others, organize events, and make decisions
Security	To have protection and security in personal and financial situations
Spirituality	To have inner peace, an understanding of life and death, and communion with God
Tranquility	To enjoy peace and quiet and a life with few personal conflicts
Variety	To have a life with many different experiences, but few rules and set routines
Wealth	To achieve financial independence and control in personal and business realms

Your top 7 values in order of priority.

1. _____
2. _____
3. _____
4. _____
5. _____
6. _____
7. _____

What's Motivating You?

Values should be anchor points for living life. After conducting values programs (in conjunction with style programs) for more than 20 years, with thousands of individuals, I am continually surprised by the high percentage of people who are unclear or uncertain about their values.

If you are willing to change or sell-out on a value, I maintain that value was not important to you in the first place. Although values do change and are revised throughout our lifetime, such as when individuals have children, there usually is a solid foundation of core behavioral values that are non-negotiable.

When our workshop participants review the list of values, we find people often want to have 7 Number One values. But you can't. Whether you realize it or not, you are constantly choosing one value over another in your daily life. In many cases, what you state is important to you is not always reflected in your life choices, as in my example about my kids' concert.

Have you heard people say their family is important to them, yet they never spend time with them? That is a simple example of stated values being incongruent with actions.

What about You?

- Are you aware of your core values and the related needs and fears that underlie each value?

- Are you also aware of the core values of the people in your most important relationships?

Each style has key needs.

- If you score high in a particular dimension, you will tend to have stronger intensity for the needs listed in that dimension.

- If you score low in any of the dimensions, you likely will not have the same intensity for those particular needs as you will for the needs related to your strongest dimensions.

Personal Needs according to Personal Style		
	EXTROVERTED	**INTROVERTED**
Task-Oriented	**Behavioral** Achievement Autonomy Power Rewards Stimulation	**Cognitive** Affirmation Order Perfection Respect Understanding
People-Oriented	**Affective** Acceptance Attention Expression Recreation Variety	**Interpersonal** Appreciation Harmony Stability Trust Unity

For example, a person who scores high in the **Behavioral** and **Interpersonal** dimensions will have strong needs associated with those two dimensions. That individual prefers working alone, wants to achieve, and likes material rewards (**B**), but also is very grateful when others say *thanks*, are honest, and don't create unpleasant situations (**I**).

If the same person is low in the **Cognitive** and **Affective** dimensions, most likely he will not be as interested in having things organized, in getting things done perfectly, or in spending time alone with just one person (**C**). Nor will this individual have a strong desire to be accepted by others, to spend lots of time at play, or to entertain others (**A**).

If your values and needs don't match exactly with your *PSI* score, don't worry. You have permission to have flexibility in your values list.

Values Have Related Needs and Fears

Needs and fears function as apposing weights on a scale. When needs are adequately met, fears decrease. If needs are consistently unmet, fears increase. For example, if you have a high need for acceptance, you will have a greater fear of rejection than a person with a low need for acceptance.

When I use the word fear, I mean the fears common in everyday life that produce feelings of insecurity and stress and that reduce our levels of personal effectiveness and fulfillment.

Your values, needs, and fears are conveyed through your feelings and through your behavior and decisions. You have positive feelings when your needs are being satisfied and negative feelings when your needs go unfulfilled.

For example, I feel better when I achieve a goal than when I fail. Negative feelings are signals to you and to others that you are not satisfied with something in a particular situation.

When needs are consistently unfulfilled, fears develop. Those fears have their source in particular needs that, over time, have gone unmet by people or situations in a person's environment.

Note: The fears we are discussing here are quite different from phobias, which are fears deeply rooted in a belief system.

Small fears that are based on internal needs from within your personality can develop into larger ones if negative conditions prevail for a long period.

> **Individuals who have high levels of fear about something usually have a history of chronic neglect.**

High-level fears, once established, can have ongoing repercussions in a person's life; they continue to reflect the unmet, intensified needs of the past.

Needs Prompt Behavior

In contrast, fears can override or stem our natural impulse to take action. Fears also can provoke less desirable behavior, such as dishonesty and deceit.

During one of my consulting visits at an auto dealership, a sales rep said he valued *honesty*. But, according to him, if he were 100% honest during the sale, his sales manager would fire him. He insisted he valued honesty and that's why he felt physically ill when he was directed to omit certain details about some of the used cars being sold to potential clients.

My challenge to him was that he was living *situational values*—important only at certain times and negotiable at others.

Was honesty really a value for him?

Fear of losing his job threatened that sales rep's value of honesty. By his actions, he showed that his value of job security was, in this case, more important than honesty. In other words, he sold out on his value of honesty.

Many individuals allow fears to control their decisions and behavior, rather than engaging their primary needs and the values that will fulfill them.

> **We need to intentionally move toward what most meets our core needs (fulfillment); we should avoid situations where our needs will not be met (lack of fulfillment).**

If we have a low need for something, not getting it will be less of a threat to us than *not getting something else* that is important. For instance, I have little need for tranquility and, when it is not present, there are no repercussions.

The following list provides style-related needs and fears for each dimension. As before, please apply this information to yourself, looking at the areas where you received the highest scores on the *PSI*.

If you are strong in several dimensions, you will want to integrate the information from each of those areas. By examining the lists of needs and fears together, you will have a clearer picture of which ones influence your behavior the most.

Typical Personal Fears

The Behavioral Person NEEDS:	Therefore . . . FEARS:
Achievement	Failure
Autonomy	Restriction
Power	Dependency
Rewards	Poverty
Stimulation	Stagnation

The Cognitive Person NEEDS:	Therefore . . . FEARS:
Affirmation	Disapproval
Understanding	Confusion
Order	Chaos
Perfection	Incompetence
Respect	Humiliation

The Interpersonal Person NEEDS:	Therefore . . . FEARS:
Appreciation	Ungratefulness
Harmony	Conflict
Stability	Instability
Trust	Deception
Unity	Dissention

The Affective Person NEEDS:	Therefore . . . FEARS:
Acceptance	Rejection
Attention	Exclusion
Expression	Repression
Recreation	Boredom
Variety	Routine

What Happens if You Are Not Living Your Values?

It is amazing how many people are not living their core values.

In a lively discussion during one of our values seminars, a participant suggested that if people really value something other than what they are doing, they would choose to do it. He stated that each of our lives, at this very moment, reflects our true values.

Although that seems a logical concept, it assumes

1. people know their values, and
2. they are consciously (ready and willing) choosing their path.

In my experience with thousands of individuals, those two points simply are not true.

> **When we are not living in alignment with our values,**
> **our personal energy is disrupted, our internal drive is hindered,**
> **and our fulfillment is diminished.**

Year after year, people list values that are important to them, yet they don't live those values. For example, some people claim health, wellness, and fitness are their prime values, but they never work out, they eat poorly, and they are bordering on obese.

My encouragement to someone with a value that is not being fulfilled is to do something about it or get it off your list! Stop trying to fool yourself and everybody else that it is important to you. In reality, it is not. Every day that you keep it on your values list is a day you are living out of congruence. That becomes an internal drain and a burden to you emotionally, whether you acknowledge it or not.

Values oppression comes in various stripes. I was working with a father/son team on the succession planning of the family business. When I asked the son in private what he really wanted to do with his life, he said he wanted to be in the arts and acting—not in business.

I asked why he was willing to take over the family business, which he did not value. "I am from Asia," he said. "Tradition expects the firstborn male to follow his father's footsteps."

No matter what approach I tried, the cultural pressure and expectations (values) were greater than the lifestyle that would have been more fulfilling to the son and his values.

> **What about you?**
> **Are you living your values or someone else's values?**

Because there can be considerable variation in our personal values, there can be vast differences in the importance we attach to events. For example, I may rate *variety* highly. That will be manifested in the number of new experiences and activities I seek. It may be revealed in my choice—or my desire to choose, if the means and opportunity presented themselves—to travel all over the world, visiting or living in many different countries.

In contrast, perhaps you prefer *security*. You may desire freedom from debt to other people—both financial obligations and moral responsibilities. As a result, you may be more likely to avoid risks and settle for your existing circumstances and routine. That may be reflected in your being content to live in the same house for 20 years.

> **Differences in values will affect behavior.**

I may be more willing to take chances than you are, especially ones where I risk security to get variety. On the other hand, you are more likely to move cautiously when dealing with financial matters, particularly ones that have a long-term impact, such as mortgages and insurance policies.

Whether our lives turn out successfully and we achieve happiness and satisfaction is determined by many other factors, not the least of which is the amount of information we have available at the time we make our choices.

Most people learn to accept values differences in others as a "fact of life." Yet often, when adjustments cannot be made, conflict occurs.

> **Conflict can occur when there is a clash of values and**
> **a lack of understanding or appreciation of our differences.**

Anger often indicates that individuals in a conflict strongly value whatever issue they feel is at stake.

People tend to get angry only when something is important to them.

Cs, for example, value *expertise*. That value influences them to seek perfection and shapes their attitudes toward tasks and people. They want to be the expert and like to succeed at whatever they do. They get quite frustrated when that doesn't happen, because they believe others will perceive them as failures. That characteristic often leads Cs into heated discussions when they think people are interfering with their methods and their plans for doing things.

The value they place on expertise influences not only their perceptions and behavior in the work environment, but how well they are able to work with others. They can have difficulty working closely with people who do not perform to their strict work standards because they don't want their shortcomings to reflect badly upon their reputation. The **C**'s attempts to control situations often lead to conflict.

Individuals with similar Personal Style patterns are more likely to have similar values than individuals with contrasting style patterns. It is much easier, therefore, for those sorts of relationships to improve because there are fewer areas of conflict. But people with contrasting style patterns and different values can develop relationships if they make a conscious effort to understand the other person and see the environment from the other's point of view.

To develop relationships with people, it is necessary to respect their values, especially when their values are not the same as yours. Marriage coaching often focuses on the differences in values between the two partners. Helping each partner learn how to be more considerate of what is important to the other is often necessary before discussing particular issues of concern.

Is, for instance, need to accept and respect **A**'s strong values for pleasure and friendship. If **A** invites home many more people than the **I** would like to see in the house or if **A** spends more money on recreation than the **I** would, then the **I** should understand the **A** is operating in the context of his own personal values.

A, on the other hand, has to learn to respect the **I**'s value about saving money (security) and having time alone together (tranquility). The **A** shows respect by accepting the **I**'s values as a reflection of the person she is.

> **Personal values are very powerful in directing behavior.**

Most people tend to invest their time and energy in areas that will bring them the most personal rewards.

What you consider *most rewarding* is directly related to what is most valuable to you. Consequently, values are like inner goals that each individual hopes to achieve while interacting with others and the environment. An example of this concept in action can be seen when groups of people get together for a collective effort. Teamwork is accomplished when the individuals on the team have common goals and values.

Groups that have members with similar values and goals work better together because motivational drives within the individuals in the group are going in similar directions.

It is safe to say that, given a choice, many of us would probably choose most of the values listed. But we are limited by the amount of time and energy we have. When we work hard to acquire one value, we often eliminate opportunities to obtain other values.

For example, valuing "challenge" might encourage one father, but not another, to seek out personal experiences—such as flying alone to Africa for a safari vacation—which would take time and resources away from his family. While that meets a personal need of his, it comes at the expense of the needs of other family members.

We have linked the values to their related needs. Reflect on how your needs and values are being realized or omitted.

Personal Values according to Personal Style

The Behavioral Person **NEEDS:**	*Therefore . . .* **VALUES:**
Achievement	Accomplishment
Autonomy	Independence
Power	Responsibility
Rewards	Wealth
Stimulation	Challenge

The Cognitive Person **NEEDS:**	*Therefore . . .* **VALUES:**
Affirmation	Intimacy
Understanding	Instruction
Order	Organization
Perfection	Quality
Respect	Expertise

The Interpersonal Person **NEEDS:**	*Therefore . . .* **VALUES:**
Appreciation	Acknowledgement
Harmony	Tranquility
Stability	Security
Trust	Honesty
Unity	Cooperation

The Affective Person **NEEDS:**	*Therefore . . .* **VALUES:**
Acceptance	Friendship
Attention	Recognition
Expression	Creativity
Recreation	Pleasure
Experience	Variety

How do Different Styles and Their Values Show Up in the Game of Life?

Behavioral

Bs will play a game as long as there is a challenge and they have an opportunity to meet that challenge. They need to achieve their ambitions, and they will frequently compete against themselves to satisfy internal goals.

Bs tend to be very consistent performers and will play their hardest every time. They tend to make good team leaders and coaches because they usually understand every facet of the game and like to be in charge. They are quick to forget losses and to focus on upcoming games because they don't like dwelling on the past.

Cognitive

Cs play because they want to win and to be the best players on the best team. That would meet their strong need for respect from others. After a loss, players often can be very critical of themselves, their coaches and teammates, the umpires, and the members of the other team. They also tend to be perfectionists and have high standards about how the game should be played.

When confident, **C**s are extremely competitive and play hard, but when upset due to low-quality playing, either by them or by their teammates, they tend to sulk and may give up playing.

Interpersonal

Is play well because they enjoy being a part of the "family." These players usually strive to play their hardest for the team as a whole, rather than simply for themselves. That meets their need to give to others and is also a good way for them to be appreciated by others.

If there is conflict among team members or the coaching staff, the **I** people will try to resolve it quietly or will become depressed and withdrawn because of their strong need for unity and harmony. They remain consistent performers, even when feeling upset because they don't want their feelings to weaken the rest of the team.

Affective

As are out there for the pleasure of playing the game. They like to have fun, thus they can be very poor players during practices. They tend to show up late and can horse around when they do arrive. Yet during the game, **A** often gives 110%.

Public recognition is very important to **As**; the glory of winning is a strong motivating force for them. They love to rise to the occasion when the pressure is on and a large audience is watching them play. They also will make time to help other players improve their skills and excel to do their best because **As** like to influence others to achieve.

Applying the Time and Energy Test to Your Top Values

Much of our personal and professional fulfillment in life comes from living and embracing our top values.

You would think that the way people invest their time and energy would reveal what is important to them. But as I mentioned, many people's lives/actions are not congruent with their core values. Based on research, that is more common than we would like to think. Many individuals, for whatever reason, are living lives that do not reflect their core values and needs.

What about you?

Have you been proactive and intentional in all your values choices or have you been living someone else's values?

> **The only person who can confirm whether YOUR values are being met is YOU.**

I suggest you use two measures to confirm that your values and needs are being met—time and energy.

For example, even though two people value friendship, the amount of time required to feel fulfillment in this value is intensely personal.

One individual may find that seeing good friends for a couple of hours once a week is enough to satisfy that value and have his or her needs met. Another person might require double or triple that amount of time to meet the friendship need.

The energy we invest also influences our needs level. Going to a private dinner with close friends is much different than attending a large party or a BBQ with them.

As you proceed with the next step, please be as honest as possible in determining whether your personal needs and values are being met from the perspective of both time and energy.

During our values seminars, we get individuals to confirm whether their values are being met by using the time and energy test on each of their top 7 values.

> **Even if two people have the same value,**
> **they each might require different time and energy**
> **to have that value fulfilled.**

During this exercise in one of our workshops, a 23-year-old male at the back of the room was in tears. I went to talk to him at the break to find out what was happening for him. He had concluded that not one of his top 7 values was being realized. I asked if he had any insight into why that was the case. He said he lived at home with his parents and that for his whole life, he had been doing what his parents wanted, not what was important to him.

His tears came from the realization that his life did not reflect his core values.

> **The power of values clarification means you can make the right decision**
> **in most circumstances in the future.**
> **Why? Instead of making situational decisions,**
> **you will make values-based decisions.**

Use your top values and your style as filters to make your choices in life.

One of my top values is independence. When I got a job opportunity to join a successful organization, I used my values to screen its potential. I quickly realized that no matter how much money they would offer me, my core value of independence would not be met. I would not be able to sustain my interest in the job without compromising my values and I was not willing to do that.

It also is important to learn the values that are important to the people in your close relationships. If their values are different than yours, are you accepting their need to live their values while they accept yours? That can be a freeing and powerful exercise.

Personal Exercise

Instructions: Values, Time, and Energy Exercise

Review or transfer your top 7 values to the following blank list. Place your Number One value in the first position and so on, up to 7. Once you have completed the transfer, carefully reflect on each value to establish whether you honestly feel that your needs related to that value are currently being met, from both a time and an energy perspective.

Make sure you consider your entire life—not just work and/or home.

- If your needs are being met, answer Yes and place a (+) in the status column.

- If No, then place a (-) beside that value.

If you wish, you may rank your values from 1 to 10.

1 = Not met at all

10 = Being completely fulfilled

Once you have confirmed your current time and energy status, summarize for each value what you need to do to continue to keep a (+) there. Or, if you responded with a (-), what you need to change to turn it into a (+).

1. _____

2. _____

3. _____

4. _____

5. _____

6. _____

7. _____

Notes

_____

_____

_____

_____

If you placed a (+) beside each of your top 7 values, you likely feel satisfied with your life. You will feel fulfilled if your life is a reflection of your values. You could feel even more aligned with your values as additional opportunities arise.

Having mostly (-) signs beside your values might indicate 1 of 2 possibilities.

1. You are investing time in areas not related to the values that are important to you. If so, you may be dissatisfied with what you are doing. Perhaps situations and/or others have sidetracked you from what is really most important to you. In that case, re-assess your priorities and your decisions about your current activities.

2. You are investing your time in areas that are valuable to you but those particular values are not on your list. If so, the values you selected on the inventory may not be your main values. You may have chosen values you feel are more socially acceptable or you selected *family values*—values based on what other people want, not what you need.

Note: A forced-choice matrix is part of the assessment process in the *Values Preference Indicator*. This is where you rank each value against every other value 5 times. That requires you to make over 300 decisions. The result of this exercise is that many people's top values from the forced-choice matrix process do not match the top 7 values they selected from the list provided in this book.

There are many reasons for the differences. The key is for you to filter through all the outside pressures and get connected to the core values that *truly* motivate and fill your needs. If this process is of interest to you or others, please go to www.crgleader.com to learn more about the *Values Preference Indicator*.

CHAPTER 9

Finding the Job/Role that Matches Your Working Style

Real success is finding your lifework in the work that you love.

DAVID MCCULLOUGH

> **Do you realize that 70% to 80% of people dislike their jobs, from a feeling of mild irritation to downright loathing?**

Most of us will spend more time at our work than anything else during our lifetime, so having 4 out of 5 people dissatisfied with their job or career is simply not acceptable.

Why are so many individuals dissatisfied with their work?

Because, the style of the job—the nature of the role or responsibility— does not match the Personal Style or values of the person.

I was conducting an evening Personal Style Workshop for a professional development organization. As part of the final section of the seminar, I discussed the importance of job-style compatibility to individual, team, and organizational performance.

At the end of the evening, the supervisor took me aside to thank me for giving her insight. She had intended to fire one of her employees the next morning.

A few months back, one of her best employees had been answering the phone, connecting clients with coaches, and doing an excellent job. She was promoted to run the client database and manage all the information for the coaching program.

Her performance and interest in this new role dropped consistently, to the point she was about to lose her job! Instead of understanding the root cause of the performance decline, the supervisor assumed the reason was the employee's poor attitude (Willingness). The supervisor felt she was no longer a valuable asset.

That was not the case. The employee had a High **A** and Low **C** style pattern. She loved people and had great energy around them, yet she had been promoted to a position that was mostly task and data. **C** was her lowest score on the *PSI*.

Quite simply, her new job did not reflect her working style requirements. The supervisor had been oblivious to that fact.

In our short chat, I was able to persuade the supervisor to reverse her decision to fire that person. Instead, she decided to promote her, and put her in charge of all the coaches in their network. Not only did she thrive in the new position that focused mostly on people, she eventually started her own coaching business.

Although the staff member had been successful in her first job, once she was promoted to a job that was incompatible with her Personal Style, she could not sustain her efforts.

How many others are in positions that have a job style that is not compatible with them? Thousands, millions, maybe even billions?!

**If you are in a position—or take a position—that does not suit
your Personal Style pattern, you will not be able
to function at your peak performance.**

A Visual metaphor to Illustrate My Point

Envision four empty glasses on a table in front of you.

Beside the glasses is a pitcher full of water.

- The water represents the 160 points that are allocated when you complete the **Online *PSI*** response sheet.

- Each glass represents one of the four dimensions: **Behavioral** ACTION, **Cognitive** ANALYSIS, **Interpersonal** HARMONY, and **Affective** EXPRESSION.

The amount of water you pour into each glass represents your scores in each dimension.

- The more water in the glass, the higher the score in that dimension.

- The less water in the glass, the lower the score in that dimension.

- The water represents the amount of personal energy you have available to engage in that style dimension.

- A full glass represents the *strengths* on which you should focus.

- An empty glass represents jobs, roles, or responsibilities you should avoid.

Scenario A

One of the glasses doesn't have much water in it. Let's say it's the **Cognitive** ANALYSIS glass.

You arrive at work to find that your boss has a lot of detailed reports, budgets, and analyses for you to do. By the first morning break, you have finished drinking all the water in your **Cognitive** ANALYSIS glass. In other words, you have consumed all your **C** energy.

But you have much more detailed work to do for the rest of the day. How would you feel by the end of the day after "working from an empty glass"? Stressed, for sure!

Scenario B

Let's say your **Affective** EXPRESSION glass is full of water. In this example, you meet with customers all day, sipping water from the **A** glass to keep you connected with people. At the end of the day, there's still some water left in your **Affective** EXPRESSION glass.

When your boss asks you to take a few clients out for dinner, you say *Sure!* You can do it because you still have more water (energy) in your glass to keep you going.

Unless you have enough water in your glass to sustain you for the specific responsibilities of your job, stress will build up in you, and your fulfillment from your work and in your life will decrease. That is especially true when you completely drain your water glass or if it stays empty for an extended period of time.

> **It is impossible to sustain your work effort or energy in a role or responsibility that does not match your Personal Style preferences.**

One of the main reasons that 80% of people dislike their job is they have not matched their Personal Style with the job style of their position. Many times, individuals and managers blame poor performance on a lack of willingness or a bad attitude. In reality, they may not have the style orientation (the water) to do the job. Many people make the mistake of criticizing themselves or feeling guilty for not enjoying their work, when in fact their discontent is the result of job-style incompatibility.

In his book *Good to Great*, Jim Collins identified that the best organizations *intentionally* have the right people, on the right bus, in the right seat, doing the right things.

He does not, however, offer a system to achieve that.

I will, right now!

What is Job-Style Compatibility?

Most employers want to hire a superman or superwoman who can be all things to all people. The reality is ***we don't need to do that***. We simply need to hire the right person for the position.

All positions and responsibilities have a style orientation. When you understand the nature of the work, you can align it with the nature (the Personal Style pattern) of the person who will best fulfill the position.

> **It is essential to identify the style requirements of the position or role before you attempt to place someone in it.**

The ***Job Style Indicator*** is an assessment process that measures the style pattern needs of a position, not a person.

Hiring or operating without understanding style compatibility is much like flying blind in a fog bank.

Note: Applying the process of job-style compatibility does not exclude the typical elements in any job screening or selection process, such as a person's education, experience, references, skills, abilities, values alignment, gifts, and talents.

Let's look at the core elements that make up work and roles.

Work Tasks

Every job contains a combination of work-related tasks that must be accomplished if the job is to be completed successfully. Most of us prefer certain work tasks over others. We have strong personal preferences for the way we would like to spend our working hours.

For example, you might like working outdoors doing manual labor tasks rather than working indoors at a desk and talking to people.

Work-related tasks can be divided into four main categories.

1. Things
Many daily tasks involve the use of objects and/or things invented to alter the amount of work we must do. The shovel is a simple example. With it you can move dirt more easily than if you use your hands, but not more easily than if you use a bulldozer.

This category includes preferences for working with machines, animals, plants, raw materials (such as wood or metals), technological equipment, robotics, large corporations, and so forth. Individuals with a strong preference for the **Behavioral** Personal Style dimension often prefer careers in this category because they call for high levels of physical energy.

2. Data
This category includes all tasks involved in the use of information. Information comes in many different forms, such as facts, numbers, statistics, and dates. It encompasses all data-related activities that involve information, for example, programming, recording, filing, planning, or editing. Individuals who have a strong orientation in the **Cognitive** Personal Style dimension are often interested in those kinds of work activities because they involve mental concentration and energy.

3. People
The work world is made up of various jobs that require people-related tasks such as teaching, selling, motivating, accommodating, supporting, and helping. Work positions in this area focus on assisting people in some part of their daily lives. Because **Interpersonal**-type individuals

are usually strong in their orientation to people, they are often interested in those types of work tasks.

4. Ideas

The fourth category of work activities deals with ideas and all activities related to thinking and performing creatively, including activities like coaching, artistic endeavors, writing, entertaining, and designing. Jobs that primarily focus on ideas require original thinking and the ability to work independently.

People with a strong natural tendency toward the **Affective** dimension are usually very inventive and intuitive as a result of their high level of creative energy. They like jobs and occupations that allow them to be imaginative, with the freedom to express their ideas and abilities.

Job Strengths and Difficulties of Each Dimension

The dynamic of job style is that each dimension has natural aptitudes and strengths **and** limitations and difficulties. Suppose you have a position where there is a high level of independence, problem-solving, fast decision-making, and risk-taking. Based on style, those elements would best be fulfilled by the **Behavioral** dimension, but the position also requires working with a team, leading others, and communicating with groups—activities that don't come naturally to a **Behavioral** style.

When individuals are confirming the style pattern of a position using the *JSI*, the following grids help them indicate the characteristics and abilities they feel are important to that role. They also review and indicate potential difficulties that need to be minimized to ensure the success of the position.

You can use this framework to outline any role or responsibility, from household chores for your children, to volunteering, to developing a job description for a VP of an international organization. The principles are the same.

Behavioral ACTION

Changing Things

Job Strengths and Difficulties

Strengths
*Individuals who are strong in the **Behavioral** dimension
tend to have abilities in these areas.*

Learning quickly	Making decisions
Working well under pressure	Taking risks
Helping situationally	Delegating tasks
Working hard	Handling responsibility
Problem-solving	Working alone
Being time-efficient	Setting goals
Planning for the future	Being dedicated to a cause

Individuals who score low in this dimension most likely
will be naturally weak in the above skills areas.

Difficulties
*Individuals strong in the **Behavioral ACTION** dimension
can have these tendencies.*

Insensitive to feelings	Poor team players
Stubborn about	Resistant subordinate workers
changing viewpoints	Ineffective communicators
Belligerent when upset	Socially aggressive
Authoritarian, rigid	Prideful, unapologetic
Unappreciative	Humorless

Cognitive ANALYSIS

Handling Data

Job Strengths and Difficulties

Strengths
*Individuals who are strong in the **Cognitive** dimension
tend to have abilities in these areas.*

Calculating figures	Analyzing details
Organizing data	Researching information
Attending to details	Following instructions
Proofreading	Getting quality results
Maintaining standards	Being loyal
Making in-depth presentations	Using deductive reasoning
Clarifying information	Creating charts and visual aids

Individuals who score low in this dimension most likely
will be naturally weak in the above skills areas.

Difficulties
*Individuals strong in the **Cognitive ANALYSIS** dimension
can have these tendencies.*

Daydream frequently	Blunt
Pessimistic, picky	Slow decision-makers
Give advice	Dominate conversations
Stress when overworked	Poor listeners
Too inquisitive	Freeze under pressure
Forgetful of people's names	Overreact when angry
Live in the past	Can be loners

Interpersonal HARMONY

Relating to People

Job Strengths and Difficulties

Strengths
*Individuals who are strong in the **Interpersonal** dimension tend to have abilities in these areas.*

Working consistently	Greeting the public
Serving others	Organizing events
Recordkeeping and filing	Finishing projects
Driving vehicles	Answering phones
Ordering supplies	Being patient
Conserving materials	Listening to others
Taking care of others	Fixing things

Individuals who score low in this dimension most likely
will be naturally weak in the above skills areas.

Difficulties
*Individuals strong in the **Interpersonal HARMONY** dimension can have these tendencies.*

Overly sensitive	Shy in front of groups
Generally unassertive	Slow to react
Stubborn when angry	Short-sighted planners
People-pleasers	Overly quiet, non-verbal
Easily stressed and	Reluctant delegators
overextended	Stress-avoiders
Indecisive	Weak disciplinarians
Too easy-going	

Affective EXPRESSION

Exploring Ideas

Job Strengths and Difficulties

Strengths
*Individuals who are strong in the **Affective** dimension
tend to have abilities in these areas.*

Imaginative	Inventive
Energetic	Quick to become involved
Resourceful	Enterprising
Quick to learn	Sensitive to others
Good group leaders	Funny, entertaining
Inductive reasoners	Persuasive
Motivational	Self-confident

Individuals who score low in this dimension most likely
will be naturally weak in the above skills areas.

Difficulties
*Individuals strong in the **Affective EXPRESSION** dimension
can have these tendencies.*

Start too many projects	Ignore timelines
Leave projects unfinished	Too many interests
Unreliable	Self-centered
Inconsistent performers	Poor money managers
Act recklessly	Too play-oriented
Impulsive decision-makers	Overly busy
Tend to exaggerate	Easily distracted

The *Job Style Indicator (JSI)* is a communications tool used to confirm that individuals understand one another as it relates to specific job and role expectations.

I worked with an organization where a team of three individuals was part of the hiring process, working to hire a person for a special position. I asked each team member to complete the *Job Style Indicator* on the position. To their surprise, each had a different opinion on what Personal Style pattern would best fulfill the role.

How can you hire the right person if the decision-makers can't agree on the best style pattern for the position?

You can't.

When the team talked about their *JSI* results, they could more accurately define the position. No guessing or estimations. Together, they crafted a job-style profile that reflected input from all of them. They agreed on the Personal Style of the individual who would best fit the job.

In hiring protocols, most processes and professionals don't include the critical step of matching the job style with the Personal Style of the applicant.

Understanding Job Style Saved This Company

The manager of a finance division of a large national retailer called me in because he was experiencing a 400% staff turnover. He needed help and he needed it now!

The problem was with their credit collection department, a large call center. The call center used an integrated computer and phone system where outbound calls were automated. When a credit agent hung up the phone from one call, he was immediately transferred to the next call.

Sometimes the next client's information would not flash onto the screen until after the call was connected. Many times, the credit department staff did not know the name and details of the person to whom they were speaking when they were transferred to the next call. To compensate, they had to drag out the introduction until the information appeared on their screen.

Their day was a series of non-stop calls to collect money from delinquent accounts. Added to that was the stress of the demanding telephone system they were using. You can imagine the pressure and intensity of that position.

The manager's vision was that he wanted to have the nicest credit department team in the industry so he hired people with **Interpersonal HARMONY** patterns to work in his division. The challenge with that idea is that an **I** individual dislikes conflict and generally is not assertive.

In spite of the manager's idealistic projection for his department, the job style did not match the nature of the people he was hiring. That is not to suggest that High **Is** cannot work in a call center but, with the **I**'s specific characteristics, these individuals were not physically or emotionally able to sustain the intense pace and pressure of the credit collection role. Hence the 400% turnover.

- We adjusted the hiring so the manager did not choose individuals with **I** as their highest dimension.

- I asked the technical department to slow down the rate of calls so the call center staff had a 10- to 15-second breather between calls.

- The system was reset so the data appeared on the screen before the collection people were connected with the clients.

At first, the number of outbound calls went down but the success rate of the collections went up. And the stability of the staff improved more than 10-fold.

After adjusting a few more aspects of the call process and changing the hiring specifications, in only a few weeks the 400% turnover was heading down below 40%.

Unless this organization had implemented that strategy, it was doubtful they would have survived another year. The cost of the high turnover and the poor collection performance were not sustainable conditions.

The Versatility of the *Job Style Indicator*

The *JSI* process can be used by the person hiring or the person thinking about accepting a position.

If a potential employer does not include a **Job-Style Compatibility** measurement as part of the hiring process, you can offer the employer the opportunity to use the *JSI*. Ask the hiring individual to complete it for the position you are considering.

That may seem bold, but you certainly don't want to accept a job that's not *you.* Why? Most likely, you'll end up quitting! I know though experience that a severe job-style mismatch heightens an individual's stress levels; in that case, the ability to continue or maintain high levels of performance is significantly hindered.

This suggestion also will reveal whether the firm is progressive and open to new ideas. If the potential employer is not, that may be a good reason to move to another opportunity. Imagine how inflexible the company would be once you actually started working there?

Once a job-style pattern has been established, compare your *PSI* score, if you are applying—or to the applicant's *PSI* score, if you are hiring.

Job-Style Compatibility Guidelines

Here are guidelines to help determine the degree of job-style compatibility between the individual and the position.

- When the scores of a specific dimension for the job style and the individual's Personal Style are within 5 points, there is a job-style **match**.

- Differences of 6 to 10 points in any of the dimensions are seen as a **slight mismatch** for that dimension.

- Score differences from 11 to 15 represent a definite **mismatch**.

- Differences greater than 15 in any of the four style dimensions are a **severe mismatch**.

In the following example, these two graphs will help you compare a person's style with a job's *JSI* compatibility.

The job style of this example position is **B**50, **C**40, **I**40, **A**30.

Job Style Graph

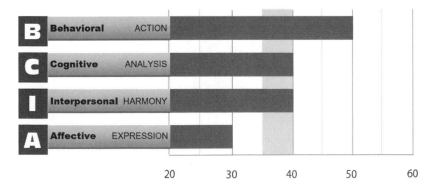

The Personal Style scores of the applicant are **B**43, **C**29, **I**40, **A**48.

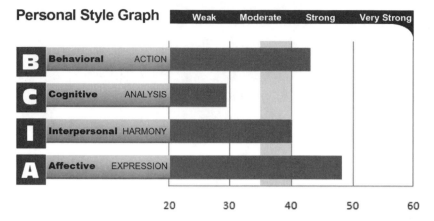

Based on this information, here are the compatibility levels of each of the dimensions for this position, compared to this applicant's *PSI* scores.

- **B** is a **slight mismatch:**   7 point difference.
- **C** is a **mismatch:**   11 point difference.
- **I** is a **match:**   0 difference.
- **A** is an **extreme mismatch:**   18 point difference.

Based on the job-style compatibility information, it appears an overall match is lacking between the person and the position. The position has a **BCI** pattern requirement; the applicant has an **ABI** pattern. Further conversations with the application would be required to confirm our initial observations of the individual's job-style compatibility.

Team Development

In the *Good to Great* research, great companies realized they had the right people but in the wrong jobs or responsibilities. You can use the *PSI/JSI* **Compatibility** process for team development and role confirmation.

Unfortunately, when individuals want to shift job roles or responsibilities, often they are not heard. By not listening and not responding, many organizations lose their best talent; those people will move on.

Ignoring staff requests also does not acknowledge the style strengths and differences each individual brings to the team. I am not talking about workers who are lazy and want to make life easy; I am referring to ongoing responsibilities that do not match a person's work style.

By having a team conversation and dialogue about each person's style pattern and the job-style pattern of each role on the team, you can intentionally adjust responsibilities to play to the strengths of each team member as much as possible. When this strategy is implemented, you will find an increase in productivity, job satisfaction, morale, and the loyalty of team members.

That applies equally to volunteers, not-for-profit organizations, education, teams, sports, and families.

Case Example: Using the *Job Style Indicator*

From Kurt Newman, Sydney, Australia

> *I had been working with one of Australia's largest labor hire companies in the area of improving sales performance. As a result of the sales development process, the weaker performers decided to leave. This left quite a gap in several key business units.*
>
> *The company traditionally hired only male ex-tradesmen. They believed only a salesperson with a trade experience could effectively communicate to their prospects and clients who also had trade backgrounds. That criterion presented other problems; some of the tradespeople were not trainable in the art of sales.*
>
> *I introduced the* **Personal Style Indicator** *and* **Job Style Indicator** *compatibility model. Their top-performing salesperson, branch manager, and regional manager completed the* **Job Style Indicator** *independently.*
>
> *The three individual graphs were drawn on a whiteboard; any major difference—5 points or more on any of the four dimensions—was highlighted. We referred back to the response page and discussed why the scores resulted in the differences. Through consensus, they agreed what an ideal candidate would look like on the* **JSI** *graph. That was used as a guiding benchmark.*
>
> *An agreement was reached to open the hiring to females and nontradespeople. Applicants, during their second interview, were asked to complete the* **PSI***.*
>
> *Prior to the final interview, the hiring team noted the major differences between each applicant's* **PSI** *score and the* **JSI** *score; we reviewed their résumé and developed behavioral-based questions to reflect all these inputs.*
>
> *One manager informed me that the process had prevented him from hiring the wrong person on numerous occasions. The company, during the next 12 months, increased sales by 45% and*

a female was the top sales-producer. Today, there are more non-tradespeople on the sales force than ex-tradespeople.

*The company has extended the **PSI/JSI** methodology to hiring branch managers, operations personnel, and administration staff.*

Kurt Newman
Sydney, Australia
www.salesconsultants.com.au

Occupations and Style

Many individuals and professionals attempt to link *occupational* suggestions to each style dimension.

I don't agree with that process.

- **Style does not predict success in an *occupation*.**
- Style compatibility applies only to a specific role or position that needs to be filled.
- Jobs that our children will enjoy in the future have not been invented yet!

Contrary to many career developers, I do not subscribe to Standard Industry Codes (SIC), National Occupational Codes (NOC), or any other fixed list of careers or roles from which individuals may attempt to determine a career based on their type or temperament.

Too many combinations and possibilities are not included in most "career interest" inventories. Style should be used to outline the qualities and characteristics required of a specific job opportunity and to confirm style compatibility, which is a very powerful and practical application. Personal Style, however, does not measure interests, gifts, talents, or your natural intelligence.

> **Temperament or style patterns should NEVER be used to determine a career path or the occupation that will best suit you.**

For example, there are no SIC or NOC codes for my personal career. Many "interest" inventories tell me I should be president of a company—but where, doing what? Should I be running a manufacturing plant, a farm, a school? I lead a publishing company, certify and train professionals around the globe, and write content and resources that change people's lives. That profile usually is not on any *interest* inventory.

Career guides can help you consider a career direction. But they are only thought-starters, not ends in themselves.

> **A friend got a list of 650 career suggestions**
> **after completing an MBTI assessment.**

One of the career assessments I completed years ago measured my interests and skills compared to other people in specific careers or positions, such as a bank manager or insurance agent. The career assessment then listed professions where I had the most similarity of interests and skills with individuals already working in that profession.

It seemed like a good idea at the time but, if 80% of individuals dislike their jobs—from a feeling of mild irritation to downright loathing—that means I am similar to the 80% of people who don't like their work and who are not living *on purpose*.

In the past couple of decades, technology has transformed the world of work and the nature of opportunities. Today, an auto mechanic needs strong IT abilities or an electronic orientation. Just a few years ago, the focus was mechanical only.

> **No occupation can be defined by a single style or style pattern.**

If I mention accounting or finance as a profession, you may immediately think **Cs** are best for the position. In reality, several disciplines are necessary for success in accounting and finance. For example, management accounting, mergers, and acquisitions require the strategic nature of a **Behavioral** style. I worked with a CFO (Chief Financial Officer) of a very large insurance agency; he had a **BA** pattern with a low score in his **C** dimension. His job role required strategic and creative approaches to expand, leverage, and invest on behalf of the firm.

> **Prejudging that certain professions or careers are suited to a specific style**
> **is a dangerous and damaging practice.**

Review the chapter on values to ensure you are using your core values as a filter to confirm that a job opportunity aligns with your core values.

Before I entered the professional development profession, I always selected positions with a lot of freedom and flexibility. Even as a teen-ager, I had a sense—more unconscious than intentional—that unless independence was part of a position, I simply could not function. That assisted me to work in the right job style.

Given the information you have gathered so far, you can progress to a place where your job/career will pick you, not the other way around.

When you are clear about the work style of the right position for you and you are aware of your core values, as the right opportunity crosses your path you will know that you know that is the place for you! It will also be obvious which jobs or opportunities don't fit you—you simply will no longer be interested in them.

Many Factors are Needed for Work Success

Numerous factors contribute to an individual's success in a position. Job style is only one factor. Therefore, it is not appropriate to use only the *JSI* when determining whether a person could or would be successful in fulfilling specific roles and responsibilities.

The *Job Style Indicator (JSI)* outlined in this chapter measures the style needs of a specific position or role. The results of the *JSI* are compared to an applicant's *Personal Style Indicator* results in a separate compatibility report, to establish the level of style-matching between the person and the position. Go to www.crgleader.com to learn more about the *Job Style Indicator* and the *JSI* **Compatibility Report.**

Note: The *Job Style Indicator* can be used with each of the CRG style assessments to establish work/job-style compatibility. The other CRG assessments include the *Quick Style Indicator* (the shorter, simpler version of the *PSI*), the *Sales Style Indicator*, the *Instructional Style Indicator*, and the *Entrepreneurial Style and Success Indicator*.

ONLINE
JSI COMPATIBILITY
REPORT

CHAPTER 10

Using Style to Increase Success in Entrepreneurship and Self-Employment

I'm convinced that about half of what separates
the successful entrepreneurs from the non-successful ones
is pure perseverance.

STEVE JOBS

Have you been thinking about starting your own business (or becoming self-employed) instead of working as an employee for someone else?

A doctor friend called one day to share a personal dilemma. He had spent the better part of 10 years in school to become a medical doctor. He said he disliked his work.

I asked the obvious, "If you don't like medicine, why are you in it?"

"It's what my parents wanted. And I have half my life invested in it so what am I to do?"

I asked if he was planning to be miserable for the second half of his life . . . ?

During a few phone calls, I coached my friend on the implications of his choices. He managed to muster the courage to leave his medical practice and started his own business. He now operates a successful real estate investment and property development firm and enjoys it. He wishes he had made the decision sooner. I am proud of him.

Perhaps he was under enormous pressure to stay working where he was, for the wrong reasons.

Are **you** working where you don't want to be?

Maybe it's for security, a pension you don't want to lose, or fear of the unknown. Whatever the reason, I want to encourage you to make the decision now to do what will bring you closer to your calling, your passions, and your *purpose*.

Many years ago, I had to go through a transition in my entrepreneurial mindset and beliefs. I had become part of no fewer than seven business ventures at the same time. The success of my training company seemed to be attracting individuals who wanted me to be a business partner with them.

One of my values is the need for *variety*. At the time, I used that filter to justify having diverse business interests, including an RV rental business, an alarm and security company, a dairy farm, car dealership, mining company, real estate investment firm, a training and consulting firm, and on it went. (I didn't even like some of the businesses, but my friends wanted me to partner with them and I agreed.)

Now there's nothing wrong with having numerous business interests but it was impossible to sustain all those hands-on start-ups and organizations in need of my personal leadership.

My error was three-fold.

1. Instead of saying No to at least some of those ventures, I agreed to participate through the false belief that they contributed to my value of variety.
2. Mastery and success are about focus. Instead of being focused, I was fragmented. When I finally realized that all this *busy-ness* was draining me, I made the decision to disconnect from all of them.
3. I also let my Personal Style contribute to my situation. Being so extroverted, I felt I could handle all the responsibilities and control the environment, but even extroverts need to acknowledge that some expectations are simply not reasonable. I came to realize that my profession of building a publishing business and writing, speaking, training, coaching, and consulting provided all the variety I needed.

> **Your ability to say No is as important as your ability to say Yes to your success in life.**

If so many people are dissatisfied with their work, surely owning their own business would be better. Unfortunately, the stats for entrepreneurs aren't much better. According to Industry Canada (and it is similar in other countries), over 75% of new small businesses are out of business in less than 5 years, and 92% don't make it past year 10.

Why so much failure? You need a business that matches your Entrepreneurial Style and your core values. If that is not present, there's no way to sustain the personal energy required to successfully launch or run a venture.

In the book *Millionaire Next Door*, Dr. Thomas Stanley confirmed that less than 10% of businesses successfully make it to the third generation. Why? The ***purpose*** and interests of the founder don't align with future generations. Or the next generation has a mindset of entitlement, not understanding the real passions of a true entrepreneur.

Many individuals reading this book don't have a traditional job or oc-cupation; they are self-employed or they own their own businesses. The same principles of job-style compatibility apply to self-employed indi-viduals and businessowners—possibly even more than to an employee.

Why?

In their quest to save money, self-employed or startup entrepreneurs attempt to do everything themselves, which can be far more costly than hiring people to help them.

I am guilty of that myself. When I first started my sales training firm in the late '80s, I operated from a spare room at the house and I did everything. That included bookkeeping, proposal writing, and all the other administrative tasks.

I have few style strengths for details regarding data, like bookkeeping. I dislike it intensely.

Of course, as a good entrepreneur, I sucked it up and did the tasks. But that drained my energy and kept me from doing what I do well, which is selling (influencing), writing, and speaking. It cost me money to do everything myself. How? Not only was I slow and miserable while doing that work, it hardly put me in the right frame of mind to sell or develop anything.

I now hire excellent, gifted individuals who are interested in the various disciplines required to operate the organization successfully. That's the way it should be in every establishment—for-profit organizations and not-for-profits.

Knowledge of entrepreneurial style helps entrepreneurs focus on their strengths and uncover the characteristics of a partner(s) and/or staff member(s) who will complement their work. Businessowners tend to hire individuals just like themselves, and that might not be what the business or partnership needs to grow . . . unless of course they confirm the job style of the positions in advance, and hire the style patterns that will fulfill the roles specific to their organizational needs.

> **I am here to suggest that we need more successful entrepreneurs.**

Why? Because entrepreneurs care about their organizations and companies, unlike some of the overpaid CEOs of many publicly traded companies whose only consideration is getting a bonus, regardless whether the business makes money.

Although in the past, the extroverted styles of **B** and **A** were seen as more adaptable to the primary needs of running a business, that no longer holds true. What if you are running an online business? Hundreds of Internet millionaires or application developers have harnessed the power of technology to serve others. In many cases, they never left their home or office to achieve their success.

According to Larry Farrell, expert on entrepreneurship, if you want to ruin an organization, hire an MBA or increase the number of managers in your organization. Why? Most MBAs are managers, not entrepreneurs.

> **We require less management training**
> **and more focus on entrepreneurial leadership.**

What Makes Small Businessowners Tick?

According to the research conducted by The Spirit of Enterprise, Larry Farrell's organization, four simple truths set successful entrepreneurs— and their ventures—apart from mere managers and executives.

1. Sense of Mission

The entrepreneurial way to deliver product/market winners

Entrepreneurs are passionate about their product and their cause. Just ask one about his or her company and you won't have to say a word for the next few hours. That same sense of mission will ensure that organization will make a difference in the world, no matter the product or service. Rarely is the discussion about the money. It is about vision.

2. Customer/Product Vision

Creating entrepreneurial passion to produce continuous growth

Small businessowners are constantly connecting the dots between the product/service they offer and their consumers. Even though Apple is a large organization, Steve Jobs continues that hands-on tradition. Apple operates like the IPad—personal, innovative, and efficient.

3. High-Speed Innovation

The entrepreneur's secret weapon for beating the competition

Entrepreneurs are dedicated to faster and quicker, unlike huge multinational companies that are buried in bureaucracy. Have you ever worked with a city planning department? Often, their process slows things to a pace that will discourage most developers and visionaries.

4. Self-Inspired Behavior

The power of loving what you do and becoming very good at it

True entrepreneurs and ***on purpose* people** do not need supervision because they are fully engaged in the tasks at hand, and they know who they are. They are connected to their responsibilities and their work roles.

The Life Cycle of All Organizations

Entrepreneurial Practices		Managerial Practices	
Startup	High Growth	Decline	Survival

Source and Copyright: The Spirit of Entrepreneurship

Change is inevitable. *Why Aren't You More Like Me?*™ is providing you a roadmap so you can be intentional in your life choices. Success is an ever-moving target; it can be fleeting if you are not paying attention.

Here are some stats that may surprise you about the temporary nature of success.

- Of the top 100 companies operating in the year 1900, only 16 were still in business in 2000.
- Of the organizations that made up the Fortune 500 companies in 1955, only 25% were on the list in 2005.
- Over 90% of all new job creation is done by small business and entrepreneurs.
- Of the current S&P 500 companies, 25% are family-run. Their total wealth exceeds that of all the other companies on the list.
- Most of the companies mentioned in Tom Peters' book *In Search of Excellence* are either no longer operational or they don't demonstrate the excellence they once had.
- One of the best-researched books on leadership—*Good to Great*—cited Fannie Mae as an example of star leadership. Most of us now know Fannie Mae was one of the major contributors to the financial meltdown of 2008.

Quote from Larry Farrell

Beating the natural life cycle of organizations is tough. In the beginning, the entrepreneurial spirit fuels the startup and creates high growth. Growth brings size and the passage of time brings new leaders. These shifts in size and leadership produce a new set of objectives.

Planning, streamlining, and controlling the enterprise become the new order. Managing this and that becomes more important than making this and selling that. Meetings, reports, and self-perpetuating bureaucracy erupt on every front. Decline sets in and, unchecked, you're on your way to demise.

The only way to fix this mess is to start over with the entrepreneurial basics. If you're looking for the bedrock fundamentals of high-growth enterprise, look no further. The key to growth in the hyper-competitive 21st century will be old-fashioned entrepreneurship!

LARRY FARRELL

The following research on the global dynamics of Entrepreneurship was conducted by the London Business School.

- About 75 million entrepreneurs operate globally, representing a labor force of about 784 million.
- Countries are ranked by their **TEA: Total Entrepreneurial Activity.**
- Over 99% of entrepreneurs launch their business without any formal venture capital or business angel investors. In fact, 65.8% entrepreneurs personally provided the startup capital. The remainder tapped into family and friends. Banks and government development banks provide only lip service to their desire to provide venture funding.
- Over 88% of fast-growing private companies never received financing from business angel investors.
- The greatest shift is required by the most socialized countries where high taxes, high employment protection, and high unemployment benefits have resulted not only in the lowest TEA, but in attitudes that suggest only 2% of the population believes entrepreneurship is a good choice.

What is the Purpose of a Small Business?

Most people will answer that question with the following.

- Make money
- Serve clients and potential clients
- Provide employment and economic activity
- Support the local community

Marketers will declare *find a need and fill it*. That's fine in theory, but what if I have no passion for that marketplace need? How will I sustain my energy to operate a business in which I have little interest?

Most people don't. That is one reason for the 75% failure rate in the first 5 years of small-business startups.

I want to suggest that these should be the real objectives for any small or privately held business.

- Serve and fulfill your gifts, talents, style, and ***purpose!***
- Support your dreams, wants, and desires!
- Have a business that provides a lifestyle that reflects your requirements!

With information and technology at the core of any developed or emerging economy, new entrepreneurial opportunities present themselves every day. If you have already started your own business or are thinking about starting one, make sure your venture meets your lifestyle requirements.

Of course there should be a need in the marketplace for your service or product, but that's not the main reason for choosing a certain business. Your venture must reflect and use your gifts, talents, style, and *purpose*.

Here are some comments from Professor Thomas L. Rodgers, PhD, Educator and Consultant to Entrepreneurs.

Most entrepreneurs do not plan before starting a business—they just do it!

There are three things every entrepreneur should do.

- *Write a business plan,*
- *take some business and industry classes, and*
- *use the* **Entrepreneurship Style and Success Indicator (ESSI)** *assessment.*

The easiest and arguably most important is the third point: Using the **ESSI**.

Entrepreneurs come with all types of personalities, but successful entrepreneurs are few and tend to have specific personality styles and success indicators. **ESSI** *assesses and informs you concerning your entrepreneurial style and success factors.*

Even though I teach entrepreneurship and innovation at the graduate level and have started several companies, my **ESSI** *was mixed with regard to entrepreneurship.*

In the class syllabus, I introduce myself as an "entrepreneur groupie" who writes about or teaches entrepreneurship. Lawyers, accountants, and consultants who help entrepreneurs are included in this category.

That is exactly what I am. **ESSI** *confirmed what was already stated in the syllabus.* **ESSI** *also summarized succinctly key personality issues and success factors in a manner that facilitates self-reflection.*

ESSI *is a great first step before moving along to business plans and formal training. This step either affirms a propensity for entrepreneurship or helps steer you into a more appropriate role.*

In addition to the **ESSI**, *the use of other CRG assessments affirmed and facilitated a self-reflective process. Over the years, I have taken numerous personality assessments and found most to be informative, and worthy of a caution when they are used inappropriately.*

What comes immediately to mind is the partner in an accounting firm who stood up and declared that everyone who was not a "thinker" should be fired.

What makes the CRG assessments unique is their self-reflective nature using pattern descriptions and narratives that are self-descriptive and helpful.

Many years ago, I was labeled off-the-chart "Intuitive." Now the **ESSI** *pattern descriptions show me as "Balanced" and "Synergistic."*

Not only are those terms a better fit for who I am, the **ESSI** *narrative helped me to reflect on how to provide a consistency in my approach to others, thus reducing mixed messages and affirming other personality styles. The emphasis was less on the categorization and more on interpersonal engagement with style and substance.*

Taking such a self-reflective journey is worthy of doing, periodically and intentionally. Life and circumstances have a way of changing us. It is good to re-affirm who we are, what we value, and how we interact with others.

Thomas L. Rodgers, PhD, Certified Public Accountant

Adjunct Professor, Trinity Western University

www.twu.ca

If you think your calling is to be self-employed or to start your own business, I recommend CRG's *Entrepreneurial Style and Success Indicator.*

First, you will discover your entrepreneurial style and learn how to play to your strengths. Second, you will rank yourself on 28 critical entrepreneurial success factors confirmed in research on 4000 successful entrepreneurs. To learn more, please go to www.crgleader.com.

CHAPTER 11

Do You Want to Live, Lead, and Work *On Purpose?*

Purpose is something bigger than goals. It is the picture you have of yourself—the kind of person you want to be— the kind of life you want to lead.

KENNETH BLANCHARD AND
NORMAN VINCENT PEALE

My son is a gifted musician. At age 8, he had the entire school rocking to his keyboard skills and abilities. Since then, he has taught himself to play three other instruments.

During a Christmas dinner at my parents' home, my aunt asked Tim what he wanted to do when he grew up. He said he was going to have his own band and play music, which I thought was a great answer. My aunt said, "That band idea is nice but you can't make any money at that, so what do you plan to do for a real job?"

I just about jumped out of my seat. My aunt's caution to Tim about her perceived perils of the music business was well meaning, but her response was inappropriate. She has no first-hand knowledge of that career. She was projecting her unfounded fears onto his choice.

Motivation is a Myth.

Now no one can clearly state why certain things inspire some people and not others, but we do know that we each have underlying behavioral values and interests that energize and fulfill us.

When I speak at conferences, some individuals call me a motivational speaker. I disagree with that characterization. In reality, no one can motivate anyone else to do anything.

The pursuit of things that interest us requires no motivation because we enjoy those activities. Interests *compel* us. Compel means to be pulled or attracted. That precludes any need for motivation.

> **We require motivation only for those things that don't interest us.**

What's Your *Purpose*?

The majority of this book is about your Personal Style, the Personal Style of others, and values. *Purpose* is also an integral part of understanding the self and others.

> **Your elements of purpose and passion are separate from your style.**

Two people reading this book could have identical style patterns—one desiring to become a fighter pilot, the other a police officer. Just as we all have unique Personal Styles and personalities, we also have distinctive passions and *purposes.*

It is possible that although the job style of your current position perfectly matches (is compatible with) your Personal Style or entrepreneurial style, you are still not engaged at work. In that case, we must look deeper. The problem might be the work environment and the lack of leadership where you work, or maybe you are simply doing something you don't enjoy—it is not your **passion**.

Just as you are wired with a specific style at birth, you are also given specific talents, abilities, and interests that intertwine with your values and style to provide your life direction.

In addition, many of you have deep faith or spiritual values that underpin or influence your life's work. Once you have clarity and understanding on all those fronts, you can confirm what you must have to achieve a sense of fulfillment and meaning in your career and life.

Caution: Share your vision for your career and life with people you can trust to encourage you! Only **you** can live your life. No one else can or will, so take full responsibility for it. Don't let pessimists like my aunt into your inner circle.

You are the only one who can confirm whether a career or calling is right for you!

> **Research suggests that most individuals in the developed world will have between 10 to 15 jobs or careers in their lifetime.**

At first glance, that seems great—individuals get to experience the variety of life—but that research is in conflict with research Malcolm Gladwell discovered while writing his book *Outliers*. Studying success, Malcolm wanted to determine which factors helped certain individuals be successful. He discovered The 10,000 Hours Rule confirmed in research by Anders Ericsson of Florida State University.

What is The 10,000 Hours Rule?

Have you ever heard, "It took me 10 years to become an overnight success"?

The research suggests that no matter your career or profession, it takes a consistent amount of time—10,000 hours or 20 hours a week for 10 years—to achieve mastery.

In those 20 hours, you must actually be engaged in your craft, not just thinking about it. From music to medicine to lawyers, leadership, and sports, the career choice does not matter. It takes at least 10,000 hours to become competent.

In my late 20s, just beginning my speaking and consulting career, I was certain my learning curve would be faster than 10,000 hours—that was my confident **BA** profile speaking. Although I had heard it took years to become an expert speaker and consultant, I was convinced it would not take me very long to be successful.

In spite of my best efforts, I did not realize true mastery and proficiency until I reached my 40s—10,000+ hours later.

As a younger person, I was naively critical that all the best corporate positions were filled by old people—for the record, anyone over 40.

> **Looking back, many people don't know what they don't know and I was one of them.**

Why does every professional sport have a development program or farm team? It takes time to perfect your craft.

Hockey in Canada starts when the child can barely walk; the boy advances to rep teams, junior teams, senior amateur, professional farm teams, then the National Hockey League—or about 10 years and 10,000 hours—to reach the pros.

When swimmer Michael Phelps set all the all-time record of eight gold medals at the Beijing Olympics, it was his third time at the Games. Did he improve during the 8 years from his first Olympics to his third? Obviously!

Why would business, leadership, and your responsibilities at work be any different? The fact is they are not.

During the dot com craze in the '90s, I was in a meeting with an organization run by a 26-year-old. He was burning a million a month in seed capital and was certain he was God's gift to leadership and management, even though it was obvious to others that his leadership style and managerial capabilities were undeveloped. The company closed forever a few months later. He had not put in his time—10,000 hours—to develop his skills.

Does our society's career-development mindset embrace a 10-year time-frame to become excellent at what we do? I'm not so sure!

Hence the conflict between the number of jobs most of you will have—between 10 and 15—and becoming a master at any profession. Even if you had a work life of 50 years and you changed professions every 10 years, at most you could master only 5 professions.

And if you became a master at something, why would you want to change? The majority would not.

If you are not already dialled into your life *purpose*, it's critical that you embark immediately to discover your passions and calling.

Are you focused on immediate gratification or do you have the fortitude to achieve a level of mastery? With the norm of 10 to 15 jobs in a lifetime, many will end up being average at everything and master at nothing.

Mastery: **The authority of a master; possession or display of great skill or technique; skill or knowledge that makes one master of a subject**

Success Strategies and Mindsets

- Mastery requires time. There is no replacement for experience.
- Patience is a baseline for your success.
- If you never master anything, you will never feel the deep level of fulfillment that comes from being an authority in a discipline.
- Research confirms each person must take responsibility for the intentional direction of his or her life. Rabbit tripping—scattered, unfocused activity—has little value.

- To help you achieve true success, know your passion and *purpose* sooner than later in life. Focus!
- The principle of applying passion and *purpose* applies to everyone's development, whether you are a parent, an educator, a leader, coach, or career or HR professional.
- Your written long-term development plans and timelines should be reviewed on a regular basis and fine-tuned as necessary, as you progress.
- A mentor and a supportive environment will speed up your success.

Your Challenge?

Get on track right now
- with the right career/calling for you,
- with a job style that matches your Personal Style,
- with the right values and environment!

Occupation planning is well worth your time. Too often, individuals accept jobs for reasons related to external factors, such as salary or workplace location, without consideration for how the job will meet their main needs.

That might be required in the short term to eat, but it is not acceptable in the long term *to live*!

Promotion Is Not Always the Answer

Most organizations believe their employees want to be promoted. The Peter Principle (from *The Peter Principle*, written by Dr. Laurence Peter and Raymond Hull) maintains that "in a hierarchy, every employee tends to rise to their level of incompetence."

Here are examples of that principle in action.

A large retail client with thousands of employees decided to promote its best customer-service counter staff people to supervisors.

➔ **Management failed to ask this question:**
Does the employee wish to change jobs?

A woman who had worked the cosmetic counter for over a decade was to be promoted. Customers asked for her by name and would wait to be served by her, even though other staff members were available.

Management constantly put pressure on her to "upgrade" her position to supervisor or assistant manager of the department. She resisted every overture. I advised management to stop trying to advance her and ruin her passion for her work. She had found her calling. Why force her to change to a role she would not like . . . managing others? That lady simply wanted to serve people at the cosmetic counter.

> **Ambition does not always mean a desire to be upwardly mobile.**

In another large industrial organization, our consulting team discovered that senior managers would shift, change, or promote their employees without any consultation with them. There was no consideration of Personal Style, job style, or the preference of the employee.

As a result, the company had a very high turnover rate in the supervisor and mid-management roles. Senior management simply could not understand the dissatisfaction of people who had no input into their own job or career path. It's hard to believe some organizations still operate that way!

The principle of engagement and inclusion applies to any, leader, team, parent, organization, or volunteer group. When individuals are not embracing their strengths, their performance is reduced.

Confirming your style and values is only the beginning of understanding yourself and others, not the end. If you have not already done so, I encourage you to expand your discovery process to include your ***purpose***, calling, passions, gifts, talents, and interests.

In my book *My Source EXPERIENCE Journal™,* I provide a step-by-step roadmap and process to help you confirm your life ***purpose,*** passions, gifts, talents, and interests. If you are seeking to discover your life ***purpose,*** I encourage you to investigate this process. This is in addition to knowing your Personal Style and core values.

Learn more at www.crgleader.com.

CHAPTER 12

How to Determine Someone Else's Style

Whenever I hear, "It can't be done," I know I'm close to success.

MICHAEL FLATLEY

How to Discover Someone Else's Style in Just a Couple of Minutes through the Skill of Translating

On my second date with Brenda (we married in 1992), I handed her a *PSI* assessment and asked her to complete it. It was a bold and crazy thing to do. Perhaps I should have waited until our third date?!

You may wish to have everyone you know complete a *PSI*. Because that is not always practical, we have designed a system to help you determine a person's style within a couple of minutes of meeting the individual.

This is a powerful process. When you learn it, you can immediately enhance your interpersonal skills and effectiveness with others. Perhaps even more important, this process will help you understand the Personal Style of the people at your workplace and everyone who is close to you.

To build credibility successfully, you must achieve three steps.

1. Translating
2. Suspending
3. Style-shifting

Let's start with **Translating.**

Translating simply means understanding what is unique about each of the four style dimensions. You become aware about the way each dimension influences people's thinking and behavior. It requires that you are aware of your surroundings and that you use your knowledge of the *PSI* Model (Extroversion-Introversion, Non-Verbal-Verbal and People-Tasks) as it applies to each style dimension.

People are constantly telling you what their style patterns are by the way they approach and interact with the environment. If you base your assessment of their behavior on the *PSI* Model criteria, you have an excellent basis for identifying their style.

Note: All you can do is observe behavior in any given moment. The person might be under stress and acting in a less-than-typical manner. Nevertheless, you are taking action on what you are experiencing in the moment.

To determine a person's potential pattern, ask yourself three simple questions.

1. Is this person Extroverted or Introverted?
Remember, our definition of Extroversion and Introversion involves the way people see and interact with the environment.

- Extroverts want to tell the environment what to do.
- Introverts defer to what the environment tells them.

Decide which fits best. Then, on the appropriate line in the Personal Style Criteria grid (an example follows), circle the two letters separately.

Extroversion is **B** and **A.**

Introversion is **C** and **I.**

Go to the next line.

2. Is this person Non-Verbal or Verbal?
Remember, our definition of Non-Verbal Action-Oriented and Verbal Non-Action-Oriented denoted the amount of language each person uses to communicate and the level of action orientation he has.

If you think the person is Non-Verbal, circle the **B** and the **I** separately.

If you feel he is Verbal, circle the **C** and the **A** separately.

Go to the third criteria.

3. Is this person Task- or People-Focused?
If you feel he is Task-Oriented, circle the **B** and the **C** separately.

If you feel he is People-Oriented, circle the **I** and the **A** separately.

When you look at the letters that are circled, you will see 1 of 2 things:

- 1 letter (dimension) will be circled three times, which suggests the person leads with that dimension, or
- 3 letters will be circled twice, meaning the person has a balanced pattern, with 3 letters equally influencing his approach.

PRACTICE THE PERSONAL STYLE CRITERIA MODEL

Name

Extroversion	B +	A
Introversion	C +	I
Non-Verbal	B +	I
Verbal	C +	A
Task	B +	C
People	I +	A

Potential Style Pattern

To see the flow of this process, let's look at individuals who have had a lot of global media exposure.

Billionaire Donald Trump

To determine his potential style pattern, ask the three questions outlined in the Translating process.

1. **Is Donald Trump Extroverted or Introverted?**
    Does he tell the environment what to do or does the environment tell him what to do? For certain, he is extroverted, so we circle the **B** and the **A.**

2. **Is Donald Trump Non-Verbal or Verbal?**
    Is he Non-Verbal Action-Oriented or Verbal Non-Action-Oriented? He is action, for sure, and non-verbal, so we circle the **B** and the **I.**

3. **Is Donald Trump Task- or People-Oriented?**
    Most of us would say he is task-oriented. In this case, we circle the **B** and the **C.**

PRACTICE THE PERSONAL STYLE CRITERIA MODEL

Name **DONALD TRUMP**

Extroversion	Ⓑ +	Ⓐ
Introversion	C +	I
Non-Verbal	Ⓑ +	Ⓘ
Verbal	C +	A
Task	Ⓑ +	Ⓒ
People	I +	A

Potential Style Pattern **"B"**

Which dimension came up three times?

B or **Behavioral** ACTION!

When you observe Donald Trump, his behavior supports the suggestion that he leads with a **Behavioral** ACTION dimension—goal- and task-oriented, a man who wants results, not excuses, who is focused on the future and solutions, not the problems.

This is a **potential** style pattern. It does not replace the understanding you would have if you knew Donald Trump personally.

Let's do more examples to get a better feel for the process.

Talk Show Host Oprah Winfrey

1. **Is Oprah an Extrovert or an Introvert?**
   She definitely wants to tell the environment what to do, so she is extroverted. We circle the **B** and the **A**.

2. **Is Oprah Non-Verbal or Verbal?**
   Based on what we see on her TV show, she will use more language than less, so she is Verbal. We circle the **C** and the **A**.

3. **Is Oprah People- or Task-Focused?**
   Most would say she is People-Oriented. Circle the **I** and the **A**.

PRACTICE THE PERSONAL STYLE CRITERIA MODEL

Name **OPRAH WINFREY**

Extroversion	Ⓑ	+	Ⓐ
Introversion	C	+	I
Non-Verbal	B	+	I
Verbal	Ⓒ	+	Ⓐ
Task	B	+	C
People	Ⓘ	+	Ⓐ

Potential Style Pattern **"A"**

What dimension comes up three times?

A.

To interact with so many people and retain her interest in others for the many years she has hosted her show, Oprah certainly has a strong **Affective** EXPRESSION dimension.

I want to suggest that we look at Oprah's life a bit more closely and revise her criteria to better understand her potential style pattern. So let's review our assumptions and observations of her behavior.

She is definitely extroverted, meaning she tells the environment what to do.

B and **A** stay circled.

In addition, her verbal nature is obvious in just about every show, so let's stay with the selection of Verbal: **C** and **A**.

In previous chapters, I affirmed two critical points.

First, the majority of individuals will have a two- or three-dimension pattern and some individuals can be balanced in all four dimensions of the *PSI* Model criteria.

Oprah is not only successful in her TV show, she has several other global ventures, including the girls' school in South Africa, *O Magazine*, satellite radio stations, her ambassador program, plus many other enterprises. To achieve that, she would have to have some Task Orientation in her Personal Style.

When a person is so balanced between two criteria that it is impossible to discern if she is people- or task-oriented, I suggest you circle all four dimensions in that specific criterion. In other words, if Oprah is balanced between people and tasks, circle all four letters as they apply to people and tasks.

If we do that with Oprah, here's what happens to her style.

She has three **A**s, two **B**s, two **C**s, and one **I**.

PRACTICE THE PERSONAL STYLE CRITERIA MODEL

Name **OPRAH WINFREY - 2**

Extroversion	Ⓑ +	Ⓐ
Introversion	C +	I
Non-Verbal	B +	I
Verbal	Ⓒ +	Ⓐ
Task	Ⓑ +	Ⓒ
People	Ⓘ +	Ⓐ

Potential Style Pattern **"A, B, C"**

I suggest Oprah leads with her **A** and that her **B** and **C** are close behind, for a Triple-High pattern. That pattern is called **Productive**. Do you feel this pattern reflects Oprah's life?

Now it's your turn.

Think of someone you know well. Maybe it's your significant other, a friend, family member, or a person at work. Using the *PSI* Model, the criteria, and the blank form that follows, ask the same three questions to find out what the individual's style pattern might be.

Is that person

- Extroverted or Introverted?
- Non-Verbal (Action-Oriented) or Verbal (Non-Action-Oriented)?
- Task- or People-Focused?

PRACTICE THE PERSONAL STYLE CRITERIA MODEL

Name

Extroversion	B	+	A
Introversion	C	+	I
Non-Verbal	B	+	I
Verbal	C	+	A
Task	B	+	C
People	I	+	A

Potential Style Pattern

PRACTICE THE PERSONAL STYLE CRITERIA MODEL

Name

Extroversion	B	+	A
Introversion	C	+	I
Non-Verbal	B	+	I
Verbal	C	+	A
Task	B	+	C
People	I	+	A

Potential Style Pattern

What are you discovering?
Does the person's potential style reflect the way you see him or her?

Also use the information from previous chapters that details the traits of each dimension. People are constantly leaving clues about their Personal Style with what they say and how they do things. Through your skills of observation, even without using the *PSI* Model criteria process, you can determine a person's potential style pattern.

Once you start using the translating system, it will come naturally to you. At the core of this process, you are making a conscious decision to pay attention to others—to get out of *self* into the world of *others*. You are making an effort to understand others from their point of view or at least to realize the behavioral differences of each dimension that result in diverse perspectives, needs, fears, and values.

The knowledge of Personal Style is imperative if you want to have successful interpersonal relationships. It provides invaluable information so you can be intentional with your behavior to increase your credibility with others.

From parenting, to understanding your life partner, to your role as supervisor, you can use the translating skill to build credibility in all your relationships.

Translating is only 1 step in the 3-step process required to successfully interact with others. You now have an idea of what the other person's style might be, which is great, but unless you also engage in **Suspending** and **Style-Shifting**, you have participated in a fun process but you have not yet learned how to connect with others.

CHAPTER 13

Your Style is Not an Excuse for Your Behavior

Think like a wise man but communicate in the language of the people.

WILLIAM BUTLER YEATS

The Skill of Suspending

Many years ago, when I was traveling over 300 days a year, living in airplanes and hotels, my patience frayed from time to time. After flying all day, I arrived at a hotel where I had stayed many times. I was to present a seminar early the next morning and wanted to go directly to my room.

The trainee on the desk told me there was no reservation for me and that they were sold out for the night. Instead of suspending my frame of reference, I accused him of making a mistake and insisted there must be a room available in the hotel.

He continued to say No. Unfortunately, my frustration turned to anger and words of aggravation were exchanged.

Finally, out of principle—to prove I was right—I dug out my reservations from deep within my luggage, only to discover my team had booked me at a hotel down the street because my regular hotel was, as the trainee stated, sold out. I left, grumbling, trying to justify my emotional state instead of apologizing and admitting to myself that I had not suspended. I obviously blew my credibility with that hotel trainee. Can you relate?

One of the most difficult things for humans to do is suspend our frame of reference and enter someone else's world.

> **Suspending as a skill is your ability to put other people first and yourself second.**

The opposite of being self-centered, suspending means to set aside your opinions, agendas, wants, needs, and fears temporarily—long enough to listen to the other person's point of view. It is a high sign of respect for others. It is very powerful.

I am not suggesting suspending is an easy skill, but it is an important one.

You are born with your own Personal Style; it stays with you throughout your lifetime. For most of this book, I have encouraged you to play to your strengths and to be aware of your challenges.

Your strengths, however, can become your greatest weaknesses. If an interpersonal situation calls for something other than the strengths that your style pattern can deliver, you must suspend your style needs first so you can connect with others who are different than you are.

Credibility is in the mind of others, based on what you do and don't do. Everyone has a level of credibility with others, whether or not you wish to have it.

> **You highly influence your credibility with others, based on your ability to suspend.**

Have you ever been in a conversation with someone and—either in your head or verbally, you finish the person's sentences? Or you actually interrupt the other person and thus impede the flow of the interaction? That is not suspending.

The opposite of suspending is getting hooked. That is where you let the behavior or actions of others upset you emotionally. You let your style needs control you in the moment. The other person or persons are forgotten.

We've all been there—where we do not suspend and a confrontation ensues, if we let our emotions go too far.

Another word for getting hooked is *offended*. Offended has its roots in the Greek language, linked to the word *bait*. Being offended, getting hooked, or not suspending can bait you into emotional turmoil.

> **Either you control your style . . . or your style will control you!**

We all have preferences but, when they infringe on others, they can become our greatest weakness. In a previous chapter, I outlined how each dimension has blocks and challenges. Some of them might apply to you.

Suspending is an emotional and mental choice to stay grounded and centered. You choose not to let circumstances affect you or allow you to get hooked or offended.

In studies with couples conducted by Dr. Gottman of Seattle, Washington, he proved that once you get offended and allow your heart rate to go beyond 100 beats per minute (non-athletic), you no longer have the ability for rational thought.

The flush of biochemicals caused by the increased heart rate hinders your ability to interact with reason and renders you almost incapable of suspending while in that state.

That is why a domestic dispute is one of the most dangerous situations for a police officer; the individuals involved are no longer lucid. Calming people down, if possible, is one of the most important steps to managing an emotional situation in safety and avoiding further consequences.

Contrary to my example with the hotel clerk where I did not suspend my preferences, there is one area where I have learned to suspend my style needs almost 100% of the time . . . and that is during my seminars.

When I first started in the professional development field, conducting and facilitating workshops, I was taken aback by judgmental participants and those who can be categorized as *prisoners*—people attending because their employer has forced them to attend.

I recall two individuals who were in one of my sessions to keep their jobs, not to learn. Right from the start, they were disruptive, almost abusive, but I did not allow their comments to offend me. I chose to suspend. That's not to suggest their conduct was acceptable—it was not—but I did not let their behavior bait me.

During the first break, I calmly but firmly acknowledged that I knew they did not want to be there and, if they continued their outbursts, I would ask them to leave, which would result in their unemployment the next day. They settled down and did not upset the class for the balance of the day.

On their evaluation forms, they rated the program -10 (the possible range was 1 to 10). The class average for that program was +9.5.

Although those participants were disappointing to me, I was not affected by their negative comments. It was about their issues, not mine.

As a result, I was able to suspend my frame of reference during the entire process.

When you suspend, you are able to stay focused in the moment and interact with others. I could have let those participants affect me—sending me into some type of anger—but that response would not have served the other 80 people in the training room

Suspending is a skill you develop to intentionally defer your style preferences in exchange for other choices. We already know we don't change our preferences, but we can *suspend* them because we care about others and our relationships with them.

How Do You Suspend?

1. **First, get to know yourself—deeply**.

    *   Take the ***Personal Style Indicator*** **In-Depth Interpretations** that came with your online assessment. Study the two-page narrative closely.

    *   Create action plans to develop your specific pattern(s), based on the recommendations.

    *   Become an expert on the styles (dimensions) that are different than yours. Learning to accept differences is critical to your ability to suspend.

    *   Identify the main characteristics of all the styles so you will understand how to approach and interact with others.

2. **Manage your style so it works for you, not against you.**
    You are the only one who can control your Personal Style pattern so that it does not interfere in a negative way with your understanding of and interaction with others.

    *   Beware of blocks that can cost you credibility as an individual or a leader.

    *   Indentify characteristics from within your own style pattern that impede you from being effective. Take control of them! That is called **developed versatility skills** versus **an undeveloped style**.

Here is a story from Natasha Suvorova on the benefits of working with style.

> *I did some work for a software development company in Russia, where the engineers' communication style left much to be desired. The engineers were required not only to develop software but get buy-in from sponsors, promote the tools, and communicate with various audiences worldwide, but they failed at that responsibility.*
>
> *After several catastrophes in trying to connect with our stakeholder groups, the engineers stopped communicating and retreated to their developer's box. That is not what the company needed or wanted. As the Organizational Development consultant, I had a lot of work to intervene and turn around the situation. We used assessments. I specifically used CRG's* **Personal Style Indicator** *as a substitute for DiSC. I was looking for style differences so we could work out a plan and goals for improvement.*
>
> *We needed to improve the relationships with stakeholders, person by person. Senior management wanted to be kept informed at each specific step and wanted to provide input and to see each strategy implemented.*
>
> *As a result of the* **PSI** *assessment and a group session with the engineers (who mostly had High* **C** *in their patterns), we were able to raise their self-awareness of their personalities and the way the world reacts to different Personal Style dimensions and patterns.*
>
> *We expanded the information to help them understand which other styles existed (different than theirs) and what they needed. They developed a follow-up plan for those critical situations.*
>
> *Moreover, they learned an algorithm (a simple and powerful process using the* **PSI***) for tackling their communication problems (engineers love algorithms). That resulted in subsequent successful communication events!*
>
> Natasha Suvorova
Russia

That is a simple yet powerful example of suspending.

Before the software engineers learned to suspend their frame of reference, their communication style resulted in failure. After they were taught how to suspend and connect with others who had different Personal Styles, the engineers embraced success.

What are the implications if you don't manage your Personal Style as it relates to others' styles and you are not in control of your responses?

- You take things more personally.
- You become upset or offended more easily.
- You are less effective, both personally and professionally.

That means you must take full responsibility for your responses and your reactions.

And unless you are willing to suspend your frame of reference and your needs, you will miss connecting and/or building credibility with a large part of the population. Yes, you still need to play to your strengths in your daily work life, but everyone interacts with people who are different than they are. There really is no option; you must suspend . . . if you want to be effective with others.

For those who are married or in a committed relationship, you know that some of your most intense negative moments can be with the person you care for the most. Brenda and I are no different.

One Saturday morning, when our household chores were stacked up, our kids' events required a parent taxi, and errands needed to be done, my playfulness and hugs to Brenda were quite frankly not welcome.

Although I had a full list of outdoor projects to do that day, I had made it a priority to connect with her and that was what I was doing. I felt that my demonstration of fondness was not appreciated. I stopped suspending my frame of reference—and took offence at her rejection of my love. At least that is my side of the story.

Brenda, with her **BC** pattern, was on task (**B** and **C** are both task-oriented). She also had a full schedule and felt my affection was infringing on her tasks and the goals she needed to achieve. Brenda did not suspend her need for space and tasks and I did not suspend my desire to be affectionate.

The result was two offended individuals. We both decided not to suspend.

Although later on we were able to calm our emotions and listen to each other's point of view, that demonstrates how quickly relationships can go sideways when we choose not to suspend our needs and let ourselves become offended.

All of us have met individuals who are offended at the drop of a hat. They are toxic to the people around them—and to themselves, too. If you are one of those individuals, you are killing yourself with the stress your emotions create in your body when you let yourself become offended.

On the other side, don't let the offended nature of someone else bait you into being offended as well, in spite of how difficult that might seem.

> **One of the most difficult truths**
> **is that no one can make you angry or upset unless you permit it.**

On occasion, you still will mess up in your relationships. The fact that you are better today than you were yesterday is something you should appreciate in yourself, as you develop your style flexibility and the skill of suspending.

Personal Exercise

What situations or behavior do you find most difficult to suspend, where you are emotionally hooked or most easily offended? List some thoughts or situations that come to mind.

_____

_____

_____

_____

_____

What has your lack of ability or your lack of willingness to suspend (you let yourself get hooked or offended) cost you in your personal and professional relationships?

Example, before I learned to suspend, I would get upset with suppliers that did not keep their delivery promises. Although I might have been justified in having those feelings, getting upset with them did not help build my credibility. In fact, it created tension. Upset is the opposite of being calm and firm, with reasonable expectations. When I shifted my approach, I was much more successful in successfully communicating with our suppliers.

_____

_____

_____

_____

_____

CHAPTER 14

Style-Shifting is Foundational to Your Success

*Human beings, by changing the inner attitudes of their minds,
can change the outer aspects of their lives.*

WILLIAM JAMES

What is Style-Shifting?

Style-shifting is the act of intentionally changing your approach to fit another person's style pattern. It is changing your behavioral response to meet the other person's needs ahead of your own.

In short, it is entering someone else's world and speaking his or her style language. Style-shifting happens when you change behavior from one Personal Style dimension to another, to respond to the style pattern of the person with whom you are interacting.

Most, if not all of us, at some time or another have style-shifted—consciously or unconsciously. Remember when your elderly relative came to visit and you had the patience (at least for a little while) to listen to him? Perhaps you walked together across the room at a pace slower than your normal gait. Rather than yelling "speed up," you accepted the style differences between the two of you and you modified your behavior.

Life is like that. Every day, we meet people who don't match our style and our values. So what do we do? Do we try to craft a life that excludes anyone who is different than we are or do we embrace and accept those differences and adjust our approaches to build credibility with others?

For the most part—not always—I would like to think we can embrace the latter.

As you learn the steps and processes to style-shift, the fact remains that you can control only you and your style; you cannot control other people. Many times in life, I wish I could have snapped my fingers to change someone's attitude or behavior, but people have free will to do what they want to do.

Style-shifting is a powerful interpersonal skill but it is not a magic pill. You could respond to someone exactly as suggested in the following pages, and the reaction might not be what you want or expect.

Thankfully, that will be the exception, because developed and mature individuals will appreciate your willingness to adjust your approach to meet their style needs first, ahead of your own.

> **You style-shift by developing strategies to target the other person's primary needs and style preferences.**

You must successfully implement the skills of **Translating** and **Suspending** before you can effectively **Style-Shift**.

Awareness is everything. If you are not aware of your Personal Style and the other person's style, none of these steps will work. You must be paying attention to yourself and others.

As you become able to recognize behavioral style patterns in your own actions and in the actions and behavior of others, you will be better prepared to develop your social awareness and versatility.

Each of us already has the capacity for a certain amount of flexible behavior toward another person, depending on the needs of the moment. The further development of your conscious understanding about your self and other people will allow you greater freedom to be more *deliberate* and *mindful* in your dealings with others, for your benefit and theirs.

Style-Matching to Avoid Style-Clashing

We can clash with others simply by virtue of our natures. People naturally get along with some people better than others. We can better respect and value those with whom we have style clashes if we are willing and able to shift into behavioral patterns with which they are more comfortable.

That is not to say we should stop being ourselves, but we can learn to be ourselves in ways that are more effective in adapting to the styles of others. That creates a more favorable climate for problem-solving and relationship development.

Five Steps to Successful Style-Shifting

The next model illustrates the five steps for effective style-shifting. The guidelines on the following pages can assist you to become more aware of how you might behave with various types of people who, in some situations, exhibit and prefer behavior that is different than yours.

For each of the four style dimensions, you may wish to note the names of people with whom you want to style-shift. You might even put their names into more than one dimension, because most individuals are Two-High in their style patterns.

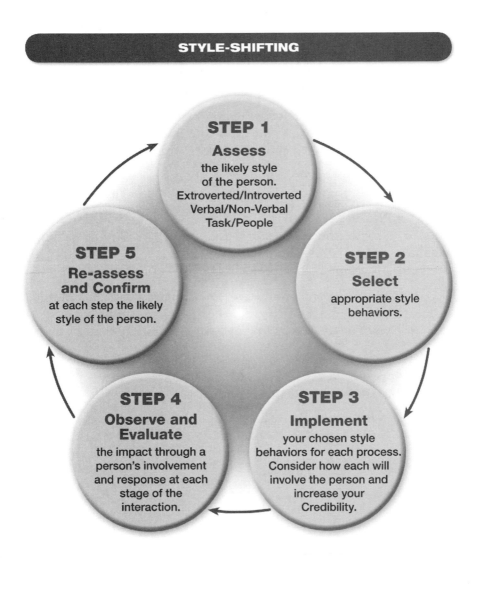

STYLE-SHIFTING

STEP 1
Assess
the likely style
of the person.
Extroverted/Introverted
Verbal/Non-Verbal
Task/People

STEP 2
Select
appropriate style
behaviors.

STEP 3
Implement
your chosen style
behaviors for each process.
Consider how each will
involve the person and
increase your
Credibility.

STEP 4
**Observe and
Evaluate**
the impact through a
person's involvement
and response at each
stage of the
interaction.

STEP 5
**Re-assess
and Confirm**
at each step the likely
style of the person.

The Five Steps to Style-Shifting

1. Assess the Style of the Other Person

For the skill of Translating, we talked about how to assess other people's behavior patterns. By observing the way people behave, according to the criteria specified in the **Personal Style** Model and the details outlined in each of the four dimensions, you can begin to get an understanding of what their Personal Styles might be.

Assessment is the first and foremost step to successful style-shifting. Some individuals may be very easy for you to translate but others, who are more balanced in their pattern, may be a bit more difficult.

One of our clients has a large medical facility with several thousand employees. As part of their leadership- and team-development process, every supervisor and leader completes the *Personal Style Indicator*.

The size of the organization makes it challenging for employees to get to know others well. Because of the reporting structure, interactions take place infrequently between and among some individuals.

To improve communications and team performance, each team member's *PSI* score is posted on his or her secure and private Intranet.

Team members are required, prior to meeting with an individual or a team, to reference the *PSI* score of each person involved. They must take into account the style differences and note the differences as part of their communication plan and process.

The result? Much more productive interchanges and a harmonious workplace. It has been so successful, they have been implementing the practice for more than 10 years.

2. Select Appropriate Style Behavior that Fits the Individual's Primary Style Dimensions

In the past, the Golden Rule said you should treat people the way **you** want to be treated, but that does not take Personal Style differences into account. The best way to treat others is the way they wish to be treated! That is called the Platinum Rule.

Assessment Criteria

	Behavioral	Cognitive	Interpersonal	Affective
Extroverted	Yes	No	No	Yes
Introverted	No	Yes	Yes	No
Non-Verbal	Yes	No	Yes	No
Verbal	No	Yes	No	Yes
Task-Oriented	Yes	Yes	No	No
People-Oriented	No	No	Yes	Yes

Let's say you determine a certain person's behavior pattern is primarily task-oriented and non-verbal. Using that knowledge, you modify your behavior to suit that individual.

Most likely, he or she will prefer action rather than talk. On the other hand, if an individual is introverted and people-oriented, demonstrate behavior that is sensitive and thoughtful, and allow the person to have his or her personal space. People feel more secure with individuals who perceive and interact the way they do, and less sure of those who behave differently.

Again, it should be stressed here that if you do not have a good working knowledge of Personal Style differences, trying to accomplish style-shifting will not be easy. It may not be sensible for you to try.

Your time will be better spent on becoming more familiar with the characteristics of each dimension. Learning what makes each of the style dimensions unique in its influence on human behavior is the foundation for building more effective relationships with others.

3. Implement Your New Style Behavior with the Person

Once you feel you understand the person from a style perspective, and know the dimension or pattern to which that individual will best respond, it is time to take action.

- Assertiveness is the key to being successful here.

- Having the confidence and courage to attempt to style-shift with others who are different from you allows you to try new behavior.

- Keep your expectations realistic. When you start, don't expect that everything will automatically work out.

- Look for opportunities to try new approaches rather than

attempting to behave for an extended period in a Personal Style dimension that isn't *you*.

- Be especially careful with the dimensions in which *you* score lower. Only implement the new behavior as long as the situation has relatively low stress.

I started in the professional development field as a sales trainer—a natural transition from my role as a top sales performer. During a sales training and coaching workshop with a couple of dozen sales managers, one asked this question: *What if the client is so different from the sales rep that continuing the relationship becomes stressful, instead of a* building situation?

Good question; it applies to constant style-shifting.

His industry requires ongoing, long-term relationships with clients. What I recommended is not always possible, but that sales manager had several sales reps he could direct and lead.

I suggested that if there were a major style difference between a sales rep and a client, the manager had the option of switching sales reps so the needs of both sides would be better met. That seemed to work with his team and the circumstances.

Sometimes, however, significant differences might be the main reason they should **not** switch the sales rep.

Let's say the client has a **CI** profile and is in IT, and the sales rep has a **BA** profile. Although they are opposites, the different style patterns actually complement each other in the critical-decision and buying process.

The **CI** buyer would be great on the details and specs needed for IT equipment or software and the **BA** sales rep would have creative and strategic perspectives that could help the client make the right decision. So if they understand their differences—and can accept them as part of their interaction—the differences will benefit both parties.

4. Observe and Evaluate the Impact of Your Behavior on the Other Person

When you are using new behavior, watch to see the impact it has on the other person. If the effect seems positive, continue with the new behavior; if the result seems negative, stop the new behavior.

Remember: The purpose of style-shifting is to develop better relationships with others, not make the situation worse.

If your style-shift was not successful, that person's style may not be what you assumed it is or perhaps the person also shifted styles when you changed your behavior.

Mentally record your observations. Look for patterns the other person displays on a regular basis in similar situations. For example, does the individual tend to behave in a particular style whenever you go out for dinner together and in a different style in a purely work situation? If so, try to develop patterns of behavior that might work when you go out to eat with the person, but don't use that behavior with him at other times.

Changes can surprise people and catch them off guard.

While conducting marriage counseling, I recall that the wife wanted the husband, who was high task-oriented, to be more friendly, gentle, and affectionate toward her. Being a High **B**, he took up the challenge and set a goal to style-shift for her.

During the next visit, the couple said his style-shifting was not very well received. The wife had rejected the new attention. Her reason? It was so foreign to her, she found it difficult to accept. Yes, he had successfully style-shifted, but his track record was so opposite to his new behavior that she found it strange at first embrace.

I had them work out a way to communicate levels of connection that were acceptable to both parties. Over time, this new way to being was more easily implemented by the husband and accepted by the wife.

5. Re-assess the Results, Make Adjustments, and Repeat the Process as Often as Necessary

Style-shifting is a process of trial and error. If at first you do not succeed, try, try again. Over time, things will begin to click into place as you consistently shift to fit the other person's particular style.

Style-shifting also takes work. My example in step 4 above shows that improved relationships are not built in a day. You have to make a commitment to continue to work on style-shifting, regardless of what others do in return.

So often when we attempt some new behavior or attitude with others, they respond to us in an undesirable manner. When that happens, our first response is to stop the new behavior and give up on trying to make a difference. It is more productive to continue the new behavior for an extended period or to ease into the shift to determine how effective it can be with a particular individual or situation.

The other non-negotiable fact is that **it takes practice to successfully style-shift.**

Start with baby steps.

I had conducted a workshop using the *PSI* with a group of teachers. They were excited about being able to connect with their students better. One of the teachers went over the top with her desire to style-shift and tried to implement everything with everybody the first week. Of course that was overwhelming and stressful for her, rather than a positive experience.

The guidelines form a cycle of steps for style-shifting to help you improve your relationships with others. In most cases, you will experience immediate results, but do allow yourself time to become proficient in the process. As with any new skill, it will be awkward at first and will progress to feeling natural and easy. With persistence, you will reap positive results.

CHAPTER 15

Coaching and Style-Shifting Guidelines for Each Dimension

*If there is any secret of success, it lies in the ability to get
the other person's point of view and see things from his angle
as well as from your own.*

HENRY FORD

Coaching and Style-Shifting Guidelines for Each Style Dimension

Understanding the guidelines for style-shifting is one thing; knowing what to do with them is another. Remember that *most people prefer to be treated in a manner similar to their style pattern or the way they treat and interact with others.*

That is the secret to successful style-shifting. By watching how people relate to others, you can pick up tips on how they like to be treated. For example, individuals who are high in a particular dimension tend to enjoy being around others who are also strong in that dimension. If you can shift into a pattern similar to theirs, they will react in a more positive manner than if you shift into a style pattern that is quite different from theirs.

The following pages outline the responses that each dimension, in its purest form, prefers. I also provide information to help coach others in becoming more aware of their style tendencies and the impact their style might be having on others.

I remind you that 90% of the population is a blend of more than one dimension. Take that into account as you observe behavior and plan your coaching and style-shifting accordingly.

Coaching and Style-Shifting with Behavioral ACTION Individuals

Once you have assessed a person's style as being predominantly **Behavioral**, you need to concentrate on what is characteristic about individuals who demonstrate that Personal Style. It involves taking into consideration that a **B**'s needs are strongest in the areas of *challenge, independence, responsibility,* and *achievement.*

First, these individuals are usually *extroverted.* That means **B**s prefer to initiate action in the environment rather than react to it. As much as possible, you should allow that person to be the leader and set the course in whatever you are attempting to do. When you do not like what he is doing, you should confront him with it very directly and confidently, presenting the facts and stating why you do not approve.

Second, **B**s are action-oriented toward tasks. **B**s focus more on obtaining results than on the process of ensuring quality. They don't care so much how something is done as long as it is done quickly and efficiently. The more you can help **B**s achieve what they want to achieve, the better you will impress them as a person worth their consideration.

Third, **B**s are non-verbal. You want to keep in mind that **B**s are not talkers. They are not ones to just sit around and "shoot the breeze." They say what they mean and mean what they say. They generally are not interested in more discussion than the situation calls for. They prefer conversations that get to the point and that focus on solving problems.

With that knowledge clearly in mind, you would approach **B**s from a task perspective rather than a people perspective. In other words, don't try to be overly friendly or intimate with **B**s unless they initiate it. Focus on tasks and objectives, rather than on personal opinions and feelings. Ask them how they would like to get things done.

If you need to express your point of view, use as few words as possible. You should stand your ground with **B**s without saying they are wrong. Don't let them intimidate you into thinking what they are thinking.

Don't waste time when interacting with **B**s because they are more conscious of time than most people. Don't tell **B**s that you are going to attempt to do something unless you know for a fact that you can and will achieve it.

Coaching and Style-Shifting Guidelines for Behavioral ACTION

Common Personal Characteristics

Aggressive	Determined	Responsible
Bold	Decisive	Self-reliant
Competitive	Domineering	Strong-minded
Courageous	Productive	Tough
Direct	Restless	Unemotional

Preferred Work Tasks

Buying	Enforcing	Planning
Debating	Judging	Problem-solving
Deciding	Managing	Supervising
Delegating	Negotiating	Visualizing

Preferred Working Conditions

Want to have impact by creating new environments
Like to exercise power and authority
Prefer large and challenging projects
Want freedom from external controls
Want opportunities for financial success

Want Others to

Give summarized facts
Respect their judgments
Support them to reach goals
Cope with unwanted details
Cooperate with them

Get Most Upset when Others

Are too slow
Get in their way
Talk too much
Try to be in control
Waste time

Respond Best to

Direct, honest confrontation
Logical, rational arguments
Fair, open competition
An impersonal approach
Getting results quickly

Sometimes, people like to create a stereotype for a High **B**—insensitive, judgmental, and my-way-or-the-highway, which is not always true. If you get results and are an individual of action, they give more freedom to you than any other style will.

Why? They value independence so much, they freely give it to others— in many cases, to a fault. They will pass responsibility to others with little orientation or instruction, expecting you to *get it*. In those cases, be firm in asking for the training or information you require, in a respectful manner. If your request seems like an attack on them, the conversation will be over immediately and your credibility will sink very low in their eyes.

Bs can be very direct but, in their direct nature, they don't blow smoke or sugar- coat their messages. In other words, you get the straight goods. So rather than feeling intimidated, be thankful for this characteristic. You will know exactly where you stand. You won't have someone skirting around the issues or pretending things are fine when they are not.

Coaching and Style-Shifting with Cognitive ANAYLSIS Individuals

If an individual is High **C**, he is predominantly task-oriented, verbal, and introverted. Keep in mind his strongest needs are for *respect, organization, safety,* and *intimacy.*

Since **C**s are introverted, you must remember they are highly sensitive to environmental stimuli. That means they experience stress from environmental stimuli more easily than individuals who are extroverted. Being too extroverted when around **C**s may simply turn them off or shut them down.

For example, if you went out to dinner with a **C**, you would want to keep extroverted behavior to a minimum at the table. Talking too loudly during your conversation or inviting others to join you might tend to upset him.

Also, you would want to pay close attention to **C**s orientation to tasks. Remember that people with **Cognitive** styles are perfectionists and prefer organization. If you could help them achieve quality results, they would react to you in a positive way. If you invite them to your office to work on a project, you would be wise to clean up your office—and be sure you are prepared (organized) to start work when they arrive.

Take into consideration that **C**s are verbal. Learn how to listen to **C**s and how to debate the topics they think are important. If they are strongly interested in a specific topic, you might ask their opinion about items and issues related to it.

You should expect **Cs** to be somewhat opinionated about what they discuss. Be prepared for them to dominate the conversation. When **Cs** become upset, they either become critical of others or stop talking and become angry. When **Cs** are not talking with you, check with them to ensure they are not upset.

Based on this information about people with Cognitive styles, you should spend more time with them on a one-to-one basis, rather than in a group setting. That will better meet their need for intimacy. People who have Cognitive styles prefer private discussions of a personal nature over normal chitchat. Carefully listen to what they have to say and ask questions about why they believe what they believe. That will make them feel important and respected.

Although you might want to overlook, to a point, their criticism of others and complaints about the world in general, you will have to address those tendencies if it becomes toxic to relationships. **Cs** can be "the glass is half-empty" individuals who negatively affect their own health and the health of others and thus increase everyone's stress levels. Helping them learn that their language could be depressing to others is an important coaching point.

With some **Cs**, getting them to say nothing at all, unless it is positive, is a reasonable expectation for long-term style-shifting. **Cs** have high expectations that often are not met by others. As a result, disappointment and anger could become common—but unacceptable—emotions for **Cs**. You need to understand their need to vent their feelings during conversations and learn not to personalize their words.

If you want **Cs** to do something for you, provide very clear and detailed information on how you want it done, and by when. Do not expect them to do too many things at once because that could create stress for **Cs**.

Coaching and Style-Shifting Guidelines for Cognitive ANALYSIS

Common Personal Characteristics

Accurate	Indecisive	Strict
Analytical	Loyal	Structured
Cautious	Organized	Theoretical
Conscientious	Perceptive	Unsociable
Critical	Perfectionistic	Worries

Preferred Work Tasks

Analyzing	Classifying	Proofreading
Appraising	Computing	Recording
Calculating	Editing	Reviewing
Clarifying	Measuring	Tabulating

Preferred Working Conditions

Seek quiet, organized working spaces
Want to work with competent co-workers or alone
Prefer to work on specialized, task-oriented projects
Expect to have an impact on the quality of products
Like positions with limited responsibilities over others
Need structured activities and clear directions

Want Others to

Give them detailed information
Ask for their opinions
Not interrupt their work
Treat them with respect
Do quality work the first time

Get Most Upset when Others

Move ahead too quickly
Don't give them enough time
Are vague in their communications
Don't appreciate their efforts
Are too personal or emotional

Respond Best to

Diplomatic, factual challenges
Arguments based on facts
Freedom from competitive strain
Friendliness, not personal contact
Doing tasks well and completely

As mentioned earlier, **Cs** have the gift to see what is not there! In other words, if you have a 100-page report and just 1 page is out of order, which page will they no doubt mention?

We need **Cs** in our society to keep order and to focus on details and data-related activities. The ongoing challenge, however, is getting them to own the effect of their words on relationships and interactions with people.

If they can be coached to be aware of that tendency and to limit their critical comments about others, they can become very effective individuals. **Cs** do have a high need for control of their workspace and area. If they have a supervisory role, they tend to micromanage others. We suggest that until a **C** has developed versatility and interpersonal skills, you might want to limit the number of people that report to him or her.

David Wright from Ireland shares a story of how style-shifting helped him with a client.

> *I had been using the* **Personal Style Indicator** *and related resources to aid the skills of influencing and sales by recognizing the needs of the receiver. A typical tutor and coach, I had an experience of ignoring my own advice.*
>
> *I was selling core skills and appraisal training to a training manager of a pharmaceutical company, which required a 260-mile round trip from my office. I wanted the sale to happen* **now**, *but the harder (more direct) I tried to sell, the more questions were being asked.*
>
> *I had made two visits without success. I was being faced with extreme caution and the possibility of being replaced by a new supplier.*
>
> *On my third visit, I reflected on my actions and what was blocking the sale.*
>
> *My* **PSI** *profile is* **AB;** *my style was short and direct and I saw no issues in resolving any of the objections being raised by my client. The person I was trying to influence was* **CI,** *cautious and needing support for the statements being made; he wanted facts rather than broad sweeping statements. He also was very conscious of how the training programs might impact people.*
>
> *I resolved to listen and be patient and factual in my answers, and develop the benefits of the program to the participants and the*

organization. While the meeting took a long time, we dealt with all his concerns in a detailed way. The outcome was that I was awarded the business and retained it for 5 more years, until the retirement of the training manager.

Without knowledge of style and the framework of the **PSI***, I would not have been successful in earning this business.*

David Wright, Ireland
www.consultwright.com

Coaching and Style-Shifting with Interpersonal HARMONY Individuals

People with **Interpersonal Style**s are most often non-verbal, people-oriented, and introverted. Their strongest needs are for *security, acknowledgement, harmony* (the opposite of conflict), and *honesty*.

People strongest in the **Interpersonal** dimension are introverted toward people, which simply means they are reserved and respond/react to environmental stimulus. Their introversion does not interfere with their ability to be sensitive or caring toward others.

They often put others before themselves and, when focused on helping others in need, they tolerate short-term negative response to their actions. Although they tend to be *people-oriented*, they can easily become upset by negative opinions, feelings, and behavior that are continually directed toward them.

Because people with **Interpersonal Style**s are non-verbal, they usually don't express their concerns to others because they don't want to be a bother to anyone. They are most verbal when they are happy and usually stop talking when under stress or when around hostile individuals. They let their actions speak for themselves and tend to judge others by the way others treat people, rather than by what they say.

If you know people who are strong **I**s, you must be sensitive to their need for appreciation. When they do something for you, make an effort to let them know you are grateful for what they have done. In doing so, you would want to remember that since **I**s tend to be non-verbal, they probably would be uncomfortable with too much verbal praise.

In this situation, a simple thank you when no one else is listening might be best or a card expressing your appreciation.

Since **I**s are predominantly people-oriented, you would want to do things for them and with them. For example, because they often go out of the way to do things for other people, you should look for opportunities where you might do the same for them. People with the **I** style dimension don't forget those who help them.

If possible, you should do things with **I**s that they enjoy. Those activities might not be your first choice, but the **I**s would feel appreciated if you chose to spend your time doing them together. For example, if they like to golf and you don't golf yourself, go sit at the golf driving range and talk with them while they practice. That would mean a lot to them.

If **I**s were upset about something, you would need to let them have time to think about what they wanted to say. Knowing that people with **Interpersonal Style**s do not respond well verbally under pressure, allow them more time to formulate their response to you. Also, listen closely to the way they feel about things. Listening is very important to those who are strong in the **Interpersonal** dimension.

Coaching and Style-Shifting Guidelines for Interpersonal HARMONY

Common Personal Characteristics

Careful	Hardworking	Slow
Calm	Lenient	Stubborn
Dependent	Likeable	Understanding
Faithful	Unassertive	Warm

Preferred Work Tasks

Arranging	Mediating	Relating
Assisting	Organizing	Serving
Balancing	Processing	Supporting
Filing	Reflecting	Typing

Preferred Working Conditions

Prefer surroundings that are harmonious
Seek team-member and support-role positions
Work toward practical and useful results
Like organized living and working environments
Want to work with others to improve things
Need guaranteed security

Want Others to

Make them feel as if they belong
Appreciate them for their efforts
Be kind, considerate, thoughtful
Trust them with important tasks
Value them as persons

Get Most Upset when Others

Get angry, blow up, or are mean
Demand that they be too mobile
Take advantage of their goodness
Are manipulative or unfair
Are judgmental of others

Respond Best to

Measured approach to challenges
Factual, practical methods
Comfortable, friendly times
Respect for their boundaries
Conventional, established methods

The **I** has the gift of compassion and caring for others, but he also can have a very stubborn, judgmental streak that can surprise others.

Here is an example of that response.

One of our training contracts was conducting sales training nationally for an automotive manufacturer. In a workshop, we designed the **Why Don't You Sell The Way That I Buy?**™ sales process to teach sales reps how to manage their selling style while intentionally responding to the various buying styles of clients.

An automotive sales professional in the workshop shared his experience of selling a van to a younger couple. My interactions with him indicated he was a very professional individual.

As part of the purchasing process, the couple was to return later in the evening to pick up the vehicle when it was ready for delivery.

The couple returned with their 12-year-old daughter to complete the final paperwork and get their new van.

The sales rep took some time to orient the couple to the vehicle and most of the operational details. Once that was finished, the couple proceeded to the finance office where the final paperwork would be signed and the couple would drive away happily in their new van. Unfortunately, in the finance office, the couple tore up the paperwork and promptly left the dealership.

The sales rep was bewildered. No harsh words had been exchanged and everything seemed to be going okay.

What happened?

The sales rep had committed the sin of omission. He had not acknowledged or included the daughter in the orientation process. Those were High **I** buyers. To them, the way you treat others is more important than the way you treat them. They were so offended that their daughter was not directly included in the delivery process, they were willing to walk away from the deal.

For individuals with very little **I**, that seems like an excessive response to a minor oversight, but **I**s are constantly watching how you treat others and deciding the level of credibility they will give you. In many cases, instead of being open and verbalizing their feelings, **I**s can, to their detriment, suppress their feelings and become bitter because they are introverted and non-verbal. That is why I earlier recommended assertiveness training for this style dimension.

Coaching and Style-Shifting with Affective EXPRESSION Individuals

A people prefer to talk. They are much more people-oriented than task-oriented. As are strongly extroverted in their approach to the environment. They need *variety, recognition, acceptance,* and *friendship* more than anything else.

As are strongly extroverted toward people, especially in groups; the more people with whom As can interact, the better. They are very verbal and like to talk with people in person and over the phone.

Their need for attention drives them to place themselves in situations where they can be seen and interact with as many others as possible. For that reason, they tend to work better in groups than alone. Being alone feels like punishment for people with **Affective** styles.

Because As are so people-oriented, they spend most of their energy working on influencing others. Their need for recognition makes them hold back their best efforts unless they are sure they can receive some kind of praise for them. They often do their best work amid the most pressure and when others are expecting them to fail.

They are motivated to gain other people's recognition. For instance, when As are on a sports team, they don't put out a 100% effort during regular practice sessions. In, fact they really dislike practices. Yet during the game, because the crowds and the media are watching and it's a real game, they will make the superb catch or goal that wins the game.

If you need to shift your style toward As, do fun or exciting things with them; tell jokes or be light-hearted. Connect with them often and try not to put restrictions on them or your relationship.

Acknowledge their talents and praise them for the things they can do well. Doing that in front of others would be best. Give them praise for their creative abilities and ideas and don't point out their faults. You should not expect them to be highly reliable, especially in matters related to time and everyday tasks.

Whatever they are attempting to do, they probably will be late or slow in getting it done. Getting angry at them will not make them speed up, but it could discourage them so much that they will stop putting out any effort.

Coaching and Style-Shifting Guidelines for Affective EXPRESSION

Common Personal Characteristics

Appealing	Flexible	Open-minded
Compassionate	Friendly	Restless
Convincing	Impulsive	Talkative
Creative	Intuitive	Undisciplined
Enthusiastic	Loud	Unproductive

Preferred Work Tasks

Coaching	Entertaining	Selling
Counseling	Performing	Training
Creating	Promoting	Traveling
Demonstrating	Speaking	Writing

Preferred Working Conditions

Want to have impact on people by selling ideas
Seek positions of mobility and recognition
Dislike having to account for details
Like opportunities for creative expression
Prefer unstructured activities and routines
Work best with a boss who has a democratic style

Want Others to

Give them opportunity to speak
Admire their achievements
Be influenced in some ways
Take care of details for them
Value their opinions

Get Most Upset when Others

Are too task-orientated
Confine them to one place
Are not interested in them
Compete for and win attention
Seem judgmental of them

Respond Best to

Being challenged in a kind way
An influencing sales approach
Enjoyable competitions
Affection and personal contact
Having a good time

As are eternal optimists, which is great but many times it leads them into overpromising and underdelivering. They don't mean to be irresponsible but they can appear that way. If they don't manage their time and organize their space, chaos can ensue.

Their personality can be overwhelming and can fill a room when they arrive, at times to the irritation of others.

I recall one holiday dinner when one of our relatives, a High **A,** joined us. When we sat down to visit after dinner, he would not shut up. He would ask questions of people, then answer the question himself.

When I directed questions to his son, the relative answered the question for him. No one could get a word in edgewise. Finally, I told him to please shut up and let his son answer.

Since **A**s are extroverted, you have to be direct, yet friendly, otherwise they are not going to hear you. When **A**s are working with individuals who have much less **A** than they do, they probably need to turn down the energy a notch or two. Otherwise, their energy can overwhelm others.

Here is a story from Anne and Brian Bercht, marriage coaches.

> *Our story is about understanding Personal Style and how practical it is to our everyday life.*
>
> *We had the privilege of working with a particular couple years ago and have kept in touch with them. Randy and Roxanne have been married more than 25 years. Both have full-time jobs, are active in their community, and have two adult children who live nearby.*
>
> *We first talked over the phone; they shared some of their story and said we were their last-ditch effort to save their marriage. They said they could not communicate and had little in common; each did things that really annoyed the other—"if she/he **really loved me**, he/she wouldn't do things that annoy me!"*
>
> *Working with them in person, we reviewed their marital history and asked what had initially attracted them to the other. Having to put aside the pain of why they were seeing us, Roxanne was first to speak.*
>
> *"I found Randy's silent confidence and direct actions very attractive, even sexy, as I think back. I was excited that he did not waffle or appear uncertain about what he wanted or about the decisions he made. He was sort of the Cool Hand Luke type of guy who did not get flustered by many things.*

"He also had a very warm side toward certain people that I noticed early on. Like the time he helped this messed-up person get a job and located a place for him to stay. Randy checked in on that guy for the next 3 to 4 months, just to make sure things were going okay. I was really uneasy about that behavior at first, but found his character to be very attractive; I was proud to be around him and to be his girl."

Randy was a bit surprised to hear that from Roxanne because most of their conversations lately had little to do with expressing compliments or appreciations, but he went on to share what he had found attractive about Roxanne.

"Well, the very first thing that caught my eye was that she was attractive. After that, I was attracted to her warm, outgoing personality and her willingness to try new things and to speak up about those things. It was like I had met someone that actually had an opinion and was not afraid to talk about it. I also liked how 'together' she seemed—she was one of the first women I knew who had some organization in her life. She would mostly do all the things she said she would do, which has played out even to today."

*I told Randy and Roxanne that to understand and work through the devastation of an affair, we would need to establish some ground rules to prevent perceived personal attacks or character judgments being made by the other. The way we did that was to review the **Personal Style Indicator** with them, which they had completed before our first meeting, and to highlight the strengths **and** the weaknesses of each style.*

That was one of the first times anyone had spelled out for them not only the attractions they felt for each other, but also the areas of aggravation or irritation.

They were able to see things for the first time.

- *Randy's silence was not a passive-aggressive way to punish Roxanne;*
- *Randy's direct way of addressing what he wanted was not rude, uncultured behavior;*
- *Randy's drive to accomplish a task was not a way for him to avoid talking about "feelings" or things "really" important; and*
- *Randy's "short" answers were not a brush-off; and that*

- *Roxanne's verbal outpourings were not a devilish scheme to drive Randy crazy;*
- *Roxanne's focus on the details was not a form of interrogation;*
- *Roxanne's involvements with other people were not a sign that she was not interested in Randy or unconcerned about what he liked; and*
- *Roxanne's system to "really" deal or discuss things was not a form of torture.*

Within an hour or two, this couple was able to see that the spouse was not the enemy and that they were both on the same side.

Pointing that out did not change all that had gone wrong up to that point. It took some time for them to really grasp how their Personal Styles played out in their lives every day. In addition, time was needed to figure out whether the negative issue they were facing was about Personal Style or something else.

When it was about style, one or the other would try to style-shift or at least voice that "this thing" could be about style. That removed much of the personal attack or character assassination that been taking place previously.

Here are their numbers, if you haven't guessed them already.

- *Randy:* **B**52, **I**44, **A**34, **C**30—**BI** *profile*
- *Roxanne:* **A**49, **C**47, **I**37, **B**27—**AC** *and* **CA** *profiles*

More recently when we worked with them, not only did we see them heal the marriage after her affair, they have moved into another dimension within their relationship, using their understanding about their style to their advantage.

*You only have to talk with Randy and Roxanne's kids to understand how valuable Personal Style has become to them. The kids have said to us, "Mom and Dad are still going around their house, and our homes, too, talking about who is a **BCIA,** and so on, or saying things like 'Remember, Bill is a **C** so you better be on time and make sure to give him enough information'—or 'Kathy is an **I**, so don't steamroll over her; be gentle.' It's like our parents are using a secret code, which they have now imprinted on us."*

Anne and Brian Bercht
www.beyondaffairs.com

A Final Word of Caution

We have outlined the dynamics of the styles in their purest form, yet most patterns are blends of the four dimensions.

The best process is to review the *PSI* **In-Depth Interpretations** of all the people with whom you closely interact. The **In-Depth Interpretations** take into account the behavioral impact of the different combinations and provide the participant and others with a roadmap for development and specific coaching strategies to increase effectiveness.

As you apply this style-shifting information in your lives, it is important that you do so in a respectful way when you interact with others. Your credibility with others is determined by the way you behave. Personal Style assessment and style-shifting are critical to your success in life, but they are not the answer to all of life's challenges.

Using Personal Style concepts can greatly improve relationships, but other factors are just as important to consider when working on your associations. Relationships are complex because people are complex. Neither can ever be reduced to a single theory, be expressed in a single approach to life, or be contained in a single book.

CHAPTER 16

Credibility: Don't Leave Home or Work Without It!

You can make more friends in 2 months by becoming interested in other people than you can in 2 years by trying to get other people interested in you.

DALE CARNEGIE

Early in our marriage, Brenda was coming home from teaching at our local college. It was late at night and I was sitting at the kitchen table, reading the paper. From my seat, I could see her arrive home. As she got out of the car with an armful of books, I waved and kept reading, not thinking any more about it.

When Brenda came in the front door, she was not happy with me (I had low credibility with her) because I **did not do** something—get up and open the door for her.

Credibility—yours and mine—can change because of *what we don't do.* Was I intentionally wanting to lower my credibility in our relationship? Of course not—but my lack of awareness and my style behavior did exactly that. Yes, I now get up and open doors!

Every moment you are interacting with others, you are leaving an impression with them. Are you aware whether you are leaving a positive, negative, or indifferent impression?

> **We judge our own credibility levels by our intentions.**
> **Others judge us by our actions.**

Our behavior—what we actually do and don't do—builds credibility with people, not what we had *hoped to do.* Our good intentions and especially our verbal messages are valid only if they consistently match our behavior, and if our behavior also demonstrates respect toward the **style pattern and values of others**.

Your Personal Style and values are continuously shaping your view about yourself, but that doesn't mean other people have the same opinion about you. For instance, while the school bully may have a big reputation on campus, he does not have any credibility with the students. He isn't liked, trusted, admired, or befriended.

He may control situations and events, but he is lonely and will be deserted as soon as the students figure out how to get away from him. His actions destroy his credibility with the people that he wants to follow him.

All too often, the same results occur for individuals, at work and at home.

What is Credibility?

Credibility is your reputation for being fair, open, compassionate, inspirational, positive, competent, honest, and trustworthy. It determines the level of respect you will receive. If you don't know a person and he doesn't know you, there is no issue of credibility because no information is available to make a decision.

Reputation is established based on the behavior you express and the behavior you *don't express*.

> **Whether you like it or not, everyone who knows you
> has assigned you a level of credibility—low, medium, or high.
> That's the price you pay for showing up.**

You cannot avoid people's judgment unless you cease to interact with others—like Tom Hanks in the movie *Cast Away*.

- You have a credibility level with the people with whom you work and at the places where you are a purchaser or a seller.
- You have a credibility level with family, friends, and all others.
- Whether or not you wanted to do it, you have established a level of credibility with just about every person with whom you have interacted.

What Does Credibility Do?

Credibility determines the level of respect you will receive from others.

Note: Credibility is not about people liking you; it is about people *respecting* you. Keep that in mind as you review your credibility levels in your relationships.

What does Credibility measure?

It measures how trustworthy, honest, and reliable others think you are.

Where Does Your Credibility Exist?

It exists in other people's minds, not in yours.

Credibility is lent to you from others. You cannot demand credibility from others or force them to think highly of you. Your credibility is in the mind of others; you must earn it by conducting yourself in a way that meets their needs, not yours.

Why Should You Care about Credibility?

Your credibility influences how much others

- Communicate to you,
- Cooperate with you,
- Learn from you,
- Are influenced by you,
- Buy from you, and
- Support you.

Credibility is a core factor to your ongoing success.

> **Building your credibility means to intentionally increase your success and impact.**

Discounting that fact—or being in denial of it—does not lessen the impact that your level of credibility is having in your life. You are simply operating without awareness or acceptance of a critical part of any success model.

Think about it. It takes weeks, months, and years to build credibility, yet you can lose it in a heartbeat. When I mention Wall Street or AIG, what thoughts do you have about credibility? What thoughts do you have about Disney?

Credibility levels and opinions are unavoidable.

What Makes Credibility Increase and Decrease?

If your behavior, as perceived by others with whom you are interacting, is deemed to be *appropriate* for time, tasks, people, situations, and values, your credibility will increase. Behavior perceived as *inappropriate* for the same factors will make it decrease.

In other words, your style, the styles of others, your values, and your Personality Development Factors are the filters through which you judge others and others judge you.

Each moment of interaction with others causes your credibility to go up, stay the same, or go down. And note that I mean *behavior seen as appropriate or inappropriate* **by the other party**, not by you.

Credibility applies equally to the sin of omission. We are being judged by what we don't do as well, as what we do.

> **I remind you that it is our behavior—what we actually do and don't do— that builds credibility with people—not what we had hoped to do.**

Before you get too confident, every style and style pattern has its blind spots or sins of omission.

- **B**s can forget to praise,
- **A**s forget appointments,
- **I**s withhold important information if conflict is anticipated, and
- **C**s can overlook feelings on the way to completing a task.

Your success at developing credibility in different environments can vary from situation to situation. For instance, you may have struggles in your role as a teacher, a police officer, or a mechanic but you may get along really well within the family unit. Or just the opposite may occur; you may be highly esteemed at work as an executive, yet you are going through a divorce or separation at home.

The same could hold true for your levels of credibility in the many other roles you play in life—as a neighbor, Board member, parent, church member, and so forth. Some levels may be high, while others are low.

The bottom line is that each one of us earns our credibility by what we say and do.

Credibility has three levels.

- Self
- Others
- Organizations

Credibility with Self

I have mentioned interactions with others but we also have a level of internal credibility with ourselves. You have met individuals who are perfectly capable of fulfilling a task or a request but they actually discount their own worth (credibility) and suggest they are not competent or worthy enough to assume such a responsibility.

Some individuals don't accept their style, values, and personality as okay. I have had individuals complete the *PSI* assessment and not agree with their results. After further discussion, we realize they completed the assessment with the mindset of "the way they would like be," not "the way they really are."

That can come from a lack of acceptance of self. Perhaps it stems from feedback from an authority (parent or boss) who suggests they need to change and become someone different than their natural style preferences. They feel and think they are not okay the way they were created. In those cases, we want to encourage individuals to embrace their natural style preferences and refuse to accept what an external environment factor is trying force upon them.

Yes, we all have stuff to work on and improve, but accepting your style as okay is the first step to building credibility with others. If you don't like who you are, others likely will follow your lead.

Credibility with Others

Too often, our own point of view (style and values) determines the way we will act in a situation. That is generally ineffective in building credibility, unless the wants and needs of others are identical to ours—which we have proven to be unlikely.

> **To intentionally increase or maintain credibility with others, we must be aware of what others need and want.**

If you really want to be successful in life, no matter your professional calling or job, your roles will require you to interact with others.

- Are your relationships important to you? If your answer is Yes, then implement the three steps to building credibility: **Translating**, **Suspending**, and **Style-Shifting.**

Do you know your credibility levels with the people with whom you interact on a day-to-day basis? If I were to ask your co-workers, friends, significant others, children, volunteers, clients, suppliers, and others, what would they say about your credibility?

> **Many individuals are oblivious**
> **of the actual impact their behavior is having on others.**

Rarely do we get up in the morning thinking about all the ways we can offend the people around us, but often our behavior does exactly that, even though we never intended that outcome.

Are you willing to find out what people really think of you?

A few years ago, an individual on our IT development team was insistent that his style pattern included a **B** in the 40s, which infers a strong orientation to results, with the other three styles just below 40. That meant his Secondary pattern was **Four-Even** or **Synergistic**.

In spite of his insistence, that is not the way the CRG team experienced him, at least not in the work environment.

He never completed or finished a project. In many cases, he did not even get the project started because he was always thinking or talking about doing something—and not doing anything. His behavior did not reflect the style pattern he said he had. There was a disconnect between his perception of himself and his actual behavior; the result was that he had a very low level of credibility with his team members.

As part of our development process, we had each CRG team member complete the *PSI* on him, to confirm how they experienced him (from a style perspective) at work. We call this process the *PSI 360°*.

Note: The *PSI 360°* tool is available online. You have the option of using the print-based versions to achieve the same outcome.

The CRG team members wanted to provide their feedback and found this a very engaging process. After the entire team completed the *PSI 360°* on this specific team member, without exception the lowest score was always the **Behavioral** dimension . . . in the low 20s, meaning that dimension had a very weak influence on his style pattern. Yet the individual felt his **Behavioral ACTION** dimension was strong and in the mid 40s.

As part of our values system, we cannot argue with a person's perception of himself. The scores from the team, however, reflected what they experienced from him, not what he thought of himself.

You might be thinking this process could create conflict, but in fact the CRG team already had that opinion of him (low credibility) before they completed the *PSI 360°* on him. The *PSI 360°* simply provided a language and a communication system that captured the team's experience of that individual. The process did not create the results; it simply documented what was already true.

Even after this feedback from the team members and from me, he insisted—and in our opinion, was in denial—that he had a strong **B** dimension and was results-oriented. Although we could not argue with his perceptions, the facts were clear: If he had **B** in his profile, he did not use it at work.

Many times, we attempted to get him to "own" his lack of performance but he would not or could not. Obviously, we no longer have him on our team.

The *PSI 360°* process was my way of confirming my thoughts—*Am I the only one feeling this way about his lack of results?* I wondered if I had I biased my assessment of him.

In the non-judgmental *PSI 360°* method, the team simply confirmed the style pattern they felt he used at work. Although the style pattern was not positive or negative in itself, it showed he did not have the style pattern required to be successful in our IT position.

That example can also be used to show how many individuals in leadership positions lose credibility. The leader acknowledges that someone is underperforming or operating outside of company policy, but he doesn't do anything about it. He ignores the problem.

What many people don't realize is that the other team members are observing and they pass judgment on the leader's lack of action. I would have lost credibility with my team if I had not taken action with that non-performing team member.

A leader's credibility is eroded by inaction.

The leadership style of the supervisor influences his decision-making process. If he is highly introverted, the external pressures of the environment such as conflict or the compliance of others can hinder his ability to take action.

Learning to style-shift and to deal with such dynamics is critical to being effective in any leadership role.

There are many other powerful applications for the *PSI 360°*.

We have had parents complete the *PSI 360°* on their kids, students on their instructors, employees on their supervisors and/or leaders, clients on their sales reps, players with their coaches, couples on each other, and other applications.

The *PSI 360°* is a very effective communicating and development process to help you become more intentional with your behavior. It increases the awareness and understanding between two or more parties. If acted on, the outcome is *increased credibility with each other*.

Whether you like it or not, your behavior is increasing and decreasing your credibility with others.

Organizational Credibility

Every organization—from retail establishments, manufacturers, political parties, government agencies, not-for-profit organizations to countries, religions, and cultures—creates a level of credibility in the marketplace; there's no avoiding it.

Isn't it wiser to establish and build your credibility than to destroy it?

Dysfunctional Individuals and Credibility

Even though your goal is to have the highest potential credibility with each person you meet, it is important to acknowledge that it's impossible to have high levels of credibility with *everyone*. That is not a reasonable expectation.

In fact, it would be dysfunctional to try to please everyone. No matter what you do, some individuals will feel you are not credible. Some people—regardless of what others do with or for them—are never satisfied.

In *The Road Less Traveled*, M. Scott Peck discusses one of the most difficult physiological conditions to treat—Character Disorder—where people blame everyone else. It is never *their* fault. Since they take no responsibility for their condition, or the impact of their behavior, why would they consider changing?! They are unaware and often unproductive individuals.

During one of our **Assessment Systems Certification** training sessions, one individual was constantly complaining about everything in the program. We had just taught the section about credibility. The lady went on to state that nobody in the program was credible. She restated our teachings that credibility is based on the other person's opinion. Her opinion was that we all stunk.

I stayed in a professional mode, allowing her to express herself in the morning session. By the afternoon, she was so disruptive and poisonous, I had to ask her to leave. So . . . no matter how intentional you are at building credibility with others, sometimes you just have to let it go.

We later learned that her co-workers did not care for her. She was able to keep her job only because she was an expert in a special software program used in the organization. That is not a good enough reason to keep a toxic person, but they did.

The objective then is for each of us to intentionally build credibility—the best we can—and accept the fact that there will be some people—such as a dysfunctional person—with whom we won't be able to build credibility.

A Study on Leadership Credibility

James Kouzes and Barry Posner conducted an in-depth study on leadership credibility, which they published in their book *Credibility*. Through extensive research with large groups of employees from several organizations, the authors identified the attributes that employees consider essential for leadership credibility. The research revealed several predominant qualities or characteristics. Here are the top four qualities that are non-negotiable if you want to have credibility in the workplace.

1. **Honesty:** The Leader tells the truth and is behaviorally ethical.

2. **Competence:** Each Leader is capable and effective and gets things done.

3. **Foresight:** Leaders set and define vision and provide direction; they clearly know where they are going.

4. **Ability to Inspire:** Leaders connect team members' personal and professional *purpose* and passions to the vision of the organization, and they show how individual contributions matter.

Other qualities high on the list include being **supportive**, **fair-minded**, **dependable**, and **courageous**.

CHAPTER 17

Are You Ready and Willing to Change?

*Change has a considerable psychological impact on the human mind. To the fearful, it is threatening because it means that things may get worse. **To the hopeful, it is encouraging because things may get better.** To the confident, it is inspiring because the challenge exists to make things better.*

KING WHITNEY JR.

Change: The quality or power of inspiring belief; capacity for belief to make different in some particular way; alter; to make radically different; transform; to give a different position, course, or direction; to replace with another; to make a shift from one to another; switch; to undergo a modification; to become different; to pass from one phase to another

If you want to increase your success and improve your conditions, it will require change.

Are you **Ready** and **Willing** to change?

What's the difference between the two?

Are you **Ready (have the ability)** to change?

You have noticed a growth on your right knee. Tests confirm it is benign, but no doctor is available to operate for several weeks.

But don't worry; I've always been interested in medicine—I recall dissecting frogs in high school. I've never been to medical school but I've watched a lot of medical programs on TV and I have tools in my shop. Come to my home on Saturday around 10 and we'll get that growth taken off!

What is your confidence level in my ability (Readiness) to operate?

None, right? I don't have the skills or the abilities to do it.

I am not *ready* to operate, even though I am *willing*.

Are you **Willing (have the right attitude)** to change?

Many years ago, I worked in sales for an agricultural company as a dairy specialist. My sales tripled in my first 3 years; I was the top sales performer.

During that time, I became engaged to be married. Although it was a long-distance relationship—I was living in Vancouver, BC, and the lady was in Brisbane, Australia—it was manageable. I was in love and successful in my work and I had even started a small business on the side.

Everything was grand . . . until Valentine's Day. My fiancée called from Down Under to say she had accepted a better offer.

I was devastated. I lost 15 pounds in 15 days—the fastest weight-loss program in the world, but not recommended.

My sales performance started to slide.

- Did that have anything to do with my sales abilities (readiness)? No. Because of my personal issues, my **willingness** level had dropped.

- If my sales manager had sent me to a sales-training refresher program on how to close the sale, would that have done any good? Not at all!

When you think of your success (and the success of others), are you **aware** of your levels **of readiness and willingness** to change and succeed?

Have you met or worked for a nice, enthusiastic, well-meaning person who was borderline incompetent at his job? How did you feel about hanging out with him? You probably had very little confidence in his abilities and even less willingness to engage him.

On the flip side, do you know a highly competent person with great work skills who is not willing to be a team player? He is the cause of much strife and hinders the progress of others at every step. You probably don't want to hang out with him, either.

Are you one of those two individuals?

Were you ever in over your head and unable to fulfill your responsibilities from a skills point of view? Perhaps you had the skills but no longer enjoyed your position because you had lost your passion for the job.

Our Readiness and Willingness Model outlines a process to help you better understand the contributing causes for a person's success or failure.

Awareness of the potential reasons for lack of progress is as important as the process of fixing the issues. When you or someone else is failing, or not achieving what you would like, we simply ask the question: *Is this a **readiness** issue, a **willingness** issue, or both?* Once you answer that question, you can take the appropriate steps to improve your situation.

Let's examine **Readiness** and **Willingness**.

1. Readiness

In our **Readiness and Willingness to Change© Model**, I define Readiness this way: **Readiness** is the measure of a person's **ability** to succeed in a given situation. It reflects and reveals how prepared and competent the person is to succeed before starting.

A person may be aware of a problem and yet does nothing about it. He sees the option of using round wheels but, for whatever reason, intentionally decides to keep his square wheels.

- Is it possible that he does not know how to change wheels?
- Is he ill equipped in some way?

Areas to Consider Regarding Readiness for Change

Social	Does the person have the interpersonal skills required for change?
Intercultural	Does the person have the cultural knowledge to change?
Emotional	Does the person have the emotional strength to change?
Spiritual	Is the person ready to search for the meaning of life, the truth?
Mental	Is the person cognitively able to learn what is needed to effect change?
Education	Does the person have the education required for the change?
Physical	Is the person physically ready to go through the change process?
Special Skills	Does the person have the skills and training to successfully complete the responsibilities and tasks that are necessary for the change?
Style-Match	Does the individual's Personal Style match the roles and responsibilities of the new situation?

2. Willingness

Willingness is the measure of a person's **attitude** and commitment toward success.

Areas to consider regarding Willingness to Change

Cooperating with others	Does the person work collaboratively as a team member?
Learning from others	Does the person agree to let others teach him or her how to perform a task?
Helping others learn	Does the person agree to teach others how to perform a task?
Accepting self and others	Does the person show caring for self and others?
Being appreciated by others	Does the person let others show recognition and caring to him or her?
Being friends with others	Does the person enjoy spending time with others?
Giving of self	Does the person permit others to benefit from his or her experiences?
Being authentic	Does the person permit others to know his or her feelings, opinions, and beliefs?
Forgiving self and others	Does the person commit to solving conflicts?
Letting go of habits	Is the person willing to let go of what he or she has been doing—the status quo—and embrace new behavior that may be more acceptable to others?
Letting go of excuses	Is the person willing to stop using multiple reasons— excuses—for not participating in opportunities or implementing change?

Ready and Willing to Work Together

If things are not going as well as you would like, is the lack of success a **Readiness** issue, a **Willingness** issue, or a combination of both?

Here is a critical question surrounding the **Readiness** of an individual.

- Is there evidence that someone can do what we have asked? Is there proof of readiness? If not, why would we assume he or she has the abilities to fulfill any new roles or responsibilities?

Frequently, couples are told in marriage counseling sessions to communicate better, but they have never learned communication skills.

Do you recall times when people—perhaps you—were promoted into jobs or roles without the proper training? Worse, they had few abilities (readiness) to fulfill the responsibilities and little interest in the new job (willingness). Rather than being forthright by saying they had no idea what they were doing—perhaps fear or pride put them into a sense of denial—they struggled in their position.

I have witnessed supervisors criticizing individuals for poor performance, yet the leader has never equipped the employee with the readiness skills to succeed. The irony is that this type of behavior on the part of the supervisor reflects a lack of readiness to lead others.

There is also the issue of willingness. Have you encountered someone who was very effective in a role but, over time, that individual's willingness levels kept dropping?

Let's say a person who was once energized and very productive in her role loses interest (willingness). Our quest is to find out why. Maybe she is disappointed to learn her job is not what she expected; perhaps the job style required by the position doesn't match her Personal Style. As a result, her willingness decreases.

There could be numerous other reasons that a person's willingness drops. They could have health concerns or they could be struggling in their personal relationship.

Suppose a new leader is placed in a department and he is incompetent. That lowers morale in the team that in turn reduces others' willingness to engage and change.

Are you paying attention to these clues for yourself and others?

What if one of your children was doing well at school, but lately his grades are slipping? Do you go *deep* with your questions to find out the real reasons? It could be that a bully at school is picking on him. Maybe a new teacher is less than encouraging, causing the child to withdraw. Perhaps it is both.

I was incorrectly labeled a poor learner all through high school. It was not until I was completing my Master's Degree that it was discovered I had mild dyslexia. The lack of awareness about my readiness (abilities) caused me a lot of pain that was avoidable.

To change or improve, you must be aware of what must be addressed. Ask yourself this question: *Am I (or is someone I oversee) not succeeding because of a lack of Readiness (ability) or a lack Willingness (attitude) to change . . . or both?*

Situational Readiness and Willingness to Change

Sometimes, the levels of readiness and willingness depend on the context of the question.

- You might be highly ready and willing at work in your current job but score low in readiness as a new parent.

- You may do parts of your job very well, but there may be other work responsibilities where you are not so ready and willing.

When conducting marriage counseling, I have seen people ready and very willing to suspend and style-shift at work but, once they get home, they cannot suspend or style-shift. Neither person is ready or willing to change for their significant other.

To better understand the levels where you and those with whom you interact might rank, use our development grid and the descriptions.

Four Development Levels (D-Levels)

D-Levels	1 Resistant	2 Reasonable	3 Responsible	4 Resourceful
Ready to Change	Not ready; unable to proceed	Ready to consider change, to think and talk about it	Ready to get involved and learn how and what to change	Ready to develop full potential and skills levels
Willing to Change	Not willing; insecure; fights help	Willing to listen to alternatives	Willing to take action now	Willing to help others develop

The following information expands each D-level.

Level 1: Resistant

Not ready or willing to change or succeed
Self-focused, self-centered, self-destructive
Uncooperative, non-compliant, disruptive of the team, unmotivated
Unable and/or unskilled to perform
Critical, verbally abusive; an accuser, a blamer
Angry, argumentative, non-trusting
In denial; refuses to change; doesn't think he or she needs to change

Level 2: Reasonable

Somewhat ready and willing to learn, change, succeed
Only ready and willing *to think and talk* about learning,
	changing, succeeding
"What's in it for me?" attitude
Agreeable to negative feedback and change but
	behavior remains the same
Motivated by others; a team follower
Overcontrolling of self

Level 3: Responsible

Ready and willing to learn, change, succeed
Self-motivated to improve self, situations
Cooperative; a team-player, a contributor
Capable of performing responsibilities
Verbally positive; an encourager, supportive
Confident, assertive; respects self and others
Transforms potential into production
In control of self

Level 4: Resourceful

Ready and willing to learn, change, succeed, **and**
	to help others do so
Personally functions at Level 3
Driven by the vision of people-development
Motivates others to improve; inspirational
Able to teach others the required skills and knowledge to succeed
Leads others from the present into the future; honest and ethical
A professional leader in control, **and** helps others
	increase control of self

Please note that Level 4 infers you are ready and willing to succeed AND you are also ready and willing to help others do the same. Leading others to success requires quite a different skill set than does personal success. Unless you are able to teach and inspire others in their success, consider Level 3 as your target.

> **When you think about the level of your success and the success of others, keep in mind the concept of Readiness and Willingness.**

Personal Exercise

How Ready and Willing Are You to Succeed?

Think of a specific situation or role in your life that you are currently evaluating, then answer the following questions. You can use this grid in multiple and specific applications, from leading a new department at work, parenting, your personal relationship, or a new volunteer role, to gauging how prepared you are to engage your new healthy-lifestyle goals.

1. On a scale of 1 to 4, how ready to change do you think you are?

   ☐ D1 Not ready

   ☐ D2 Ready to think or talk about it

   ☐ D3 Ready to learn how to do it

   ☐ D4 Ready to teach others

2. What blocks or challenges may be in the way of your readiness to change?

   _____

   _____

   _____

   _____

   _____

3. On a scale of 1 to 4, how willing to change do you think you are?

   ☐ D1 Not willing

   ☐ D2 Willing to think or talk about it

   ☐ D3 Willing to learn how to do it

   ☐ D4 Willing to teach others

4. What blocks or challenges may be in the way of your willingness to change?

   _____

   _____

   _____

   _____

   _____

CHAPTER 18

Advanced Knowledge of Each Style Dimension

Change your thoughts and you change your world.

NORMAN VINCENT PEALE

Discovering Each Style's Unique Orientation to Time, Decisions, Communications, Learning, and Money

To help you deepen your understanding of style and its impact on every part of our lives, I am including a summary of each style's orientation toward time, making decisions, communicating, learning, and money.

Because most people's style patterns have more than one dimension, you must merge the information from one or more styles to get a full and complete perspective.

Behavioral ACTION: Extroverted, Non-Verbal Action, Task-Oriented

Time, Decisions, Communications, Learning, and Money

Of the four styles, **B**s place the highest value on time—*Time is money* and *time's awastin'*. Slow-paced individuals, meetings, traffic, or projects behind schedule can particularly irritate **B**s.

They think in the present and look to the future and really don't care about the past. The past is past, so get over it. Because of this time orientation, they tend not to hold grudges; people who keep bringing up issues from the past will not be appreciated by **B**s.

When **B**s are in a buying mode and making a decision about a purchase (or a person), typically they have already made a decision before they call or leave their home or business. They are looking for the best value and competent sellers. If you speak slowly or don't have complete and correct information for them, they will abandon the process and seek to buy from someone else.

Most High **B**s reading this section have been in a retail store situation where either the clerk or the process was too slow for them, so they put down the product and left to go to another store—even though that would delay their purchase even more.

For them, it becomes the principle of the matter. "If you are that slow, you don't deserve my business." That applies to any meeting or business or personal decisions. They say, "Get the facts and let's decide now." In their mind, there is no benefit to delaying a decision.

You also must appear to respect them in their decision-making process. Disrespect them and look out! There could be fireworks. They will pay or invest more into something or someone if it will save them time, which means saving money in the long run, in their mind.

How will they communicate in interactions? Use the criteria to predict their behavior. They will be focused on the task at hand, and they will be in charge of the conversation . . . so it will be direct and to the point. They won't need a lot of details or information, just the main points or facts. Anything more will frustrate them.

They can send a one-word answer to an email requesting a detailed response. They might just say okay. Since they are extroverted, they will resist people who tell them what to do. You must ask—*not tell*—them what to do, and even allow them the option of saying No. Anything else might cause them to resist, just on the principle of the matter.

They can be accused of undercommunicating (non-verbal) and not providing all the information others might need to successfully complete a task or fulfill a responsibility. In many instances, others will have to ask a **B** for more details, to get the full picture.

Note: Learning Styles in our model are different from Personal Style; they are covered in detail in our ***Learning Style Indicator***. Learning styles also will be covered in my upcoming book ***Why Don't You Teach The Way That I Learn?*** and its accompanying programs.

One of the unique elements of our Learning Style Model is that we recognize **B**s as **Independent Learners**. They want control of the pace, time, and content of any learning experience and really dislike anything that is not real and factual.

When I took my Executive MBA from a non-traditional educational institute, local universities tired to discredit the distance-learning process as not being valid. Today, if you don't offer distance learning or blended-learning options, you are behind the times.

Why are so many potential learners interested in distance-learning options? Many individuals need the freedom to study and learn in their own time, and not have the university dictate their schedule.

I almost failed high school, but not because I was stupid—although one teacher told me I was. The reality? I was bored. I understood the concepts in the first 5 minutes of class and did not need the rest of the hour to go over and over them.

When I completed my MBA with honors, I proved that when I am interested and the structure of the learning allows me to engage—when and how I want—I can achieve outstanding results. That applies to High **B** staff, students, and children. They learn best in independent learning conditions and environments.

Finally, money or wealth can be important to High **B**s but for a different reason than most people think. Wealth is a measure of achievement and is seen by many **B**s as part of their need for challenge. Wealth simply benchmarks success. **B**s tend not to worry about money because they know they can turn up the jets and earn more whenever they decide to do it.

Cognitive ANALYSIS: Introverted, Verbal Non-Action, Tasks

Time, Decisions, Communications, Learning, and Money

Cs see time as something to be respected. If you have an appointment at a given time, you better keep that appointment and not be late. To them, 3 PM means 3 PM—not 3:05 or 3:10. Your credibility will go down immediately if you don't honor their time orientation.

Oddly, even though keeping commitments is important to **C**s, they can lose time by getting bogged down in details.

They think in terms of the past and the future. The **C** has orientation to the past; they bring up former issues again and again and even project them into the future, which can make them seem pessimistic. Learning to let go of past hurts—while not omitting the learning from the past—is one of their best development opportunities.

When it comes to decision-making, it's about collecting ALL possible information to make a quality decision. They will not be rushed into any decision. If they don't have their questions or concerns answered in detail, there is little chance they will feel comfortable making a decision.

Their decision process is all about your respect for their need for information. I remind you that **C**s are verbal (lots of data), yet non-action-oriented; they will collect quantities of information but may not act on it.

Because they are introverted, the time needed for making major decisions can be weeks and even months. They can be more focused on making the right decision than on making any decision at all. That pace can frustrate others, yet if they feel pushed, they will dig in their heels more and further resist any decision.

Their quest for information must be respected or you will not earn their trust.

During a live coaching session, I was working with a sales team in a retail environment. Their greatest fear as a sales team was being "stuck" with a High **C** buyer. They knew a lot of time would be spent with that person; numerous questions would be asked and the chances the High **C would** purchase something at that moment was low. In the sales team's view, it was a waste of time.

How do they know a High **C** buyer? Many times, the buyer is carrying a clipboard or sheets of paper containing research from the 'Net. The pace of the High **C** is methodical, which includes an intense focus toward tasks. The High **C** is not friendly and warm.

Sometimes, **C**s standards are so high, they can't find anything that meets their expectations so they don't buy. Yet many **C**s do eventually buy from *someone.*

The **C**'s communication style is focused on the task at hand, with the quest to acquire additional information. Because they will be guarded and defer to the environmental stimulus, safety in the relationship and the environment are paramount for them.

They don't like last-minute important discussions without time to reflect on their thoughts or ideas. Even though their communicating style can be the most critical of others, **C**s can be very sensitive to feedback or critical comments toward themselves.

Sometimes, requests from others will be received by the **C** as information, instead of items for action. Make sure clarification and agreements are part of the communication process. To keep communication open, avoid making comments the **C** can take personally. They communicate more freely in a low stress environment.

Cs are visual learners.

They have to see it through their eye-gate to understand it. You could have a great discussion with a High **C** but, if nothing is put in writing, the meeting did not exist.

Let's say I am a trainer, teaching students about a new software program. I am giving directions verbally. If I want the **C** students to understand the lesson, I must support my verbal information with visual aids.

If I am selling a product to a High **C**, it is best to show them print materials or to source the information online so the **C** can review the information via the eye-gate. **Cs** want to deal with experts who know their products! Making false claims or exaggerated statements will instantly kill your credibility when dealing with **Cs**.

As a **C** buyer, I ask you, the seller, the horsepower of a new car I am considering. You respond that you think it is around 200. By using the words *think* and *around*, you cause me to doubt any further information from you. If you don't know the answer, don't try to guess. Simply say you *believe* it is 200 horsepower and that you will check the documents so we know the exact number.

Cs learn best in a structured environment with well-organized methods. Because of their introverted nature, they prefer learning at a slower pace so they have the time to process the details or the concepts.

Cs for the most part are cautious and can worry about money. They do like deals. Many **Cs** will compare prices and be excited about saving 10 cents on a can of soup. And they will tell others about their achievement.

They will invest more to create the perception of safety. They may buy a Volvo vehicle because of its safety rating or purchase a security alarm system for their home before people of other styles might.

Although you would think all **Cs** would have budgets and be organized around their finances, we have found that is not always the case. Some **Cs** have little interest in money and others **Cs** do, so we have no predictive behavioral observation on this matter.

Cs do have a personal sense of fairness or equality that is seen as a feeling of entitlement as it relates to group dynamics and money. **Cs** would be the first to be upset if someone else got a bonus at work and they did not. If someone else got a raise, the **C** would want one as well, whether or not the **C** deserved it.

Interpersonal Harmony: Introverted, Non-Verbal Action, People

Time, Decisions, Communications, Learning, and Money

Is are the best at being present in the moment. That is one reason they are such good listeners; their orientation toward time is with you, not thoughts from the past or the future.

For them, time is secondary to relationships; generally, they will go with the flow. They strive to be seen as reliable and will keep their time commitments but not at the expense of a relationship or if the commitment will create a conflict.

Since they are introverted and action-oriented, they will move forward to get things done but at a comfortable pace. Just as with **C**s, intensity or constant time pressure can wear down the physicality of the **I**. That can cause more stress for the **I** than for the extroverted styles.

Is take their orientation toward time into their decisions, meaning they need time for thoughtful consideration before making a decision. They are the most practical of all the styles and also will use time as their filter for making decisions.

If it is an organizational decision, the impact on others will be more important to the **I** person than the organizational issue itself, such as a merger or a new computer system.

As much as possible, the **I** might frame the decision to avoid conflict or avoid putting stressful change on others. Because of their practical nature and their introverted style, they can take the longest amount of time to make a major decision. If they are considering the purchase of a new vehicle, it might be years from the time they start thinking about it until it actually happens.

In every seminar I have conducted, the **I** is the dimension that keeps their current vehicle the longest, in many cases over 10 years. After all, in their mind it works just fine; they really don't need a new one.

When it comes to important group decisions, this lack of urgency can play havoc on getting things done or moving forward, especially if there is a lot at stake. They might even decide ***not to decide***, given all the pressures.

Of course, that can become counter-productive if not addressed. In terms of their preferred seller, they are looking for someone they can trust who is willing to warmly guide them through a purchasing decision. They want a person to help them with their decisions and show them the potential options available, while having their best interests in mind.

Because they are so sensitive to feelings and motives, they can tell if you have their best interests in mind—or not.

To get the full picture, communicate with the **I** in private. Large-group interactions can cause them to withhold important opinions or perspectives. As I mentioned earlier, before **I**s will fully disclose their views, they must trust the people with whom they are communicating.

Because **I**s are introverted and non-verbal, you likely will have to ask several questions to get the answers you seek; they might not be forthcoming at first. Being their friend will help increase authentic communications.

Is value honesty very much but, under stress, they would rather not tell the whole truth if that will stir up conflict. Keep that in mind when communicating with an **I**.

If you are an **I,** the idea of avoiding conflict at all costs is not always beneficial to relationships. In fact long term, that might create more strife than being honest upfront.

If hurts or conflict have occurred as part of your communication with an **I** person, the **I** can quickly withdraw and become bitter and untrusting. In those situations, unless you can rebuild your credibility with the **I**, you cannot count on getting the full story.

Is **are auditory learners.**

They learn though their ears—listening, lectures, and presentations. They don't like large-group presentations but appreciate small-group work and partner work. Some like to listen to music while they work or learn.

They don't like stress in their learning environment. Excessive pressure, criticism, or aggressive instructors will cause them to withdraw and shut down. They require clear, concise instructions so they can fulfill what is expected of them.

Regarding money, the **I** is the most conservative of all the styles. They are practical; they don't spend unless it is a necessity. Even then, they might come up with reasons why the leaking dishwasher is still okay. On average, **I**s dislike debt and avoid debt whenever possible because owing money can create stress for them.

For the most part, money is simply a means to live and help others, not something to acquire. Savings are important to them for security purposes, not for the accumulation of wealth.

Affective EXPRESSION: Extroverted, Verbal Non-Action, People

Time, Decisions, Communications, Learning, and Money

As move between being present in the moment and thinking about the future. Their orientation to time is generally a lack of consciousness of time as a measurement.

Often, they can be late for appointments or events, not appreciating how much time was really needed to get there. They will do things last-minute, cramming everything into a compressed time frame. Because they are extroverted, verbal, and people-oriented, the **A** will negotiate for more time to submit his research paper or deliver a work project.

For some reason, time gets away from **A**s. They so enjoy their activities or engaging in an important relationship that 2 hours go by and it feels like 2 minutes to them.

Notice I said *enjoy*. The opposite can be true for an **A** if the activity is not agreeable to them. When that is the case, the passage of time is painful and feels like forever to them.

As tend to be the most spontaneous of the four style dimensions. They can make decisions in the moment, depending on how they are feeling about things. They are motivated by the experience the decision might bring to them or to others about whom they care. They want to have fun and enjoy the process.

As can be involved in complicated and detailed decision-making processes—as long as they don't become bored. If they do, they will disconnect from the process. If they are in a meeting that is dragging out or going slowly, they will become frustrated.

In many cases, their decisions are based on emotions. They can walk into an electronics store to buy a 9-volt battery and walk out with a new 60" flatscreen TV.

A buyers need to have fun in the purchasing process and experience the enjoyment of whatever they are considering. If it is a new dress, the **A** needs to put it on and see herself in it. If it is a new car, she must enjoy the dynamics of driving the car.

As want only the information that is important to them. Forget the rest of the details—you will bore them. The **A** can and, in many cases, does, make the decision to purchase in seconds and minutes, not days or weeks.

The **A**'s communication is full of language (verbal) and of an influencing nature (extroverted). For the most part, they will speak their minds, many times out of turn, not waiting for others to finish. Because they like stories, many of their responses will include stories related to the topic.

They can also stray off topic fairly easily and move into something totally unrelated to the first part of your conversation. You might need to help them get back on track because their mind internally moves to numerous topics quickly. Because they are people-oriented, they can become more animated and increase their verbal nature when in larger, higher-energy environments and groups.

Even though **A**s can be bold and courageous in their communications, they also like to be liked. If criticisms or judgments are directed toward them in harshness, or without care, they can withdraw and be wounded in their heart. That can shift their emotional state very quickly, from the life-of-the-party to a moping person in the corner of the room.

As need to learn how to manage their extraordinary level of communication energy so that others will be able to speak and be heard.

As are experiential learners.

They need to do it to get it, while having fun in the learning. The **A** extroversion also means they need to physically move to learn. Sitting for long periods will hinder their ability to focus or absorb information. That is evident even in High **A** children. No matter how many times you tell a High **A** 2-year-old not to touch something, he will go back to it.

Why? The **A** style is tactile. The interaction of their touch with the item helps them understand and connect to learning about it. If you are an instructor training an **A** person in a new software program, the **A** needs to be *in* the program with you, not just watching you work on your screen.

One of our friends is a medical doctor who works with kids with ADHD. (His opinion is we don't need drugs to medicate our kids into a stupor. We need to change their diet and get rid of all the sugars that make them hyper—but that's a topic for another book, on health.) He wants kids to be in an exciting learning environment that allows them to *move*. That is especially true for High **A** learners.

Although I am cautious in making general statements, I have found that **A**s—unless they have developed discipline—can have the greatest challenges in managing money. Because they are spontaneous and may purchase items on impulse, for the enjoyment of the buying experience rather than for practicality, they can get themselves into debt.

Budgeting requires structure and **A**s prefer to avoid structure. They can spend without weighing or even knowing all the consequences. They can go out with friends and offer to buy, because **A**s naturally are very generous. They might not be able to afford it, but that's not the point. Their friendships and having fun are the point.

Some **A**s play a game to motivate themselves into action. They take on debt to force them to act to pay it back.

Another dynamic around money is the tendency for **A**s to change their minds and ventures. They may be investing money in a project and then, without warning, they get bored and move to another venture—abandoning all their investment in the first project.

In personal and business partnerships that can become contentious so, with an **A**, set your monetary guidelines upfront to mitigate those issues.

Nancy R. Harris, MSS, tells how style helped her client become clear about his future

One of my clients is a man who had been divorced for 9 years. He really had no idea why his wife had left him. Using the **PSI***, we learned that for 20 years, when she had said things like, "The kids need to be picked up at 3 pm" or "The bathroom needs to be painted" or "Sex would be great," he did not see them as requests. He heard them as facts and information.*

So he never did anything, always expecting she would ASK when she needed or wanted his help.

She left, believing he never really loved her and the kids. When he would say Yes, he was acknowledging she had given him information. She thought he had agreed to do it and he NEVER kept his agreements!

The transformation of my client and the changes in many others I have witnessed and helped is because of CRG's **Personal Style Indicator** *and the content of this book!*

Nancy R. Harris, MSS
www.nancyharris.com

**Nancy R. Harris, MSS, shares a client's response
to the realization of style differences.**

> *One of my favorite examples of a client's transformation is of a mother and daughter who came to me for help. The daughter was adopted so there were **many** differences. Mother and father were introverts (**I** and **C**) and college professors who truly believed Saturday night was best spent at home reading a good book and listening to classical music.*

> *The daughter was an extrovert and a High **AB** pattern. When I looked the mother in the eye and told her that her daughter needed to be on stage with an audience and lots of people contact, and that a good safe PARTY on Saturday night is what she needed as a reward for long hours of studying all week, the reactions were profound.*

> *The daughter looked at me with great thanks and said, "Are you telling me my mother is always going to be like this? Is she always going to be against and the opposite of what I want?" When I answered Yes, they both just laughed and said, "Oh, well. We might as well get used to it, instead of fighting about it!"*

Nancy R. Harris, MSS
www.nancyharris.com

CHAPTER 19

Applying Style and Values in Your Everyday Life

Many of life's failures are people who did not realize
how close they were to success when they gave up.

THOMAS A. EDISON

Someone once asked me who could benefit from the knowledge of Personal Style and where could it be applied. I said if you are walking and breathing and a teenager (or even younger, with the help of adults), you can gain from the knowledge of style.

In other words—Everyone!

In terms of applications, if you are interacting with a person or you have a job, role, or specific responsibilities, you will benefit from implementing the style strategies in this book.

Here are samples of areas where the knowledge of style and the *PSI* have been successfully applied.

Career Development	Mentoring
Change Management	Parenting/Family
Communication	Personal Effectiveness
Conflict Resolution	Personal **Purpose**
Coaching	Problem-Solving
Customer Service	Sales
Dating Compatibility	Self-Awareness
Education	Self-Management
Executive Coaching	Stress Management
Hiring Process	Succession Planning
Job Selection and Matching	Supervisory Training
Leadership Development	Team-Building Development
Life Coaching	Teenagers/Students
Management Development	Time Management
Marriages	Wellness Programs

Applying Style and Values in Everyday Life

On the following pages are real stories and case studies of the power and effectiveness of using style and values to improve relationships and enhance results in various applications.

Sports and Coaching

Every sport has the dynamic of players and coaches. Regardless of their skills, we have all seen elite athletes walk out on coaches or coaches bench star players due to conflict. In some cases, the discord is based on style differences.

Here is a case where the Canadian National Junior Men's Curling team implemented the *PSI* with the help of Lynn Bennett, of Leadership Intelligence.

1. *The Who, What, How, Where, and When (the critical facts in the case)*

   - *Leadership Intelligence partnered with Curling Coach John Thompson*
   - *Junior Men's Curling Team representing Kitchener/Waterloo Ontario Canada*
   - **Personal Style Indicator** *assessment for all members of team (4 plus an alternate, as well as the coach)*

2. *The Places, Persons, Activities, and Contexts of the Situation, in Detail, in the Words of Coach John Thompson*

   - *During the 3 years I have coached, I have had each player complete a* **PSI***. It is a fairly simple assessment process that we do at my home. It can be completed in about 15 minutes.*
   - *The results offer me and the players*
     - i. *detailed information on our preferred interactions and team dynamics;*
     - ii. *insights into how each of us would prefer to interact with each other;*
     - iii. *information on how we prefer to give and receive information. This gave me as coach new insights into how to approach and communicate with each player and the team as a whole, as well as what to say and how to phrase things in a time-out or during debriefing;*
     - iv. *indications of who would step out as leader, and who and how others would follow;*
     - v. *insights into how the team should be reorganized from a style/*

team dynamics perspective to succeed (done during the 2008 – 2009 season);

    vi. an accurate prediction of how our team interactions and dynamics may result in "dysfunctional behaviors" during times of stress, such as when we experienced poor results, which we did early in the 2009 – 2010 season.

7. **List All Indicators (including Stated "Problems") that Something is Not as Expected or Desired, summarized by Lynn**

- When John came on as coach, the players had assigned positions.

    i. Skip: Leads the team, sets game strategy, calls the shot (quarterback), throws last rocks;

    ii. Vice: Assists the skip and must communicate with front end players (second and lead) as well as throw second-last rock;

    iii. Second and Lead: Both sweep; must communicate to those calling the shot/holding the broom the momentum or speed of the rock; throw the first four rocks of the game (two each). These players may be invited to offer their opinion on game strategy. That, however, is generally on the invitation of the skip.

- Position assignment was based on what members wished to play and the overall skill and confidence in throwing ability; other factors were **not** considered. They included visioning the ice, critical and forward thinking, risk assessment, stress management, self-management, leadership, communication, desire to win, adjust to changing conditions, recovery time after failure, etc.

4. **List Critical Statements by Major Parties, for example, People, Groups, the Work Unit, in the Words of Coach John Thomson**

- This team was called dysfunctional by many, after watching them in the National Finals on The Sports Network (TSN). The Canadian Curling Association representative Scott Arnold received many concerned comments on the team's poor group-dynamics.

  After working with the team in the lead up to and in Switzerland, his concerns were proved false. Had the fans and others watching understood the Personal Style preferences of each team member and the team, they would have understood us and our ability to use our styles to our benefit.

5. *List All Goals of the Major Parties that Exist or Can Be Reasonably Inferred.*
   - *Win the Ontario Championships.*
   - *Win the Canadian Championships.*
   - *Get to the final four at the Worlds.*
   - *Win the World Championships.*

6. *Application of the* **Personal Style Indicator**
   - *Existing team members asked to revisit* **PSI** *and new team members asked to complete the* **PSI.**
   - *Lynn Bennett prepared a Team Profile.*
   - *Lynn Bennett debriefed each individual team member, the team, and the coach on the* **PSI** *results and applications.*
   - *Lynn Bennett provided ongoing support, coaching, and insights to the Team Coach.*

7. *Results*
   - *Represented Ontario at the Junior Men's Canadian Championships 2010 and won!*
   - *Represented Canada at the World Junior Men's Championships 2010 in Flims Switzerland; took the bronze medal after losing on last rock in the one/two game.*
   - *Says John Thompson, Coach, Junior Men's Canadian Curling Champions and Junior Men's World Bronze Champions:* **"The Personal Style Indicator** *is a terrific tool that could really benefit coaches at all levels.* I was quite skeptical when my wife introduced me to it, but it has proven time and again to be a very accurate and helpful tool. Certainly for someone like me who is coaching a different group of boys each year, it has been a great headstart on getting to know my teams and how to communicate with them.*

8. *Outcome*
   - *John Thompson strongly recommended the* **PSI** *to the Canadian Curling Association.*
   - *CCA is accountable to assist all of Canada's top-tier teams as they strive to be the best, representing their city, province, and country at the regional, provincial, national, and international level.*

Lynn Bennett
www.leadershipintellegence.com

Many scenarios within this case study can be expanded, but the net result is that the team became national champions and earned third place in the world competitions—an achievement the coach said would not have been possible without the use and understanding of Personal Style.

With the help of Lynn, their consultant and coach, they got the team members to play to their strengths and understand their reactions to stress and leadership. It also outlined the way the coach could best communicate to each team member while understanding each member's preferences and differences as they applied to the team objectives and goals. Those principles would apply to any sports team and coaching application.

Career Development and Life Planning

> **You cannot do true career planning or career development without understanding your Personal Style and values.**

I remind you of the current stats that over 80% of individuals dislike their job, from a feeling of mild irritation to downright loathing. Speaking at a high school, I asked if the seniors had completed a Personal Style assessment as part of their career planning course. The teacher answered, "There is no budget for it. We just talk about it and leave it there."

No wonder people's "water glasses" are empty or people are dissatisfied with work. They are unaware of the best job style to match their Personal Style strengths.

Note: Career developers and programs are in the top-three client groups of CRG's holistic assessment systems that help people understand themselves so they can make intentional choices about their life and careers.

Here are stories from four clients who have found benefit for themselves or others in using the *PSI* and *VPI* in career and life planning.

> *My significant other and I each filled out the* **Personal Style Indicator** *and* **Values Preference Indicator** *and shared our results with one another. These tools have helped us design a plan for improving our effectiveness in communicating and understanding what is important and valued by the other.*
>
> *It really has been worthwhile to know our strengths and recognize the main difficulties in our styles. I'm not saying it is always easy*

for me to effectively communicate, but now I can practice shifting my style to accommodate my partner's Personal Style.

*The **Values Preference Indicator** was a particular eye-opener for me. It was a real wake-up call to discover that the areas I value most are areas in which I don't spend the most time. For example, I highly value friendship, but I was not making time to get together with friends.*

Knowing my top values and rating my satisfaction in those areas helped me set goals and make plans to spend more time involved in the areas of my life that I truly value.

*The **Values Preference Indicator** is a tool that can be used as you transition to a new life-cycle phase. My next life cycle will be retirement. I plan to revisit this assessment then.*

Jenny Lace

Several years ago, I had an experience with a man in his early 40s. His parents had been killed in a tragic car accident when he was very young and he was raised by his older sisters. As he told me, "My sisters did the best job they could, but they provided no guidance, as a parent might have, in terms of career direction."

*He went on to say he graduated from high school and went from job to job, never really enjoying any of them and never thinking he ever would. I administered the **Personal Style Indicator** as well as the Motivated Skills Card Deck. When we were done, his eyes lit up. "For the first time in my life, I see what I should be doing."*

With that, he got himself a job that was just perfect for him. He called me a few months later to tell me how life-changing the process was for him and how he always would be grateful for the insights he gained.

Fran Kelley
www.careermuse.com

*I have used the **Personal Style Indicator** and **Quick Style Indicator** (**PSI** Light) for several years in my job and career coaching business. In working with my clients, the **PSI** and **QSI** confirm known personality styles or reveal new ones. The fact that each client provides his or her own input gives credibility to the process.*

*For me, the most important fact is that the accuracy of the **Interpretations** is very consistent.*

Mike Aquino
www.mpahire.com

I first took the **Values Preference Indicator** *as part of a workplace session. Since then, I revisit the* **VPI** *every 6 to 12 months to see if my core values have shifted and, if they have, why. It is an opportunity to reflect on what each of my core values brings to my everyday life. The bottom two thirds of my values typically move a couple of positions each time I do the* **VPI**.

A common outcome for me is to identify situations that may have shifted a particular value up or down my list. Often, I can identify several events since my last **VPI** *that have affected the outcome.*

For example, a meaningful change in my financial situation, such as purchasing life insurance or creating a Will, lowered **security** *and* **wealth** *on my list, presumably due to the fact that those values had garnered new or additional attention.*

Subsequently, the values I associate more closely with my needs will move up and down the list more frequently—values such as friendship, intimacy, and cooperation. The values I always identify as my main core values—independence, creativity, and challenge—have always been my top three.

The largest benefit is to craft my life, both at home and at work, to reflect my values. Also, by frequently returning to the **VPI,** *I understand how I am developing as a person. When I review my results and I am not sure why a value is positioned where I think it should be, I can reflect on why that is. The* **VPI** *allows me to frequently check-in with myself and my personal goals.*

Clint

Leadership and Managerial Development

Leadership is about understanding self as well as others. The way we engage others and present ourselves will either motivate or disillusion our followers or team. As leaders and managers, we are responsible to lead the way. When leaders understand their leadership style and their team members' style, they can optimize their leadership and team effectiveness.

When I conducted my MBA research on employee job satisfaction, productivity, quality of work done, engagement, and staff morale, one factor came up as the number one reason for low staff morale. You may have guessed it already.

> **The number one reason for low staff morale
> is the individual or supervisor to whom the person directly reports.**

Regardless of the politics in an organization, the leader of a group sets the tone for the team. If there is low morale in a work group, there is a higher than 90% chance that the supervisor is contributing to that condition.

Style influences your ability to build credibility, productivity, quality, and job satisfaction in the workplace, in for-profit and non-profit organizations.

This case study on Developing Style Versatility in a Leader is from Dr. Terry Anderson, Co-Author of the *PSI* and founder of CRG.

Sandy is a General Manager for a paper distribution company that sells and delivers paper to printing companies.

Sandy's **PSI** *Profile*

*High **Behavioral** ACTION and **Cognitive** ANALYSIS*

*Low **Interpersonal** HARMONY and **Affective** EXPRESSION*

*Sandy's Personal Style Graph: **BC** Independent Style Pattern*

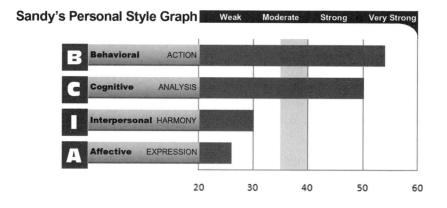

Sandy's Strengths

1. For the most part, he gets quality results the first time.
2. He can process large volumes of information.
3. He makes objective decisions using a large database of information from many sources.
4. He can challenge others toward excellence.
5. He acts as a model for others.
6. He is inventive and original.
7. He is careful to avoid pitfalls.
8. He provides guidelines others can use.
9. He ensures quality control.
10. He persists when under stress.

Sandy's Difficult Areas

1. He is impatient with lower performers.
2. He can appear smug and "know-it-all-ish."
3. He can be insensitive to others' feelings.
4. He can be lonely and fatigued.
5. He can be too critical.
6. He can get "touchy" when he gets critical feedback.
7. He can be too self-sufficient.
8. He can lack the courage to face emotions.
9. He can get lost in details before deciding.
10. He can seem manipulative or coercive.

Upon reading his **In-Depth Interpretation**, Sandy laughed. He said the description of him was better than 90% accurate and he became more aware of things about himself he often figured were "blind spots."

The Condition

Sandy is in charge of a sales force of nine people who tend to be predominantly high in the **Affective EXPRESSION** and **Interpersonal HARMONY** style dimensions.

They resent Sandy's air of superiority and demands for high performance without any promises of rewards. They need recognition and *appreciation from Sandy, but he rarely has time to give such "soft" rewards.*

He has only rewarded people for sales results that affect the "bottom line." Over the years, he has demonstrated inflexibility in his approach to others and gets really irritable at people who don't accept his domineering tactics, putting them down in front of others.

The increases in company profitability were 3% and 5% during the past 2 years, not enough to keep up with inflation (at that time).

The turnover rate in the sales division and in the secretary and receptionist positions were over 34% per year, primarily because those employees had frequent contact with Sandy. They reported that their primary reason for seeking work elsewhere was to avoid working for him.

Just prior to the time we began this coaching work with Sandy, his wife had left him.

The Intervention

*Sandy took a 1-day **Personal Style Indicator** workshop. Although he often was able to achieve short-term results by intimidating people in subtle ways, he learned that his relationships with the people in his life were negatively affected by his self-oriented and caustic approach.*

As a result of the workshop and the feedback Sandy got from the managers below him and from his wife, he decided

- *to change (style-shift) the way he treated the High **A** and **I** sales and support staff (and his **AI** marriage partner);*
- *to eliminate from his management style "put-down" statements and behaviors; and*
- *to add more interpersonal behaviors such as expressing appreciation for a job well done.*

He now hosts an awards ceremony every 6 months for those in the company who achieved agreed and reasonable levels of performance. He instituted an employee-of-the month recognition program for exceptional performance beyond what is expected, and introduced interpersonal skills training and team-building sessions for him and his management staff.

The Results

After 1 year, the turnover rate had decreased to 7% from the previous 34%. Two-way communication improved between Sandy and his employees at all levels.

Problems were solved that had previously "been swept under the carpet" because most people avoided Sandy altogether. Overall profitability of the company increased 14%. In addition, the adjustments caused Sandy's wife to go back to try to re-establish their marriage relationship.

When Sandy developed some interpersonal skills and versatility in his approach to people with styles opposite to his, it had a dramatic effect on the performance of his subordinates and it affected the organizational performance.

Dr. Terry Anderson
www.consultingcoach.com

Team Development

The fundamentals that apply to leadership and the sports case studies apply to any team development. Early in this book, I mentioned that Jim Collins' research for *Good to Great* outlined the traits of successful organizations. The organizations had the right people on the right bus in the right seat doing the right things.

How do you do that?

Analyze the style needs of the position using the *Job Style Indicator*.

What if you have what appear to be the right individuals but, as a team, they miss the mark?

Without knowledge of style and values, team members tend to be protective of their space and job responsibilities. In addition, style differences can become an irritant rather than a complement to the different styles of others. Teams that learn about Personal Style together can use style language to describe each person's preferences, strengths, and areas of difficulties.

> **You match the roles and responsibilities to the objectives the organization needs to fulfill.**

When team members see the reason for a shift in responsibilities in their job, they are significantly more open to accepting the changes.

When I work with teams, I get them to read through each other's **In-Depth Interpretations** and make note of the style pattern of each of the team members with whom they work on a regular basis. That allows them the opportunity to learn about each other so they can make choices about their interactions and the best team strategies to get things done.

Here are three stories of how the *PSI* or *QSI* transforms teams and team members. The first is from an IT Director; the second from an economic development manager; the third from an employee of a large parking facility.

> *Several years ago, I became part of a team that had a lot of infighting based on technology religion—the traditional UNIX versus the evil Microsoft Empire!*
>
> *Both groups reported to me and we all sat in the same area. Imagine that! You could feel the tension when you entered the floor.*
>
> *Through the lack of leadership over the years and the lack of trust, a snake pit of hostile technology servants had been created that tried to outdo one another at every turn.*
>
> *Entire technology-specific infrastructures had been created so one group did not have to interact with the other.*
>
> *That had to end.*
>
> *Fundamentally, I knew we had to get to the "trust" issue. But how? I started with a course that used the CRG* **Quick Style Indicator** *(shorter version of the* **PSI***) and was blown away. If I could get my team to take the* **QSI** *survey, would that help? At that point, I had nothing to lose.*
>
> *Before distributing the assessment, I looked for small projects that were cross-functional, where the two teams had to work together, usually in pairs. That enabled them to get to know each other on a more personal level.*
>
> *The magic started to happen.*
>
> *That's when I introduced the* **QSI***. (At staff meetings, I spend quite a bit of time preaching about trust and showing clips from racing teams, demonstrating the power of teamwork.)*
>
> *To my surprise, everyone enjoyed the* **QSI** *assessment, even those*

who struggled and tended to overanalyze those types of exercises. As the manager, I found it very effective; it greatly improved the work results, especially when the team was working directly with me.

You see, I'm an **AI: Versatile Pattern** *(dominated by an orientation toward people). In other words, I skim along at the 30,000 foot level, filled with enthusiasm and talking wildly with my hands.*

When I would talk with my lead software architect (we'll call him Bob), a **CB: Competitive Pattern** *(dominated by a task orientation), he'd politely listen to me, nodding his head at every gesture as if he was right there with me.*

I scheduled some time with Bob to discuss our **QSI** *results. "Wow!" I said. "With all my sign language, I bet you never really knew what you were supposed to be focusing on?!"*

No argument there.

Going forward, I started going to Bob with a list of specific concepts I wanted to address. I was sure to listen more than I talked and that we both knew where we stood before I headed for the stratosphere again. It worked wonders. He was much happier knowing what he was supposed to be doing; I was very pleased with the results . . . and have been ever since.

I definitely plan on using this style shifting method as I ease into a much larger organization and meet my new team. This has been a great help in my professional career and my personal life.

Louie Danuser
Director IT

We have used the **PSI** *a number of times with staff teams. It results in colleagues having more of an appreciation of one another, and an understanding of why some relationships seem to work better than others.*

We have used the **PSI** *to select project teams to avoid the "group thinking" that comes from choosing people from just 1 or 2 style dimensions. Different styles and perspectives working together usually result in better outcomes. Sometimes, it takes more time to accommodate all the different styles but we have found it much more thorough and effective.*

I was part of a management program that used the **PSI** *assessment.*

It helped raise my awareness of my tendencies and prompted me to be more intentional in adapting my style to each situation, rather than going with my initial reaction.

Art Lawson
Manager, Community Economic Development

I participated in a program called Team Leader University where I was introduced to the CRG **Personal Style Indicator**. *After completing the* **PSI**, *I gained a better understanding of my own Personal Style, and the Personal Styles of the individuals with whom I work on a regular basis.*

We were taught about the Platinum Rule—treating others **the way they want to be treated**, *and how knowing your Personal Style is critical in practicing the Platinum Rule. With the knowledge from the* **PSI**, *I was able to improve my working relationships with my direct managers as well as my co-workers.*

Recently, I took an Interpersonal Communications class on the topic of understanding your personal communication style. I felt I was a step ahead of the class because I had completed the **PSI**. *Unfortunately, many of my classmates had no idea about Personal Style. Many had never heard of the concept.*

Brittany Shea
Executive Assistant

Relationships and Marriages

I believe there is no place in our lives where our Personal Style is revealed, tried, and tested more than in an intimate relationship. Our true needs and self are exposed in those situations. There is nowhere to hide who you are and what you need.

Years ago, our firm conducted marriage counseling. When couples came for help, typically it was not about positive events; usually they had built-up hurts and anger.

Before we began the sessions, we required each couple to complete the *Personal Style Indicator*. Learning about style helped them better understand themselves and their partner and re-directed the negative energy that they had previously focused on each other. As they became familiar with the contents of this book, they realized that at least part of the conflict was linked to their style differences.

A lot more than style goes into a great marriage! But since each partner's personal style does not change, and will influence his or her behavior forever, it is necessary to address style differences and compatibility issues if you want to have a successful relationship.

Many professionals have dating and premarital couples complete the *PSI* and read this book, to better understand the long-term dynamics of style in their relationship.

> **Sometimes, what first attracted you to your significant other can later become the greatest irritant.**

A man marries a High **C** because he appreciates her organized and scheduled life, with everything in its place. That was attractive until her desire for organization spilled into his life. If he has little **C** in his profile, her tendency can be taken as criticism or control. So a shift occurs. What he first experienced as a positive is now a negative trait in his partner.

A woman marries a High **A** partner. At first, she appreciated his spontaneous and enthusiastic nature. Later, she viewed it as chaotic and undisciplined behavior.

> **It does not matter what style pattern you have or your partner has; there are positive and negatives to every pattern. That is the reality of life.**

Your perception of the realities determines the way you experience and respond to them.

Here is a story of a couple able to overcome the stress of an affair with the help of the *PSI* and marriage coaches.

> *I had an affair on my husband. I ended the affair and kept it a secret for 5 years while I did everything in my power to "fix" my marriage. Eventually, I disclosed the affair to my husband and started what turned out to be a very tumultuous journey toward true healing.*
>
> *After a year-and-a-half of trying to restore the marriage on our own, we realized some other barriers needed to be overcome so we could heal.*
>
> *We went to a Healing From Affairs conference where they utilized*

CRG's **Personal Style Indicator** *and referenced this book. What amazing tools!*

After taking the assessment and receiving in-depth teaching about the dimensions and our patterns, we started to understand some of the difficulties we were having in our marriage and in our healing.

My husband is a **BI: Determined** *pattern, while I am an* **AC: Inventive** *pattern. Immediately, we realized he is non-verbal (***B** *and* **I** *are both non-verbal) and I am verbal (both* **A** *and* **C** *are verbal).*

Believe me, everyone around us could see this, as could we. Most important, we now are able to see this isn't a fault of the other person, but a trait.

As we discovered our unique strengths, difficulties, and needs, I began to have a better understanding of who I was. By the end of the conference, we received many tools necessary to help us effectively develop our marriage. We both agreed the **PSI** *was the turning point for us.*

Over the years, my husband had felt I didn't know myself (therefore, how could he know what I needed?). I now realize how true that was.

What an amazing feeling to not only understand ourselves and each other, but to be able to style-shift in a way that honors and respects the other person. It is also a gift to be able to communicate with our children now that we see who they are and what they need to feel heard.

We now have a healed and fulfilling marriage where there is forgiveness and respect. Thank you for making these tools available to people like us.

Thank you,
M and K

Improvement and success in relationships *are* possible.

> **Please let people know that the information in this book can help individuals avoid needless heartache!**

The following example confirms that with the right tools, many marriages have a chance to be transformed.

Coaches Brian and Anne Bercht, CRG Licensed Associates, offer this story.

One of the primary tools that Passionate Life Seminars uses to help couples recover from infidelity is the CRG **Personal Style Indicator**, *which has been foundational in bringing about a safe environment for couples to begin dialog.*

The accuracy of this tool, combined with its ease of use, has always impressed us. More important, it has been transformational for most of our clients who have used it. The **PSI** *makes an immediate impact on couples and we have witnessed its long-term positive effect on them.*

This is a story of Karen, a woman born and raised in America, and Kenichi, a man born and raised in Japan. The couple met when Karen was working in Japan on a short-term work visa. They had been married and living in Japan for almost 9 years before I talked to them.

After our initial phone consultation, I had them each complete a **PSI**. *Our next session was to review their reports. Just before the session, I needed to spend only a couple of minutes familiarizing myself with their* **PSI** *graph, scores, and patterns. I opened that session by asking if I could share what I thought might be some sources of frustrations, irritations, or obstacles in their relationship . . . apart from the infidelity.*

I made an educated guess that some of their struggles were around these areas.

- *Having the "house" in order*
- *Not having "fun"*
- *Not "planning" enough*
- *Being too "controlled"*
- *Being too "expressive" or "not expressive enough" of "recognition" and "lack of appreciation"*

Most of the items are outlined in the various chapters in this book.

As I shared my thoughts about the struggles they had been experiencing for the past 8 years, they looked at each other in amazement and confirmation. They asked how I could know all about them without having met them and only briefly talking to them on the phone. I replied that it was all revealed in their style patterns and numbers.

I went on to share ways each of them could respond better to the other without feeling they had to give up their personal convictions or change who they were.

I shared that much of their struggle was about feeling attacked or put down for not doing things the way their partner preferred, which was mostly style-related.

After we talked for 45 minutes, Karen said she and Kenichi had learned more about their relationship and how to make practical adjustments in that one call than over the past 4 years. That included reading many books—a stack of more than a dozen.

The couple's insight came from the power of **PSI** *numbers.*

Karen's Personal Style was **A**53, **I**40, **C**27, *and* **B**20 (**AI** *pattern*).

Kenichi's Personal Style was **C**55, **I**51, **B**34, *and* **A**20 (**CI** *style*).

The majority of the conflict was between her **A** *and his* **C** *style preferences, needs, and wants.*

Anne and Brian Bercht
www.beyondaffairs.com

Relationships include siblings and all possible family interactions. As told in the following example, style can affect family relationships.

This is a true story of the interaction between two brothers. Some details were altered to maintain their privacy.

Anthony and Ian (not their real names) are brothers.

Anthony has a High **A** *style pattern; Ian has a High* **I** *style pattern.*

Anthony, who is 2 years older than Ian, moved away from home and lost touch with his sibling. When Anthony last saw Ian, Ian was a recent university graduate in his early 20s, still finding himself. Anthony was well into his career as a successful sales manager for a thriving business.

Anthony's wife saw that her husband was not enjoying his work any more and asked why.

Anthony is a very inspirational person; his customers appreciated his passion and level of service. His manager, more of a High **B** *pattern, was at odds with Anthony's style of selling, despite his record sales and high rate of customer satisfaction.*

That frustrated Anthony because he brought a unique approach to a business that needed new methods to compete better in the marketplace.

Ian, too, was developing his own experiences in the field of sales. Even though he achieved amazing sales records, Ian's work preference was not the sales profession. His heart wanted to be in a less competitive occupation—something that put people first and that would help make an important contribution to society.

Within a short period, he made a radical change in his career and got into advertising. After several years in various roles in the advertising industry, Ian felt another change was coming. He also felt he needed more control of his destiny.

One evening, Anthony called Ian to find out how things were going. Anthony was impressed that his brother had made the bold move into advertising and asked if he would come out West for a little vacation and to discuss a new business idea. Anthony's idea was simple, albeit unconventional.

- *Go through the classified newspaper ads, looking for companies who were hiring salespeople.*
- *Approach those businesses, not just as a single salesperson but as a sales and marketing team.*
- *Prospective customers would benefit from the short-term gain in sales revenue and the long-term gain of strategic marketing initiatives.*
- *Anthony and Ian would provide their services on a performance-level basis (commission).*

Ian flew to the West Coast and began deliberations with Anthony on his business idea. Uncharacteristically, Ian's excitement led to quitting his job and giving Anthony's idea a go.

A problem was slowly brewing, however. The two brothers had never worked together and neither had any idea how much they had evolved since teenagers. Although they were basically the same people, new events and circumstances helped bring out or test their natural temperaments.

For example, Anthony had heard how Ian was such a "go getter" in his last sales job so when it came to prospecting new clients,

Anthony thought Ian would be the best one to get on the phone and do the cold calling.

Ian was not comfortable with Anthony's idea and he was bewildered. He had gone into sales as a temporary measure to pay down debt; it was Anthony who had chosen to make sales a career. Anthony admitted his strength was making presentations to those who were prepared to receive them.

Other issues were coming up. Ian was annoyed by Anthony's spending on flashy business cards and dominating the conversations at networking events. Anthony struggled with Ian's lack of candor on matters and lack of acceptance for his ideas when situations changed rapidly.

One afternoon, the two brothers reached a boiling point in their relationship. Emotional discussions ensued.

Nonetheless, Anthony and Ian were fortunate to have been be raised by parents that demanded their children learn to respect each other.

After ending a tumultuous discussion with Ian, Anthony turned to a colleague who specialized in building high-performance teams to see if there was a solution to this impasse.

*Within 30 minutes, after completing the **Personal Style Indicator (PSI)** and reading the **PSI In-Depth Interpretations**, Anthony's jaw dropped.*

*Some days later, Ian reluctantly completed a **PSI** and was equally amazed with the results. As the two read each other's **In-Depth Interpretation**, they engaged in a lengthy discussion soliciting each other's feedback.*

Ian was in shock as scenes played back in his head of how Anthony had dealt with matters concerning their business venture in the past. At some point in the conversation, there was a tearful moment of release when they realized the unbelievable pressure they had put on each other.

From that point on, they were able to sort out each other's roles with respect to the business.

Anthony and Ian went on to many other business ventures together, sharing compatibilities in working and dealing with people. Ian supported Anthony's ideas; Anthony encouraged Ian to be bold and think laterally; Anthony recognized Ian's need for focus and completion.

They also recognized areas of their business that needed "The Third Man," a person with a style preference that would fill a gap so they could be **the true crack team** *they envisioned for their customers. None of this would have been possible without the knowledge of style and the contents of this book!*

Anthony and Ian

Parenting

Two of the most powerful applications of style are with children and youth. So many children and parents are at odds with each other because they misunderstand style.

Imagine you are a High **I** parent who is caring, loving, and patient toward your child.

But what if your child is High **B**? He is going to be direct and not want to be cuddled. The child will push the boundaries. If the High **I** parent gives in to the demands of the High **B** child, the child will not respect the parent because the parent is a pushover.

Remember that credibility is in the eye of the beholder.

The **B** child needs personal space and will try to tell the environment what to do.

Let's say the child wants to go to a party and the parent says No. If the child always get what he wants, he sees the parent can be manipulated. It is the parent's responsibility to mean what she says. If she says No, then changes her mind under pressure, over time the child will understand that the parent's words mean nothing. Dramatic, but true.

I recall a High **B** hockey dad who wanted his boy to be mean and aggressive while playing hockey. His son, an **I,** was not. The dad belittled his son publicly to stop acting like a girl and a wimp.

Those actions and words would be crushing to any kid, but it destroys the spirit of an **I** at the very core. The dad was trying to make his child like he was, rather than encouraging the boy to do his best within the context of the child's unique style.

Opposite to the previous example, here is a parent who, early on, realized the power of style identification in her children.

Our children were 7 and 4 when we introduced the idea of personality styles to them. They have very different personality styles.

To help them understand themselves and each other better, we used the characters of the Winnie the Pooh *stories and connected them to style concepts.*

*My husband and our older son are both outgoing, charismatic, and willing to try anything (High **A**). It was easy to identify them as the "Tigger" or the **A**s of our family.*

*Our younger son is quiet, introspective, a bit of a worrier. He was our "Piglet" (**I**). I tend to be a mix of Eeyore (**C**) and Rabbit (**B**)—practical, no-nonsense, and a bit of a pessimist. (I prefer "trouble-shooter" to pessimist.)*

The kids could immediately relate to the characters and see how different they all are, and also how they each play a part in the story as a whole. It just wouldn't be the same if any of the characters (styles) were missing.

*Each is valuable for what he brings to the group. A story with only Tiggers (**A**), Piglets (**I**), Eeyores (**C**), or Rabbits (**B**) wouldn't be as interesting. It helped the boys appreciate their differences and understand their value, just as they are.*

*There's no need for Piglet (**I**) to try to be more Tiggery (**A**) and Tiggers (**A**) just aren't as much fun if they're constantly fussing over the details that **C**s are so good at managing.*

Lisa Greaves

This professional uses the *PSI* in her parent-coaching practice and as an educational specialist.

I continually get positive feedback from the couples who have read this book and have used the CRG Personal Style and values assessments. They have reported more effective communication with one another.

Another positive outcome is they are able to assess their children's Personal Styles and practice shifting their own styles for more satisfying interactions.

In my full-time job as an education specialist in deafblindness, I have used this book and the CRG assessment tools as a resource when consulting with school districts and families. This has come in handy with the intervener team model.

An intervener is a paraprofessional who has specialized training in deafblindness and is assigned to a deafblind student to provide access to information that is typically gained through vision and hearing.

Since deafblindness is a low-incidence disability, it is not unusual for teachers, service providers, and parents to need training. It really requires a team to develop and implement specialized programming and strategies.

*Collaborating on a team is not always smooth sailing. For teams to be effective, they need tools like the **Personal Style Indicator** and other CRG resources to avoid conflict, resolve conflict, and compare personal and work styles with one another.*

It can be fun to share information about each other's styles and participate in some style-shifting activities.

Jenny Lace
Certified Coach for Parents

Those are some of the many examples and applications and the positive benefits of knowing your Personal Style and values and those of others. I think you get the idea that style and values can apply in just about any situation.

The Keys to Success with the *PSI*

- The above individuals acted on the information from the *PSI*, thus

- Increasing their self-awareness and their ability to be intentional in their behavior and their choices.

- They accepted their own unique style pattern.

- They acknowledged that others might have a different style pattern than they did.

- They tried to work with their differences, rather than against them.

CHAPTER 20

Why Aren't You More Like Me?

So, let us not be blind to our differences, but let us also direct attention to our common interests and to the means by which those differences can be resolved.

JOHN F. KENNEDY

Although it happened more than 25 years ago, I remember as if it were yesterday. I arose at 5 AM to milk my herd of dairy cows. It was a gorgeous and clear May morning. The air was fresh and the sun was just about to rise above the mountains.

As I watched the beautiful sunrise through the barn window, I asked myself this simple question: *Would it be okay if, 20 years from today, I was doing the same thing . . . getting up at 5 to milk my cows and watch the sun come up?*

I knew in my heart the answer was No. That day, I made the decision to embrace my innate gifts, talents, and interests and leave the family farm. It wasn't easy but it was the right decision; I needed to realize my potential and fulfill my *purpose*.

My *purpose* is to help others discover their *purpose . . . and live it!*

What about you?

Each of us has a choice every single day . . .

- to live a life of fulfillment *on purpose*, while making a positive difference in the lives of others, or

- to achieve something less.

This very moment, you can decide to embrace the knowledge in this book to better understand yourself and others from the standpoint of both nature and nurture.

> **Please—No more apologies for who you are!**
> **Your style pattern—no matter what it is—**
> **is the absolute best style pattern for you.**

Is your style pattern working for you or against you?

Here are a few reminders of ways you can increase your effectiveness.

Key Strategies Critical to Your Future Success

- Use your deep understanding of your style pattern(s) and the related strengths, common areas of difficulties, reactions to stress, how to work with and lead others, and what you can actively do to increase your personal and professional effectiveness with self and others.

- Recognize why you don't like or feel irritated by others who are different than you are.

- Pay attention to the clues others are leaving for you; **Translate** their behavior using the *PSI* Model of Extroversion/Introversion, Non-Verbal/Verbal, People/Tasks.

- Actively **Suspend;** do not get hooked or offended by people who are dissimilar to you.

- Control your style. Don't let your style control you.

- Accept the differences in others; serve them in their style needs and orientation.

- Intentionally **Style-shift** to increase your credibility with others.

- Be aware that you create a level of credibility with everyone with whom you interact, whether you want to or not; it is the price of showing up in this life.

- Know the job style of the work and roles that are best for you.

- Choose the working environment that reflects your values and needs, not someone else's.

- Discover and validate your interests, gifts, and talents—and make sure you use them.

- Live the lifestyle and activities (values) that are most fulfilling to you

- Encourage others—such as your children, family, friends, and co-workers—to become aware of and to embrace their unique style, values, and strengths.

- **Do not** use your style as an excuse for your behavior; take responsibility for your conduct.

- Confirm whether you or others are ready and willing to change.

- Realize your need to develop and understand the whole person, including biophysical factors, self-worth levels, environmental systems, social teachers, emotional anchors, spirituality, and your Personal Style—all of which make up your unique personality.

I can list more, but you get the point.

The research is clear. Without knowledge and awareness of Personal Style, 98% of individuals will underperform and fail to reach their potential.

I have not always accepted myself for the person I am and, at times, my environment did not embrace my individuality.

When I first learned about my Personal Style, I felt like a burden had been lifted from my shoulders. I understood why I thought and acted the way I did. I could fully embrace my unique personality.

Every day, I use my knowledge of my values, Personal Style, job style, the styles of others, and my *purpose* as a roadmap for all my decisions and interactions. I am conscious about my preferences and the implications they have in my environment.

That can be true for you, too! Use this book as a resource. Your new understanding can change your life forever—if you act *intentionally* on the information.

This is only the beginning of your transformation. Be patient and diligent in your commitment. With your new awareness, you can change the way you respond and live.

Consider yourself armed and positively dangerous! You will make a difference in your life and in the lives of everyone with whom you interact.

Go for it!

You have nothing to lose and everything to gain!

Here's to us all **Living *On Purpose!***

Index and the Interpretive Summaries of the 21 Style Patterns

When you completed the **Online** *PSI*, your report included your pattern(s) that applied to your results. The following pages outline all 21 patterns and the corresponding interpretive summary for each pattern. When you want to understand someone better, you can confirm with them their pattern and access this information.

Ultimately, it would be best if the person can confirm his or her style pattern by completing a *PSI*. Then you can review his or her two-page *PSI* **In-Depth Interpretations**.

Understanding the 21 Style Patterns

Index of Style Patterns

Behavioral ACTION Patterns	B	Commanding
	BC	Independent
	BI	Determined
	BA	Optimistic
Cognitive ANALYSIS Patterns	C	Analytical
	CB	Competitive
	CI	Practical
	CA	Perceptive
Interpersonal HARMONY Patterns	I	Harmonious
	IB	Reliable
	IC	Thoughtful
	IA	Responsive
Affective EXPRESSION Patterns	A	Performing
	AB	Idealistic
	AC	Inventive
	AI	Versatile
Triple-High and Four-Even Patterns	BCI	Ambitious
	CIA	Balanced
	BIA	Influential
	BCA	Productive
	BCIA	Synergistic

Behavioral Interpretive Summaries

B   *Commanding*

These people are often strongly self-reliant, innovative in getting the results they want, and able to use others and opportunities (not necessarily in a negative way) to their best advantage. They like control, power, and the freedom to make their own choices. They either do things the way they want to do them or prefer quite often not to do them at all.

Their creativity often manifests in hardheaded, computer-like calculations and strategies, the logic of which goes beyond the understanding exercised by most people. The confident fashion in which they approach people and problems can, in the minds of some, create the image of a cool, polished manipulator.

B & C   *Independent*

Individuals with this Personal Style are high in the **Behavioral** and **Cognitive** dimensions and tend to be more logical and analytical than people with any of the other patterns.

These people want quality results and therefore try to be in control so that no mistakes occur. There often is a war going on inside them because on one hand, they have a strong drive for accomplishment but, at the same time, are held back by their high need for quality. People with this style often show great determination and carefulness when doing tasks they consider important. They want quality results quickly.

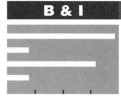

B & I   *Determined*

Because this Personal Style type has the dominant **Behavioral** tendencies, they have a certain doggedness and persistence for getting things done, even if it takes all day and night. While the **Interpersonal** tendencies in this style take a back seat to the **Behavioral** tendencies, there also is a willingness to work with others to accomplish the desired result. They will tend to the necessary details in the process.

These people can display a positive stubbornness when it comes to getting the job done. With the strong dominance factor, human relations are likely to suffer, but not to the extent of the other **Behavioral** styles, due to the softening effects of this person's desire for **Interpersonal** HARMONY—as long as the desired results are forthcoming.

B & A   *Optimistic*

Behavioral ACTION and EXPRESSION tendencies are both high in this Personal Style pattern. These types of people are energetic, confident, and willing to explore new ways of improving things.

People often show a mixed reaction to these individuals. On one hand, their energy, optimistic attitude, wordiness, and fortitude impress others, but their drive to get results might interfere with having others feel comfortable with them.

There is often a need for people with this pattern to work on balancing their results orientation with more consideration for human relations. Others are attracted to them and fascinated by them, but can feel intimidated by their high energy and unusual creativity. People with this pattern can exhaust themselves with their own energy.

Cognitive Interpretive Summaries

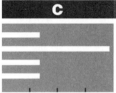

C   *Analytical*

The **Analytical** Personal Style is unique; the other three dimensions are quite a bit lower than the **Cognitive** score. The person with this style may tend toward being an introvert who is a specialist in an area that requires great attention to detail.

The **Analytical** person usually wants logical consistency; control of feelings, structure, and order in the environment; and quite often a conservative neatness of the home, dress, and work environments. They tend to keep others at some distance because they perceive that most other people are less organized, less sensitive, and perhaps less trustworthy. Others may feel overly criticized by a person with this strongly perfectionistic orientation.

C & B   *Competitive*

People with a **Competitive** Personal Style are predominately introverted (sensitive to stimulation) individuals who can draw upon a reservoir of resilience. Their non-verbal signals often show restraint in the expression of feelings, including only a scant show of emotion through the use of the face, eyes, and hands. They prefer being in control in their interactions with people and tasks because of their high needs for quality and production.

There can be a great internal pressure within these people because they are being pulled in two directions—one direction for accuracy and quality and the other direction for decisiveness and immediate action. Others may respect this type's ability to work but may seldom enjoy their friendship because they rarely relax. This person often underestimates the value of play, at work or at home.

C & I   Practical

Though concerned with **Interpersonal** HARMONY, people with this Personal Style are often more focused on getting the task done. They have a lot of energy to invest in reaching their goals and want to get there in a high-quality manner. They are likely to desire work in a positive work climate with competent others.

Their preference, however, is to work alone toward reaching specific goals.

Give a project to them and expect it to be done. Also expect to see them carve their way through any obstacles. This is one of the two most-introverted style patterns. People with this pattern seem to prefer emotional distance from others, but also tend to be pleasant and polite in work and social relationships.

C & A   Perceptive

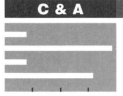

People with this pattern tend to be both critical and creative. This style pattern contains an interesting mix of analysis and the creative expression of ideas, a combination that can easily influence people. Individuals with this style tend to be competitive in proving themselves.

They want to influence others with their original presentations of facts, ideas, or products. They also can be effective problem-solvers and mediators because they can relate to the needs of people and the task demands of a situation. Their logical and imaginative capacities tend to be balanced; that mix can confuse some people.

On one hand, they seem to be telling others to come nearer through their inventive and emotional expression, but there is a somewhat clearer message of "keep your distance" in the more reserved tendencies of the **Cognitive** style. They are reserved and also can be creatively expressive.

Interpersonal Interpretive Summaries

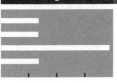

I   *Harmonious*

This behavioral style tends to be the most casual of all, the most adaptable, the most willing to be cooperative, and the most willing to serve and help others. People with this Personal Style often show warm, pleasant, even-tempered qualities in their relations with others. The images that people with this style can portray to others range from the kind, patient, helpful mother or father figure to the naive, pliant, and submissive child.

Some people perceive so much sweetness in these individuals, they can be suspicious of their sincerity but most people really appreciate the soft, relaxed qualities they tend to express. Mainly intuitive and focused on relationships with others (rather than being logical and task-focused), these types of people can be easily hurt when they feel used and can feel deeply valuable when they are appreciated.

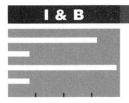

I & B   *Reliable*

People with this Personal Style tend to be somewhat compulsively concerned with producing results in a reliable and pleasant manner. You would want people with this pattern to enforce policies or rules and you would expect they would do so in a respectful manner.

People with this style are often willing to take on specific responsibilities if the tasks are well defined and if there is opportunity for challenge and some variety.

Because this pattern has both a capacity for introversion and extroversion, there is a lot of potential for style-flexibility. The conscientious and pleasant manner in which people with this pattern can get results is an often-envied ability. Under pressure, they can become hostile and impulsive.

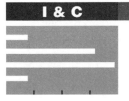

I & C   *Thoughtful*

Individuals who have a **Thoughtful** Personal Style are motivated to be correct in all they do to avoid displeasing others, especially those in positions of authority. They often have a high need for acceptance and are quite uncomfortable with personal conflict. They believe that to have security and the respect of others, they must be correct, complete, and as perfect as possible when performing tasks.

People with this Personal Style often have perfectionistic thinking patterns that can lead to unrealistic expectations of self and others and therefore disappointments. They work well in positive environments and with supportive co-workers.

Under adverse conditions, people with this style can tend to become withdrawn and depressed. When pressured by others, they can become stubborn or even caustic if pushed far enough. Once betrayed, they can be slow to forgive.

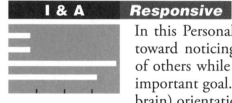

I & A   *Responsive*

In this Personal Style pattern, there is a tendency toward noticing and responding to the emotions of others while still being focused on a task or an important goal. They have a strong intuitive (right-brain) orientation to the environment. People with this pattern are often dependable, loyal, affectionate, polite, bubbly to an extent, and willing to support others and serve their needs.

Soft-spoken but spontaneous, these types of people often have a sense of humor that others enjoy. There is a more prominent creative streak in the expressive arts such as music, painting, sculpture, dance, interior decorating, or fashion, for example. The need for contact with people and belonging to or even leading social clubs or organizations can be pronounced. These individuals seem to need to be with others.

Affective Interpretive Summaries

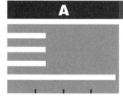

A   *Performing*

Sometimes, in school years, the person with this style is called the class clown. Quite often, people with this style will do unexpected things to call attention to themselves. It's as though they are saying, "Hey, everyone look at me," in much of what they do. They tend to be unrestrained in the expression of eccentric jokes or other unusual behavior that can irritate or embarrass others.

Their refreshing spontaneity and natural manner of self-expression can be very funny and can influence others, for example, the inspirational speaker, teacher, or salesperson. If they could develop greater style-versatility in the ACTION and **Interpersonal** areas, their talents likely would be even more appreciated.

A & B   *Idealistic*

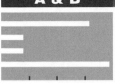

People with the **Idealistic** pattern tend to be high in energy, creative, and focused on the achievement of immediate objectives. They are perhaps the most extroverted (indicating a resilient nervous system) of all patterns. They also can be unexpressive at times and overly focused on getting results. They can handle a lot of stimulation before they feel overloaded.

Their determination to accomplish their goals by persuading others to follow their verbal influence and strategic plan is stronger than most. Some people think they are attempting to convince or sell others, rather than just influence them.

They can be highly expressive while pushing ahead to reach pre-determined goals. Both soft-hearted and hard-headed **Idealistic** types often will be seen selling ideas to people they care about or selling products they believe in.

A & C   *Inventive*

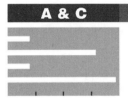

People with this style pattern tend to be strong in both the **Affective** EXPRESSION and **Analytical** areas. This unique mix of style tendencies often manifests in the form of creative practicality.

People with this pattern are likely to come up with creative ideas, do their homework (research the details or the background of their idea), then communicate their findings to others they would like to influence to implement the idea. They tend to have an unusual versatility of both right- and left-brain capacities.

While they tend to be expressive, they are very concerned about quality. Musicians or actors dedicated to putting on good performances or artists who seek to sell their work/ideas to others could exemplify individuals with this type of Personal Style.

A & I   *Versatile*

People with this Personal Style pattern tend to be both receptive and expressive at the same time. They are often patient people and good listeners who express themselves in a way that promotes harmony with others. They are active personal and interpersonal problem-solvers.

They tend to express themselves for the purpose of facilitating acceptance, resolution, and clarity. They are intuitive yet practical because of the capacity of their harmonious tendencies toward being useful to others. They often are fairly high in energy when it comes to working with people, but can get sidetracked when it comes to getting tasks done on time.

Triple-High and Four-Even Interpretive Summaries

B, C, & I   Ambitious

People with this Personal Style are generally intense, highly motivated people who are conscientious and dependable. Complex and somewhat unpredictable, they may tend to push toward their goals, be concerned about producing high quality, and also show concern for the welfare and morale of others.

They tend to get results by combining analysis with practicality. They often are concerned that others will fall below their own standards. They can be so motivated to improve things; others admire their ambition and their drive for accomplishments but potentially feel intimidated, overwhelmed, or even jealous of their energy, drive, and creativity.

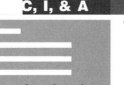

C, I, & A   Balanced

These people tend to be good problem-solvers in relationships and with tasks. Being both analytical and expressive, with a balanced tendency toward promoting harmony, they often are energetic and highly competent when working with people to get tasks done. They are so committed to both quality performance and quality relationships, they can make good team members and even good team leaders.

Sensitive (introverted) and resilient (extroverted), they often have an interesting and effective mix of receptivity and expressiveness in their styles. That is perhaps the easiest pattern for others to work with, because of its natural versatility.

B, I, & A   Influential

People with this style pattern tend to be complex individuals who demonstrate a wide range of style-flexibility in their behavior. They can be quite naturally task- and relationship-focused. Their relationships, however, often can be too task- or results-focused. They may tend to work on their relationships or be involved in situations where they can develop people.

They may be parents, teachers, or sales managers who naturally seek to influence others in positive ways, for the benefit of all concerned. They may be interested in business results. They treat people with more sensitivity than many businesspeople who focus on results but tend not to notice others' feelings.

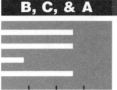

B, C, & A *Productive*

The **Productive** pattern is characterized by a dynamic balance between the rational and intuitive tendencies. There is a keen insistence on quality results and a searching sensitivity regarding new perspectives and the unexpected.

This pattern is both unusual and complex in nature, due to the demanding and conflicting qualities of Triple-High dimensions. Not many people are willing or able to be results-oriented, perfectionistic, and emotionally and intuitively sensitive at the same time. Style-flexibility is a major and distinctive mark of this unique pattern. The productive pattern is generally characterized by simultaneous intensity and insistence on creative quality and results.

B, C, I, & A *Synergistic*

People with this pattern are extremely flexible and adaptable. With equal strength in all four style dimensions, they have the natural ability to see the world the way all other styles do.

When they are in control of their pattern, they tend to be good team players and can mediate among diverse groups of people. If they aren't in control, they can have difficulties with others. They can be good leaders and team members when their drive toward being task-oriented is balanced with their strong people orientation. When it isn't balanced, they often become confused and unsure of themselves.

They tend to feel "style crazy" because all four dimensions are equally strong. Having to constantly please all four dimensions at the same time often leaves them feeling very divided inside. They can feel very challenged when it comes to problem-solving and decision-making because they are seldom totally satisfied with the outcomes.

Example of **PSI** In-Depth Interpretation Report

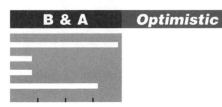

Strengths

Often, these people are called the movers and shakers in an organization because they push to get innovative ideas initiated. They are very good at influencing others to join in to get things done. They often are successful salespeople, good at making the hard or difficult sale because, intuitively, they are receptive to the non-verbal cues of others and highly motivated to influence them.

They usually possess strong verbal skills and can be very action-oriented toward both tasks and people. They sometimes appear to be very political because they are often concerned about how well they do and how others see them.

These individuals often exude strength and confidence, causing many people to be astonished at their courage and daring when attempting difficult tasks. They are quick to seize positions of authority and leadership, preferring to lead rather than follow.

They are good at keeping on the move and somehow manage to get others to look after all the details and the follow-up on a project, especially people with **Cognitive** and **Interpersonal** Styles. Optimistic individuals tend to be stereotypes of the classic, hard-driving, we-can-do-it-no-matter-what type of person.

Common Areas of Difficulty

In their personal relationships, Optimistic people often are described as bull-headed and sometimes selfish. They can appear self-oriented and busy with their own projects and usually listen to others with understanding only when it helps them reach their own goals. The Optimistic person can idealize people, put them on pedestals, and idolize them as role models, yet when the idols fail to live up to expectations, they are soon discarded or replaced.

People who work slowly and carefully frustrate the Optimistic person who tends to respond by criticizing, patronizing, or belittling their efforts in various ways. Their mottoes might be, "the ends justify the means" or "I don't want excuses; I want results." Because they tend to be forthright, courageous, and outspoken, they expect others to speak out or quietly acquiesce.

Some people find their forceful character and drive for independent accomplishments very difficult to handle. To many, they appear cocky; they attempt to convince others that they can do a job or a task quite easily and that they are willing to try difficult things.

People with the Optimistic Personal Style often underestimate how difficult and time-consuming things are but, because of their self-confidence, will throw themselves totally into a project just to prove they can do it, sometimes at the expense of health, family, or work relationships.

Reactions to Stress
Under stressful conditions, expect people with this style to double their efforts. They may display an increase in impatience with perhaps some flare-ups of temper and a more aggressive attitude toward others who do not support their plans.

Because they are such hard workers, they seem to get even more demanding about getting their way when they are under pressure; they are more likely to express their irritation with others when the results aren't achieved or the standards aren't met.

People with this pattern have the most difficult time knowing when to relax, call it a day, and try again tomorrow. Even on vacation or during leisure time, this style of person works hard at playing.

Team Functioning and Compatibility with Other Styles
Generally, they don't make very cooperative team members because they are in a hurry to get results and teamwork slows down their fast pace. They have a hard time sharing the stage with other team members. They can be so stubborn and immovable at times, others feel intimidated or are reluctant to speak up and participate while the Optimistic person is around.

When it comes time to pull together in a crisis situation, however, they can emerge as heroic leaders who can help others rally together around a common cause, as in team sports, crises, or even wartime situations. When things seem the least hopeful, these people are the ones on the team to give up last, and often convince others that they should continue to press forward toward success.

At work, they tend to like to surround themselves with the more compliant **Cognitive** and **Interpersonal** Styles whose introverted natures—meeker and quieter—allow the Optimistic person the freedom of movement and unopposed authority he or she craves.

When they have to work with others who also are dominant and expressive, they experience more difficulty because they prefer the "limelight" to be on them. They don't like their positions or views to be challenged unless it helps them achieve their goals. They do, however, enjoy being competitive and often participate in sporting events.

In intimate relationships, they tend to be attracted more to the introverted styles (**Cognitive** and **Interpersonal**) because of those individuals' abilities to adapt appropriately to the Optimistic style's strong-willed, assertive, even aggressive approach to human interaction.

Their insensitivity and dominance sometimes leads to bitterness springing up in their **Cognitive** and **Interpersonal** family members. In more intimate relationships, that can cause long-term difficulty.

Leadership Implications

People with the Optimistic style pattern can be successful leaders when they gather around them reliable and loyal "lieutenants" who handle the unwanted details and deal with the emotional needs of others on the team.

Since they tend to be self-focused, they often frustrate followers who are trying to be heard or noticed. Unless people with the Optimistic style can learn to listen to others' concerns more respectfully and more frequently, they eventually may find that their followers, co-workers, employees, and family members become discouraged or even demoralized.

When they integrate consideration for the strengths and contributions of others with a concerned sincerity toward helping others overcome personal limitations, in the eyes of others their status as leaders is raised considerably. They tend to be perceived as the more visionary and charismatic styles of leaders because of their natural tendencies to see potential and possibility in situations. Rather than merely daydreaming about how things might be, they are prepared to "take the bit between their teeth" and do something to make it happen.

To do so, they are good at delivering inspirational speeches that motivate others into action. They also tend to make very productive group leaders on work projects that involve clearly formulated tasks where the procedures are straightforward and known to all. They are good at leading followers who are cooperative, supportive, and faithful.

To Increase Effectiveness

These individuals probably would have more pronounced effectiveness if they could further develop and consistently practice a more versatile approach to human relations. For lowering their internal pressures, they also could devote more effort to developing strategies for managing time efficiently and reducing stress in their lives.

To soften their somewhat cool but charming social image, they need to be more aware and accepting of their own failures and shortcomings. That would help offset the air of arrogance some people detect in them and for which some people are quick to judge them harshly.

In addition, they might wish to develop more flexibility at drawing upon the strengths in their Interpersonal dimension through communication skills training; that would enable them to pay more attention to the needs of others and thus increase the harmony in their relationships at home and at work.

They also might seek to develop more style-flexibility in their Cognitive dimension, which would lead to a more patient and measured approach to details. Or, they should ensure support will be available from others for the handling of the unwanted details.

They could practice more creative right-brain activities: Listening to music; taking up hobbies; participating in sports; being still; praying; going for casual walks or hikes in nature; sharing conversation over dinner with spouse, family, or close friend(s); and so on. They may need to develop a clearer set of ethical principles that can guide their treatment of others.

They may need to re-assess the value they put on other people and be more careful when handling people to prevent the damage they apparently can unintentionally cause to others' morale or self-worth. Those around them will likely benefit from their developing the capacity for intimacy. They need to learn to open their hearts to others and try not to remake people into what they want them to be.

People with the Optimistic style, perhaps more than any of the other styles, seem to need a physical outlet of cardiovascular exercise as a tension release for their seemingly constant level of high energy output. If they don't have this energy channeled in appropriate directions, they risk becoming targets for stress-related illnesses.

The **PSI 360°** Process

Getting Someone Else to Complete the *PSI* on You

The **PSI 360°** process can be used in many applications. We have had teams complete the **PSI 360°** on every other team member. That benchmarks the way each team member perceives the others in a non-judgmental way. The process is very effective for team-building, communications, optimizing performance, internal and external customer service, and so on.

We have had sports-team members complete the **PSI 360°** on their coaches, older children on their parents, parents on their children, business partners and personal partners on each other. We have had students use the ***Instructional Style Indicator*** as a **360°** and complete it on their teacher, instructor, or professor.

We also have had clients use the ***Sales Style Indicator*** as a **360°** on their sales rep to provide feedback on the way clients experience the sales rep's customer service and sales approach. All are strong developmental processes!

One other option we have built into the system is to have a **360°** completed by a third party.

- As a sales manager, I could send out an assessment to my sales rep's clients, get the **360°** feedback from them on my sales rep, and have it returned directly to me.

- As a principal in a school, I could send it to students regarding a specific teacher, and have it sent back to me, not the teacher.

- Sports directors can get the players of a specific coach to provide **360°** feedback on his coaching style.

- A senior manager who wants to understand the leadership style of a supervisor could have employees who report directly to the supervisor complete the **360°** and send it back to the manager.

As you consider all the possibilities of the way style can impact your life and the lives of others, keep the **360°** process top-of-mind as a significant option.

To learn more about the **360°**, please go to www.crgleader.com.

Additional Resources

Consulting Resource Group International Inc. has over 100 resources and services in 10 languages that you can access for personal and professional development.

They include leadership development, team-building, career search, placement and development, health and wellness, sales and customer service, learning and instructional styles, entrepreneurship, HR, interpersonal relationships, coaching, and more.

Assessments available in Print and Online

Personal Style Indicator
Sales Style Indicator
Entrepreneurial Style and Success Indicator
Instructional Style Indicator
Learning Style Indicator
Values Preference Indicator
Self-Worth Inventory
Stress Indicator and Health Planner
Leadership Skills Inventory–Self
Leadership Skills Inventory–Others
Job Style Indicator
Quick Style Indicator (Print Only)

For Professionals

Consider Attending CRG's **Assessment Systems Certification** Workshop.

Learn why over 80% of Professionals and Other Participants Prefer CRG Assessment Systems.

CRG was founded by Dr. Terry Anderson over 30 years ago, in 1979, because he discovered gaps—even misrepresentations—in many of the assessments offered in the marketplace.

A university professor, he could not find a single style assessment that had these important attributes.

- Was self-scoring and permitted self-interpretation.
- Honored the participant in the design.
- Was user-friendly and easy to understand.
- Had reliable research behind it.
- Did not require certification to implement.
- Considered a multi-theory approach to its design.
- Included a holistic model for development.

So, in sheer frustration, CRG created its first assessment: the ***Personal Style Indicator***.

Unfortunately, many flawed assessments are still in use today. When you compare our model and resources to others in the marketplace, you'll find we are unique in the industry. If you think we are similar, the differences will be clear after you've attended our **Assessment Systems Certification** workshop.

CRG created this professional approach, "We give psychology away for the benefit of the learner." The response to our pioneering approach was so positive, CRG expanded to create a comprehensive system of assessments and support materials.

Parts of our system are available in 10 languages. Our resources are actively used in more than 30 countries.

Here's how we approach assessments.

- To use a familiar analogy, CRG assessments teach people *how to fish*. We do not create a co-dependent relationship with participants. Many other assessments have little value without a formal debriefing from a certified consultant.

- Our assessments complement one another, thus enabling fast-tracked and holistic development.

- CRG assessments yield results that make it easy for participants to respond instantly, intentionally, and independently.

- Participants don't want to take tests. They prefer communications tools that provide them with a path for living, leading, and working **on purpose**. We provide the means for people to achieve their goals.

- CRG redefines the stereotypical definition of Extroversion and Introversion and provides a new framework for describing behaviors and performance.

To learn more about upcoming CRG's **Assessment Systems Certification** workshops, registration, the program outline, and/or options for this program to be used in-house, please go to www.crgleader.com or call the CRG office: 604 852-0566.

Toll Free in North America: 1-866-852-4347

Most of the 360 people in attendance have been through other assessments such as DiSC, MBTI, or True Colors, yet they consistently gave feedback on how much more valuable and superior CRG's Personal Style Indicator (PSI) was in comparison.

Jim Janz, President
Janz and Associates

This was the most powerful workshop I have ever attended in terms of valuable content, dynamic presentation, huge practical applications, and phenomenal personal growth—coupled with tremendous business opportunities.

Howie Hoggins
Energy Shift Adventures

To learn more, please download our 52-page PDF: **Secrets of Success** Catalog.

Another book by Ken Keis

My Source EXPERIENCE Journal – A Personal Discovery Process for Those Who Want to Lead a Passionate and Fulfilling Life™

Only 10% of the population is living life *on purpose.*

This book is designed for the 90% who are still searching for their personal *purpose.*

This 88-page journal is filled with insightful questions and exercises that take you on a journey of self-discovery. It's also a perfect process for assisting your clients to determine what they really want, in all areas of life.

You will discover . . .

- Your key motivators
- Your undiscovered passions
- Your ideal career
- Your true interests
- A unique process to keep connected your Source—forever

About the Authors

Ken Keis, President and CEO of Consulting Resource Group, is the author of **My Source EXPERIENCE Journal**™, 40 programs on business management, leadership, sales, career, wellness, and personal development, and more than 400 articles. He is also the co-author of 12 CRG assessments.

In addition to writing 3 million-plus words of copy along the way, over the past 21 years Ken has conducted more than 2000 presentations, including 10,000 hours of consulting on coaching, business, and HR.

A Certified Professional Consultant with an MBA in International Management, he is considered a foremost global authority on how assessment strategies and processes not only increase *but multiply your success rate*.

As co-creator of CRG's proprietary holistic developmental models, assessments, and courses, Ken is an expert in assisting individuals, families, teams, and organizations to realize their potential and *purpose* in the emotional, mental, psychological, intellectual, interpersonal, physical, financial, and spiritual areas of life.

Called one of the most passionate presenters you will ever experience, Ken also is an Internet radio host, TV and radio guest, and seminar speaker.

Meet Ken at www.kenkeis.com or www.crgleader.com.

email: info@crgleader.com

Phone: 604 852-0566

Everett Robinson has a Master's Degree in Counseling Psychology and is co-author of CRG's *Personal Style Indicator*, *Values Preference Indicator*, *Learning Style Indicator*, *Instructional Style Indicator*, and the *Self-Worth Inventory*. An acknowledged authority on Personal Style, he wrote the first two editions of *Why Aren't You More Like Me?*

I used to wonder why people didn't get my point of view—it was so obvious to me! I would get exasperated and frustrated. As a result, I had few friends and no tolerance for people who were different than I was. Because I was unaware of other people's Personal Styles, I was ineffective in my job as a manager and saw constant staff turnover. It wasn't until my job was threatened that I became aware that the problem was me, not "them."

The many assessments I'd taken (and given) all basically conveyed the same type of information—they answered the "what" message about my strengths and weaknesses, but they didn't help me with "how" to interact with people.

Together, **Why Aren't You More Like Me?** *and CRG's* **Personal Style Indicator** *provide insights that no other book and assessment can offer. I had a "Eureka" moment when I finally understood* **how I am** *and* **how I can be** *with the way others are.*

They are also powerful tools for hiring, coaching, and training. I can see immediately that if a person's Interpersonal HARMONY score is low and Cognitive ANALYSIS score is high, this individual will be ideal for an isolated and non-supervised position.

My **PSI** *scores showed me how to communicate and provide feedback in a way likely to produce a positive response. My new knowledge allows me to choose my own path and adapt my Personal Style to work in my favor with the people with whom I interact. My social and professional status have been enhanced.*

To make this information even more compelling for you as a professional, I highly encourage you to engage the **CRG Assessment Systems Certification.**

I challenge everyone to discover how **You Can Be More Like Them.** *The information in this book should be taught in every one of our schools!*

July Ono
President, On The Beach
Education Corporation

5DV6EU5FP